TRADITION OLD AND NEW

Other works by F. F. Bruce:

THIS IS THAT

THE SPREADING FLAME

ISRAEL AND THE NATIONS

AN EXPANDED PARAPHRASE OF THE EPISTLES OF PAUL

SECOND THOUGHTS ON THE DEAD SEA SCROLLS

THE TEACHER OF RIGHTEOUSNESS IN THE QUMRAN TEXTS

BIBLICAL EXEGESIS IN THE QUMRAN TEXTS

THE ACTS OF THE APOSTLES: GREEK TEXT WITH INTRODUCTION AND COMMENTARY

THE BOOK OF THE ACTS: ENGLISH TEXT WITH EXPOSITION AND NOTES

THE EPISTLE TO THE HEBREWS: ENGLISH TEXT WITH EXPOSITION AND NOTES

THE EPISTLE TO THE COLOSSIANS: ENGLISH TEXT WITH EXPOSITION AND NOTES

THE EPISTLE TO THE EPHESIANS: A VERSE-BY-VERSE EXPOSITION

THE EPISTLE OF PAUL TO THE ROMANS: AN INTRODUCTION AND COMMENTARY

PAUL AND HIS CONVERTS

THE NEW TESTAMENT DOCUMENTS: ARE THEY RELIABLE?

THE APOSTOLIC DEFENCE OF THE GOSPEL

THE BOOKS AND THE PARCHMENTS

THE ENGLISH BIBLE

THE HITTITES AND THE OLD TESTAMENT

NEW TESTAMENT HISTORY

TRADITION OLD AND NEW

by

F. F. BRUCE

M.A. (Cantab.), D.D. (Aberd.)
Rylands Professor of Biblical Criticism and Exegesis
in the University of Manchester

"Hold to the traditions which you were taught
by us, either by word of mouth or by letter"
(II Thess. 2 : 15)

THE PATERNOSTER PRESS

ISBN: 0 85364 100 5
Copyright © 1970 F. F. Bruce

AUSTRALIA:
Emu Book Agencies Pty., Ltd.,
511 Kent Street, Sydney, N.S.W.

CANADA:
Home Evangel Books Ltd.,
25 Hobson Avenue, Toronto, 16

SOUTH AFRICA:
Oxford University Press
P.O. Box 1141, Thibault House,
Thibault Square, Cape Town

Made and Printed in Great Britain for
The Paternoster Press Paternoster House
3 Mount Radford Crescent Exeter Devon
by Cox & Wyman Limited Fakenham

TO
JOHN AND WINNIE HARRISON

CONTENTS

PREFACE

WHEN THE PRESIDENT AND FACULTY OF THE SOUTHERN BAPTIST Theological Seminary, Louisville, Kentucky, honoured me with an invitation to deliver the Norton Lectures on Religion and Science for 1968, several factors moved me to choose the subject of Tradition.

In the first place, any teacher of Biblical Criticism and Exegesis is necessarily concerned with tradition – whether it be the tradition that preceded the composition and canonization of the biblical documents or the hermeneutical tradition that finds its source in them. Again, there is the renewed interest in tradition stimulated by the ecumenical movement and the consequent dialogue between churches which statedly give a dominant place to tradition in their life and thought and churches in which it is given, at best, a subordinate place. For my own part, I had also been increasingly impressed over the years by the prevalence of tradition in churches and religious movements which believed themselves to be free from its influence. The final factor in directing my thought along these lines was an international colloquium held in our Manchester Faculty of Theology in November 1966 on the subject "Holy Book and Holy Tradition". To participate in this colloquium and later to help in preparing its main proceedings for publication was a valuable and educative exercise.

The following pages represent a considerable expansion of the four Norton Lectures delivered from March 5 to 8, 1968. Parts of Chapters VIII and IX were delivered as the Ryder Smith Memorial Lecture in Richmond College, London, on October 17 of the same year.

To my friends and colleagues in both these theological schools I am deeply grateful for the kindness which has made these occasions such happy and memorable ones for me. In particular, Dr. Harold S. Songer, Chairman of the Guest Speakers' Committee of Southern Seminary at the time of my Norton Lectures, far exceeded the formal obligations of his office in all that he did for my comfort during my days in Louisville.

Miss Margaret Hogg has typed the manuscript and helped me in other ways with her customary willingness and efficiency.

June, 1970   F.F.B.

ABBREVIATIONS

Ant.	*Antiquities* (Josephus)
Ap. Const.	*Apostolic Constitutions*
Ap. Trad.	*Apostolic Tradition*
AV	Authorized Version (King James Version)
BJ	*Jewish War* (Josephus)
BJRL	*Bulletin of the John Rylands Library* (Manchester)
CD	Covenant Document of Damascus ($=$ Zadokite Work)
CR	*Corpus Reformatorum*
E.T.	English Translation
Hist. Eccl.	*Ecclesiastical History* (Eusebius)
HTR	*Harvard Theological Review*
JBL	*Journal of Biblical Literature*
JTS	*Journal of Theological Studies*
KJV	See AV
NEB	New English Bible
Nov T	*Novum Testamentum*
n.s.	new series
NT	New Testament
OT	Old Testament
Princ.	*On First Principles* (Origen's *De Principiis*)
Q	Qumran (index letter for Qumran manuscripts)
1QM	War *(Milḥamah)* Scroll from Qumran Cave 1
1QpHab.	Commentary *(pesher)* on Habakkuk from Qumran Cave 1
1QS	Rule *(serek)* of the Community from Qumran Cave 1
4QEx^a	One of several Hebrew manuscripts of Exodus from Qumran Cave 4
4QpMic.	Commentary *(pesher)* on Micah from Qumran Cave 4
RGG	*Religion in Geschichte und Gegenwart,* 3rd edition, ed. K. Galling (Tübingen, 1956–65)
RHPR	*Revue d'Histoire et de Philosophie Religieuses*
RSV	Revised Standard Version
RV	Revised Version
SJT	*Scottish Journal of Theology*
TB	Talmud of Babylon (Babylonian Talmud)
TDNT	*Theological Dictionary of the New Testament,* ed. G. Kittel and G. Friedrich, E. T. by G. W. Bromiley (Grand Rapids, 1964 –)
Test. XII	*Testaments of the Twelve Patriarchs*
TJ	Talmud of Jerusalem (Palestinian Talmud)
TU	*Texte und Untersuchungen* (Berlin)
ZNW	*Zeitschrift für die Neutestamentliche Wissenschaft*

INTRODUCTION

L EWIS CARROLL, WITH HIS USUAL PERCIPIENCE, PUTS THE
matter in a nutshell in the trial scene of *Alice in Wonderland.*

At this moment the King, who had been for some time busily writing in his
note-book, called out "Silence!" and read from his book, "Rule Forty-Two.
All persons more than a mile high to leave the court."
Everybody looked at Alice.
"*I'm* not a mile high," said Alice.
"You are," said the King.
"Nearly two miles high," added the Queen.
"Well, I shan't go, at any rate," said Alice: "besides, that's not a regular
rule: you invented it just now."
"It's the oldest rule in the book," said the King.
"Then it ought to be Number One," said Alice.

"Tradition Old" in the title of this book is a concept which calls for no
explanation; if anyone asks what is meant by "Tradition New", or how
in fact tradition *can* be new, Lewis Carroll supplies the answer. However
new it may be, it is "tradition" if it is pronounced to be so by adequate
authority.

What interests me specially is the part played by tradition in the life
and thought of people who in theory and profession repudiate the
authority of tradition, appealing from the tradition of others to the Bible
alone.[1] If such Christians, who (like Presbyterians of the old school)
acknowledge the Bible as the only infallible rule of faith and practice but
(unlike Presbyterians) have no recognized "subordinate standards", are
called biblicists, this term is used in no disparaging sense. By heritage and
conviction I myself am a biblicist; theologically as well as academically
I am *homo unius libri.* One of the functions of recognized subordinate
standards, like the Westminster Confession of Faith and the Larger and
Shorter Catechisms in the Presbyterian tradition, is to provide guidelines
for the interpretation and application of Scripture. Where subordinate

---

[1] *Sola scriptura*, in the Lutheran phrase, denotes Scripture as the *principium cognoscendi*, the
prime source of theological knowledge. Luther's appeal to Scripture alone as the standard by
which councils, canon law and all other forms of ecclesiastical tradition must be tested was
determined as a result of his confrontation with Johann Meier von Eck at the Leipzig dis-
putation of 1519 and found historic expression at the Diet of Worms two years later (cf.
A. S. Wood, *Captive to the Word*, Exeter, 1969, pp. 69 ff.). "The distinguishing mark of the
Reformation and its disciples," says a modern Lutheran theologian, "is the exclusive particle,
the word 'alone' . . . Concretely expressed, the relationship of the community and the Word
of God is not reversible; there is no dialectical process by which the community created by
the Word becomes at the same time an authority set over the Word to interpret it, to adminis-
ter it, to possess it . . . For the community remains the handmaid of the Word" (E. Käsemann,
New Testament Questions of Today, E. T., London, 1969, pp. 261 f.).

standards are not recognized, it does not follow that there are no such guidelines: guidelines and even more precise canons are quite likely to be laid down, but because they take the form of *unwritten* tradition, their true nature may be overlooked. Indeed, in some more enclosed traditions the authority of Scripture will be identified with the authority of the accepted interpretation and application, because it has never occurred to those inside the enclosure that Scripture could be interpreted or applied otherwise.

Of an "Irish clergyman" (actually John Nelson Darby) under whose powerful influence he came at a formative period of his youth, Francis William Newman says: "he only wanted men 'to submit their understanding *to God'*, that is, to the Bible, that is, to his interpretation!"[2] The history of the spiritual successors of the "Irish clergyman" provides an adequate commentary on the consequences of such submission.

Interpretation and Translation

A group of biblicist churches in a certain country came under the influence of a few Pentecostal teachers. Their leaders were particularly concerned at the increasing practice of glossolalia which was attributed to the influence of the Pentecostal visitors. It might have been thought that, since glossolalia was a feature of some apostolic churches, it would have been acceptable in a biblicist community – but it was not countenanced in the tradition of these churches. There were historical reasons for this, arising from differences between their spiritual ancestors and Edward Irving, but they were probably unaware of this. They would not have wished to appeal to tradition: Scripture was their authority. But while Scripture discourages an over-high evaluation of glossolalia, it does not forbid the due exercise of the gift. The leaders of the affected churches, however, inherited an interpretation of I Cor. 13:10, "when the perfect comes, the imperfect will pass away", which took it to mean that glossolalia and similar manifestations of the Spirit were intended to be temporary, and would "pass away" when the New Testament canon was complete. In one circular letter which they issued on the subject they appealed to this as the "standard" interpretation in their churches. Quite apart from the validity of the exegesis – and that the concept of the completed New Testament canon was present to Paul's mind is extremely improbable – it is unwise to refer people of independent thought to a "standard" interpretation, for the very fact of its being so described renders it suspect. The leaders would have been wiser to appeal to Paul's ruling that only those utterances (in whatever "tongue" they were expressed) were acceptable in church which tended to "edification" – to

[2] F. W. Newman, *Phases of Faith* (London, 1850), p. 34.

the building up of the community and its members. But the appeal which was actually made was in effect, though not in name, an appeal to tradition, even if those who made it believed they were appealing to Scripture.

At times it is not the interpretation of a passage of Scripture, but its very rendering, that becomes a hallmark of a particular tradition. For example, when I hear Matt. 16:19 (cf. 18:18) translated "Whatever you forbid/permit on earth must be already forbidden/permitted in heaven", or Acts 2:38 translated "Repent and be baptized with reference to (or even 'on the basis of') the forgiveness of sins", I have a good idea what company I am in.

"Letting down the side"

Some years ago I spoke to a group of theological students in a British university on the subject of their choice – the principles and methods of biblical criticism. Like myself, they belonged to the evangelical tradition. I illustrated part of my talk by dealing with the structure, date and authorship of one particular section of Scripture. Some of them, I knew, had been brought up to regard as erroneous the conclusions to which, in my judgement, the relevant criteria pointed; yet these conclusions contradicted no biblical statement and could not be reasonably dismissed as arising from unwillingness to admit the supernatural element in divine revelation; indeed, they involved the acceptance of miracle in general and predictive prophecy in particular. If, then, these were the conclusions to which the evidence led, I asked, what was the objection to them? They thought the matter over and then one of them said: "What you say seems quite logical, but some of us feel that if we accepted these conclusions we should be letting down the evangelical side."[3] This, it seemed to me, was carrying loyalty to a tradition too far, but I could sympathize with them; I could only feel sorry that such a tradition should be called "evangelical", and glad for my own sake that I had been brought up to subordinate tradition to evidence.

Tradition and Counter-Tradition

It is noteworthy how often the renunciation of an old tradition is followed by the speedy development of a new one, held at least as tenaciously as ever the old one was. This is frequently found in liturgical words or orders of worship. Sometimes those who secede from the more liturgical or centrally organized churches will endeavour to get as far

---

[3] At least they did not say, "But if you begin there, where are you going to stop?" – as was reputedly said to someone who attempted a partial defence of Robertson Smith's dating of Deuteronomy by arguing that Moses, whatever else he wrote, probably did not write the account of his own death in chapter 34.

away as possible from traditional liturgy and central organization in their new church worship and order – and discover before long that they have created a new "tradition" of liturgy and order based on a regrettably negative principle.[4] The same process can be seen in the identification of sacred sites. Because the Church of the Holy Sepulchre is the *traditional* site of our Lord's death and burial, some Christians instinctively reject it for that reason, and will defend a nineteenth-century tradition (Gordon's Calvary and the Garden Tomb) as vehemently as ever those with whom they disagree have defended the fourth-century tradition. Defenders of either tradition as tradition do not take kindly to the suggestion that the site cannot be certainly located, and that its identification must ultimately be determined, if at all, on grounds of objective evidence (topographical, archaeological and the like). Or, because the traditional site of St. Peter's burial is bound up with the issue of papal primacy, certain forthright Protestants, not content with denying papal primacy, think it desirable to reject the tradition of Peter's residence, death and burial at Rome into the bargain – although this tradition is rather more solidly founded than the tradition of St. John's residence, death and burial at Ephesus, which the same people, for different but equally non-objective reasons, wholeheartedly accept. For Peter's tomb, too, a rival "tradition" has commended itself to some in recent years, for an ossuary found on the Mount of Olives in the 1950s, inscribed (possibly but not certainly) "Simon bar Jona", has been hailed as the authentic repository of the bones of the prince of the apostles![5]

"Regional Holiness"

An American theologian remarked in my hearing that somebody ought one day to write a Ph.D. thesis on "regional holiness". He had in mind various religious groups in the United States in whose conception of practical holiness attitudes to (say) tobacco, alcohol, dancing and the theatre play a prominent but varying part, and his point was that the

---

[4] As when dissenters from Anglicanism feel that it is best to keep as far as possible from the Prayer Book forms, without always knowing what it is they are keeping far from. The biographers of Professor A. Rendle Short of Bristol tell how "an unexpected feature of his public prayers was that he would use in his extempore exercises memorized sections of the Book of Common Prayer of the Church of England. There was a classic occasion one Sunday morning at Bethesda. He used a prayer from the Communion Service. When the members of the congregation were leaving an elderly member, who vigorously held that all 'set prayers' were wrong, was heard to remark to his neighbour: 'Mr. Short prayed very beautifully this morning. At times he sounded almost inspired'" (W. M. Capper and D. Johnson, *Arthur Rendle Short: Surgeon and Christian*, London, 1954, p. 162).

[5] By F. P. Peterson, *Peter's Tomb Recently Discovered in Jerusalem* (Fort Wayne, Ind., 1960). For details see P. B. Bagatti and J. T. Milik, *Gli Scavi del "Dominus Flevit"* (Jerusalem, 1958), p. 83. The first two words of the Aramaic inscription on the ossuary (No. 11) are clear; the letters of the third word are possibly (as Fr. Bagatti thinks) *ywnh* (*Jona*) but may with equal possibility (according to Fr. Milik) be read *zynh* (*Zena*, corresponding to the Greek form Ζηνᾶ occurring on Ossuary 21, genitive of Ζηνᾶς; cf. Titus 3:13).

variation in attitudes frequently depended not on denominational connexion but on geographical residence. He mentioned one evangelical
denomination in the States whose main strength lay in two parts of the
country, quite a long way from each other. Members of the denomination
in one of these regions took a strong line against mixed bathing, whereas
those in the other region had no inhibitions about it. Probably mutual
charity was exercised during recreation periods when representatives of
the two regions came together for denominational conferences. Such
"regional holiness" does not require a far-flung expanse like the United
States for its manifestation: it could be paralleled in the religious life of
Scotland. But wherever it appears, it is an aspect of tradition in the field
of conduct – although those who exhibit it would probably deprecate
its being described by the term "tradition".

Arrested Development

One important aspect of the fixing, or indeed petrifying, of tradition
often appears when a community is transplanted from its former environment to a new and unfamiliar one. It may try to preserve its sense of
identity and security by holding tenaciously to its traditions in the form
which they had reached at the moment of transplantation. The Amish
are perhaps the best known example of this – best known because their
traditions comprise their total way of life. But on a less comprehensive
scale the phenomenon is common enough. I can think of a religious
journal published in the United States which from time to time announces
Christian conventions to which those speakers are invited who adhere to
the "old paths".[6] If the conveners were asked what they mean by this
Jeremianic term, they would say that it denotes loyalty to principles of
church order and fellowship, together with certain forms of cultural
separation, which they find in the New Testament. But in practice (as
viewed from the outside) their language means that they invest with
sacrosanctity the stage to which their community's faith and life had
developed at the time when they left their original environment and
settled in the new world. Fellow-members of the community who did
not emigrate have continued to develop and change in ways that are
consonant with health and vitality, but their emigrant friends who come
back to visit them from time to time are prone to shake their heads over
their departure from the way of truth.

This is not unlike the tendency which John Robinson of Leyden
deplored in his farewell address to the Pilgrim Fathers, when he saw how
many Christians appeared to have come to a full stop in religious development, refusing to go beyond the point to which leaders of the past, like

[6] Cf. Jer. 6:16.

Luther or Calvin, had brought them. Those leaders had not received the complete will of God in their lifetime and, were they still alive, they would as willingly embrace further light from God as that which they had already received. He reminded his hearers of the solemn undertaking which they had given in their church covenant, to receive whatever God might reveal to them in the Scriptures, for that God indeed had more light "to break forth out of His holy word" he himself had no doubt.[7]

Light from the Word

To many it seems safer and more comfortable to stay within familiar and old-established boundaries. The admission of more light may show up inadequacies in cherished traditions – inadequacies that would otherwise have remained hidden – and they may be disposed to question whether what is claimed to be "more light" is in fact light. But light by its nature is self-evidencing,[8] and John Robinson's choice of this figure for the further truth that might be learned from Scripture was apt. There are those who demand authority for truth, forgetting that truth is itself the highest authority. Where the Holy Spirit guides the people of Christ into further truth, that guidance (though meeting with some initial resistance) tends in the long run to commend itself to their general acceptance. It will not conflict with truth already learned and established, even if it shows that some things previously reckoned to be truth were only imperfectly so, or not so at all. It will be acknowledged to be in harmony with the mind of Christ, as His mind is primarily revealed in Scripture and progressively appreciated in the church. The word by which tradition is to be tested and the church's faith and life continuously reformed is no mere deliverance of antiquity laying down precedents for all time to come: the Spirit who spoke in that word to the churches of the first century speaks in it to the churches of the twentieth, and does so in terms which address themselves dynamically and relevantly to our present condition.

[7] Cf. W. H. Burgess, *John Robinson, Pastor of the Pilgrim Fathers* (London, 1920), p. 240. His farewell address (1620) was summarized from memory in later years by Edward Winslow (Governor of Plymouth, Massachusetts), who heard it, in his *Hypocrisie Unmasked* (London, 1646), pp. 97 ff.

[8] "The message [of Scripture] stands in its own truth and grandeur and in this sense is self-authenticating, for no higher guarantee can be given it, no greater authority than that of the Living Word of whom it speaks and who uses it as the vehicle of his saving action" *(Conversations between the Church of England and the Methodist Church,* London, 1963, p. 15).

CHAPTER I

THE TRADITION OF THE ELDERS

TRADITION, IN SOME RELIGIOUS CIRCLES WITH WHICH WE are well acquainted, is not esteemed as a good word. Especially when it is set alongside Holy Writ, it is apt to be disparaged as "mere" tradition. Certain biblical expressions spring readily to the minds and lips of those who thus disparage it: "the tradition of the elders . . . the tradition of men . . . making void the word of God through your tradition" (Mark 7:4, 8, 13; cf. Col. 2:8). Our Lord's repudiation of rabbinical tradition, the Reformers' repudiation of ecclesiastical tradition, are felt to provide supporting precedent for the view that tradition is something to be repudiated.

Yet the word is used in other and more noble ways. In my schooldays in Scotland we had a headmaster (or rector, to give him his official title) who, at the beginning of each school year, addressed the new boys and girls and impressed upon them that they had come to "a school with traditions". Its history, he informed them, could be traced back to the thirteenth century, although he probably did not wish them to suppose that the traditions of which he spoke were as ancient as all that: in fact, before his coming to the school it had forgotten most of the traditions it ever had, and while he did what he could to revive them, I suspect that some were not so much *revived* as *created* by him – and were none the worse for that. After all, a tradition must begin sometime and somewhere.

So too in ecclesiastical life a local or national church or a denomination builds up its traditions over the years and generations and becomes so attached to them that it is very reluctant to abandon or modify them, even in the interests of a larger and more comprehensive unity. It is not that it sets its traditions up as rivals to Holy Scripture, although at times they may present an obstacle to the free advance of the Spirit. The traditions that are most tenaciously cherished are often concerned more with practice than with doctrine. In one scheme of union of which I have some knowledge, between two denominations of the Reformation order, there have arisen no complicated questions of doctrine like the maintenance of apostolic succession or the essentiality of the historic episcopate – that specially awkward impediment in the path of unity. In fact no theological problem has held up progress; but when the negotiators got down to the brass tacks of temporalities and practicalities, they found that it was here that the hitches developed. Not that these are likely to prove insuperable barriers, but people feel strongly about them, because they are the elements in their particular "tradition" of which they are most directly aware. They may not even use the word "tradition" in this connexion, but it is tradition that is involved when people say "This is what we have always done" or "This is what we were always taught".

One does from time to time meet churches or individual Christians who profess a pure biblicism and deny that they have any tradition or traditions apart from what is written. But a pure biblicism is rarely so pure as it is thought to be. Let these friends be confronted with an interpretation of Scripture which is new to them, held (it may be) by others but unknown in their own circle, and they will suddenly realize that what they had always taken to be the plain sense of Scripture is really their traditional interpretation; other people have different traditional interpretations, and the criteria for preferring one interpretation to another must be sought not in the antiquity of the traditions or in the warmth with which they are held but in a careful study of the principles of biblical interpretation and an exegetical examination of the relevant texts.[1]

On the crucial role of biblical interpretation in Christian tradition more will be said anon.[2] But first we must come to closer grips with what is said about tradition in the Bible itself. Especially if we desire to be pure biblicists – and even if we have no such desire – this is of primary importance for our theme.

Tradition in the New Testament

The New Testament word for tradition is *paradosis*, which may denote the act of handing over or the material which is handed over. Its cognate verb, *paradidōmi*, is used in the New Testament in a wide variety of senses – it is frequently used, for example, in reference to Judas Iscariot's betrayal of our Lord[3] – but what is of special moment to us is its use for the handing over or delivery of tradition. Thus Jesus, on an occasion already referred to, charges the Pharisees of His day with nullifying the primary meaning of one of the commandments of the Decalogue "through your tradition *(paradosis)* which you hand on *(paradidōmi)*" (Mark 7:13). With the verb *paradidōmi* another verb is closely associated as its correlative – *paralambanō*. This verb, too, is used in the New Testament in many contexts meaning "take" or "receive", but we are specially concerned with its use for the receiving by one party of the tradition which has been handed on by another. Thus Mark, speaking of some of the traditional practices of those Pharisees whom Jesus criticized, says: "and there are many other things which they have received *(paralambanō)* to observe" (Mark 7:4).

---

[1] Cf. F. R. Coad, *A History of the Brethren Movement* (Exeter, 1968), pp. 249 ff.
[2] See pp. 74 ff.
[3] Cf. Matt. 10:4; 26:16, 25, 46, 48; 27:3 (and Synoptic parallels); John 12:4; 13:2, 11, 21; 18:2, 5.

The Oral Law

In Hebrew there are two terms corresponding to these two Greek verbs – *māsar* ("hand on" or "deliver") and *qibbēl* ("receive"). Neither of them is frequent in the Old Testament and only once does one of them approximate the usage with which we are now dealing: "accept (*qibbēl*) instruction" (Prov. 19:20). From these Hebrew verbs are derived the nouns *māsōreth* (or *māsōrāh*) and *qabbālāh*, both of which mean "tradition" in post-biblical Hebrew – the former being used of the traditional reading and elucidation of the text of Scripture, and the latter of post-Mosaic legal material and (later) of mystical lore.

The "tradition of the elders" with which Jesus found fault may with confidence be identified with the oral law whose transmission from Moses to New Testament times is outlined in the familiar opening words of the Mishnaic tractate *Pirqē Abōt*:

> Moses received (*qibbēl*) Torah from Sinai and delivered (*māsar*) it to Joshua, and Joshua to the elders,[1] and the elders to the prophets, and the prophets to the men of the great synagogue[2] . . . Simon the Just was one of the last survivors of the great synagogue . . . Antigonos of Soko received (*qibbēl*) it from Simon the Just . . . Yose ben Yoezer of Zeredah and Yose ben Yochanan of Jerusalem received it from them . . . Joshua ben Perachyah and Nittai the Arbelite received it from them . . . Judah ben Tabbai and Simeon ben Shetach[3] received it from them . . . Shemayah and Abtalion[4] received it from them . . . Hillel and Shammai received it from them. . . .

This brings us to the closing years of Herod the Great. Mention is next made of Rabban Gamaliel, Hillel's disciple and successor as head of the school which he founded (and teacher, incidentally, of Saul of Tarsus[5] who, but for a momentous experience which befell him once at Damascus, might have succeeded Gamaliel and duly made his appearance in *Pirqē Abōt*). Simeon ben Gamaliel is recorded next, and with him we reach the end of the Second Jewish Commonwealth.[6]

This genealogical table of "tradents", or transmitters of the oral law from one generation to another, oversimplifies the process in more ways than one. In particular, the five pairs of tradents between Antigonos of Soko and Gamaliel the Elder were not, as might be inferred, colleagues

[1] Cf. Josh. 24:31; Judg. 2:7.
[2] Traditionally set up in time of Nehemiah and Ezra (cf. Neh. 8:1 ff.; 9:38 ff.); cf. quotation from John Owen on p. 161, n.2, below.
[3] They flourished in the reigns of Alexander Jannaeus and Salome Alexandra (103–67 B.C.).
[4] Possibly to be identified with Samaias and Pollion who flourished before and at the beginning of Herod's reign (Josephus, *Ant.* xiv. 172 ff.; xv. 3 f., 370).
[5] Cf. Acts 22:3. See p. 29.
[6] Cf. Josephus, *BJ* iv. 159; *Life* 190.

jointly responsible for handing on the tradition which they had received, but (at least in some instances) rivals. Hillel and Shammai (*c.* 10 B.C.) were leaders of two distinct schools of tradition which diverged quite sharply in some points of interpretation and application of the law. Yet, for all their divergence, they shared a large area of common ground: they accepted the principle of tradition as a means of adapting the requirements of the ancient law to changing circumstances, in distinction from the Sadducees who (in theory at any rate) insisted on the strict letter of the written code.[1] The data and methodology of the schools of Hillel and Shammai were similar, even if they differed in their interpretation of the data and application of the methodology.

The fundamental insistence of the genealogical table is, however, that the tradition – the *oral* tradition – of the schools of Hillel and Shammai, and especially that of the school of Hillel, perpetuated by Yochanan ben Zakkai and his associates and successors after A.D. 70, could be traced back to Moses, who received it from God on Mount Sinai at the same time as he received the written law. To both alike is given the designation Torah, meaning (divine) direction or instruction. *Historically*, the oral law is a practical commentary on the written law, growing over the centuries as the written rulings and statutes were adapted and applied to the changing conditions of life in succeeding generations. *Dogmatically*, however, the oral law, quite recent as it might be, was invested with authority by being promulgated as "Mosaic Torah from Sinai". That the rabbis themselves appreciated the paradoxical side of this legal fiction is evident from the story of a visit which Moses was permitted to pay incognito to the lecture-room of Aqiba (the leading doctor of the law in the Hillelite tradition at the beginning of the second century A.D.): Moses was frankly puzzled and could not recognize what was confidently declared to be, by implication, his own law.[2]

Growth of Case-law

The beginnings of the process of applying the basic law to a variety of situations can be readily discerned within the Old Testament itself. For example, the sabbath day was protected by a comprehensive regulation: "in it", the Israelite was enjoined in the Fourth Commandment, "you shall not do any work" (Ex. 20:10; Deut. 5:14). But what was the precise meaning of "work"? Which activities counted as work, and which did not? In a simple agricultural community the answer was relatively easy: "work" consisted of those activities which made up the daily routine of labour. But in the Pentateuchal legislation itself we have evidence of

[1] Cf. Josephus, *Ant.* xviii. 16.
[2] TB *Menahot* 29b.

rulings on the question whether this or that more occasional activity constituted work within the meaning of the commandment. What of those special agricultural activities which recurred season by season, and not day by day? The ruling was plain: even "in ploughing time and in harvest you shall rest" (Ex. 34:21). What of lighting a fire? Was that permissible or not? The answer was No: "you shall kindle no fire in all your habitations on the sabbath day" (Ex. 35:3). What about gathering fuel to light a fire? Again the answer was No – and in this case the ruling was embodied in a narrative of the category designated in later times as *haggadah*: a man who was found gathering sticks on the sabbath was kept in custody until a divine response was secured (Num. 15:32 ff.). The development of case-law is thus illustrated. In the time of Nehemiah the importation of wares into Jerusalem on the sabbath, already forbidden under the monarchy in terms of a ban on commercial transactions and the carrying of burdens on that day (cf. Amos 8:5; Jer. 17:21 ff.), was effectually prevented by the governor's order that the city gates be closed and guarded by Levites from sundown on Friday till after sundown on Saturday (Neh. 13:19 ff.). At the same time, those Levites were evidently not deemed to violate the sanctity of the sabbath by standing guard over the gates.

These later interpretations did not always aim at sharpening the original law and making it more stringent; frequently they eased its literal rigour to fit new situations.

"Yochanan the high priest" – perhaps John Hyrcanus (134–104 B.C.) – is said to have introduced certain modifications with regard to the law of tithing.[1] The Pharisees, on the other hand (as the Gospels make sufficiently plain), were exceptionally scrupulous in their observance of this law. They would not take food that was liable to be tithed unless they were assured that the tithe had actually been paid on it; and in addition to tithing the principal produce of the soil – grain, wine and olive[2] – they tithed minor garden herbs.[3]

Hillel is credited with the introduction of the *prozbul* – an innovation which in large measure nullified the ancient law that debts owed by a fellow-Israelite were to be remitted every seventh year (Deut. 15:1–16). By the end of the pre-Christian era this simply meant that a Jew in need of a loan could not find a willing lender among his fellow-countrymen if the sabbatical year was approaching. Hillel accordingly eased his plight by providing for a declaration to be made, before the debt was contracted, that it was exempt from the law of remission. Thus a regulation which was humanitarian in purpose in the context of a simple

---

[1] Mishnah *Ma'aser Sheni* 5:15; *Soṭah* 9:10; TB *Soṭah* 48 a.
[2] Cf. Deut. 14:22 f.
[3] Cf. Luke 11:42, "you tithe mint and rue and every herb".

agricultural economy was replaced by another, equally humanitarian in purpose, which was more appropriate to a developed mercantile economy.[1]

Hillel's successor Gamaliel modified the law which restricted the sabbath-day movements of witnesses of the new moon;[2] he also forbade divorce proceedings to be annulled without the wife's knowledge.[3]

Another adaptation of the letter of the law to changing circumstances appears in relation to Ex. 16:29, "let no man go out of his place on the seventh day" – a regulation which, if strictly applied, would have prevented any movement outside one's home on the sabbath. But "his place" was interpreted to include any point within 2,000 cubits' distance from a man's home, or from whatever location he might designate in advance as his home for this purpose – the 2,000 cubits being described as "limit of the sabbath" or a "sabbath day's journey".[4]

Jesus and the Tradition of the Elders

The particular interpretation which attracted Jesus' criticism was one which enabled a man to avoid the duty of maintaining his parents if he could claim that the money which he might have used for that purpose was already *qorban*, "devoted (to God)". According to Jesus, this application of the law that vows made to God must by all means be fulfilled (Deut. 23:21-23) was allowed to override the weightier obligation laid down in the Fifth Commandment:[5] "You have a fine way of rejecting the commandment of God, in order to keep your tradition!" (Mark 7:9). The "tradition" which He criticized may have been maintained in the school of Shammai; at any rate, before the end of the first century Eliezer ben Hyrkanos, an eminent Hillelite rabbi, ruled, with the approval of his colleagues, that a vow might be annulled if it adversely affected relations between parents and children.[6]

To return to the question of working on the sabbath: the Mishnah enumerates thirty-nine categories of work, all of which are forbidden on that day.[7] Since two of the categories are reaping and grinding, it is commonly inferred that Jesus' disciples incurred the stricture of the Pharisees in respect of both of these when they not only plucked ears of grain as they walked through the fields on the sabbath but also extracted the

[1] Mishnah *Shebi'it* 10:3 ff.
[2] Mishnah *Rosh ha-Shanah* 2:5.
[3] Mishnah *Gittin* 4:2.
[4] Mishnah *'Erubin* 4:3, etc. The fixing of a limit of 2,000 cubits was based on an extension of the principle of Num. 35:5.
[5] Ex. 20:12; Deut. 5:16; cf. also Ex. 21:17; Lev. 20:9.
[6] Mishnah *Nedarim* 9:1.
[7] *Shabbat* 7:1 ff.

kernels by rubbing the ears between their hands (Mark 2:23 f.). The thirty-nine categories probably represent the teaching of the school of Hillel. The school of Shammai, we may surmise, had an even stricter interpretation. Yet both of these schools would probably have agreed that a domestic animal might be rescued from a pit on the sabbath without detriment to the sanctity of the day – a situation which must have called for a ruling early in a pastoral or agricultural community.[1] Jesus assumes that no objection to an action of this kind will be raised by any of His Pharisaic hearers: "Which of you", He asked, "having an ass or an ox that has fallen into a well, will not immediately pull him out on a sabbath day?" (Luke 14:5). But the community of Qumran, to judge by the sabbath regulations of the Damascus Rule, would apparently have disagreed: "Let no one help an animal in birth on the sabbath. Even if she drops [her young] into a cistern or a pit, let him not lift it out on the sabbath."[2]

It was evidently accepted from early times that the ban on sabbath work did not apply to the sacrificial services in the sanctuary or to certain other ceremonial obligations. In the Gospel narrative, Jesus appeals to this fact in debate. "The priests in the temple profane the sabbath, and are guiltless", He says (Matt. 12:5) – that is, they "profane" it by doing their regular work on it (in fact, probably by doing more work on it than on other days). The implication is: if one form of serving God is permissible on the sabbath, why not others (which from certain points of view might be considered more important, such as healing)? Again, if the eighth day from a Jewish boy's birth coincided with the Sabbath, he must be circumcised on that day, sabbath or no. Hence the argument in ohn 7:23, "If on the sabbath a man receives circumcision [undergoes an operation affecting but one small part of his body], so that the law of Moses may not be broken, are you angry with me because on the sabbath I made a man's whole body well?"

But Jesus' fundamental principle of interpretation of the sabbath law appears not so much in these *ad hominem* arguments with doctors of the law as in His appeal to the primary intention of the sabbath institution. "The sabbath was made for man, not man for the sabbath" (Mark 2:27) – more particularly, the sabbath was instituted for men's rest and relief, not to be a burden to them. Therefore, any action which promoted the divine intention in instituting the sabbath was an honouring of that day. The satisfaction of normal human need, He held, takes priority over ceremonial requirements or the rulings of the schools. For this principle scriptural precedent was available. The "bread of the Presence" in the

[1] A stricter interpretation allowed the animal to be helped in various ways short of being lifted out (cf. TB *Shabbat* 128*b*).
[2] CD 11:13 f. Cf. Josephus's remark that the Essenes "are stricter than all Jews in abstaining from work on the seventh day" (*BJ* ii. 147).

sanctuary might be reserved by sacred law for the priests alone, but David and his man were not censured for eating it when they were hungry (I Sam. 21:1 ff.; Mark 2:25 f.).[1] As for the sabbath law, others might concede that in a case of extreme urgency, a matter of life and death, remedial measures might be applied on the sacred day – but as an exception to the general rule.[2] If there was no great urgency, then, in the words of a synagogue official who was annoyed by an act of healing in his synagogue on the sabbath, "there are six days on which work ought to be done; come on those days and be healed, and not on the sabbath day" (Luke 13:14). A woman who had suffered for eighteen years from *spondylitis deformans*[3] (if that is what it was) could easily wait another day, he reckoned. But Jesus in effect said "No; she has waited long enough, and the sabbath is the most fitting day for her to be released from her trouble. If on the sabbath you untie your ox or ass as a matter of course and take it off to be watered, how much more should this daughter of Abraham be relieved on the sabbath?" (Luke 13:5 f.).

If we turn from the sabbath law to the law of divorce, a comparable situation meets us. Jesus, together with the Qumran community, the schools of Hillel and Shammai and the Jews in general, read the same wording in the Deuteronomic legislation where it is recognized that a man is entitled to divorce his wife if, after marrying her, he finds in her "some unseemliness" (Deut. 24:1).[4]

But here too the question of definition arose. What constituted "some unseemliness"? The school of Shammai, as we know, limited it to unchastity: if a man found that his bride was not a virgin, as he might reasonably expect her to be, he was entitled to dismiss her. The school of Hillel, commonly credited with milder interpretations than the school of Shammai, manifested its "mildness" here in the husband's interest: he might divorce her (so its leaders expounded the law) for practically any feature or practice which he found displeasing – "if she spoils his dinner", for example, or (as Aqiba ruled) "if he sees a woman more beautiful than she".[5] But when Jesus was asked to say whether a man might put away his wife for any cause, He did not deal with the exegesis of Deut. 24:1–4; however "some unseemliness" might be interpreted, that whole provision, He said, was a modification of the original ordinance; it was introduced later because of the hardness of men's hearts. The original ordinance was

[1] It is interesting to find David's eating the shewbread brought into association with the sabbath law in rabbinical tradition; cf. the discussion in TB *Menaḥot* 95b, where Rabbi Simeon (c. A.D. 150) argues that the incident took place on the sabbath, the day when the old loaves were replaced by new ones and eaten by the priests (Lev. 24:8).

[2] Cf. TB *'Abodah Zarah* 27b–28a.

[3] So A. R. Short, *Modern Discovery and the Bible* (London, 1943), p. 91.

[4] In Deuteronomy the provision for divorce is assumed, not introduced as something new: Deut. 24:1–4 is one sentence (cf. RSV), with its principal clause in verse 4.

[5] See the discussions in Mishnah, *Giṭṭin* 9:10, and TB *Giṭṭin* 90a.

disclosed by God's intention in instituting marriage, as laid down in the creation narrative: "From the beginning of creation He 'made them male and female'; this is why a man will leave his father and mother and be joined to his wife, so that the two become one flesh" (Mark 10:2 ff.).[1] From this Jesus deduced that in the original institution man and woman were made for each other, being joined together by God, and divorce was not contemplated; divorce, in fact, was an attempt to undo the work of God. The practical implication of this ruling would have been a redressing of the unequal balance in favour of the wife, who under Jewish law could not take the initiative in divorcing her husband and who had little opportunity of defending herself against such initiative on his part.

Paul underlines the tradition of Jesus in this matter not only in Eph. 5:22 ff., where the marriage relationship, expounded in the light of Gen. 2:24, is treated as a "mystery" setting forth the relation which subsists between Christ and the church, but in I Cor. 6:15 f., where he uses the Genesis language about "one flesh" to insist on the vital bond established even by casual intercourse with a harlot, and thus "displays a psychological insight into human sexuality which is altogether exceptional by first-century standards".[2]

But such is the hardness of men's hearts that before the gospel tradition was finally stereotyped Jesus' ruling was modified by the reintroduction of the Deuteronomic loophole. The two exceptive clauses in the First Gospel (Matt. 5:32; 19:9)[3] may indeed represent an adaptation of His ruling to the conditions of the Gentile mission, in which a couple might before their conversion have cohabited within forbidden degrees of affinity, so that their union constituted "fornication" in a technical sense. But the history of canon law shows how the kind of approach which Jesus was careful to avoid has tended to obscure the spirit of His liberating pronouncement by treating it woodenly as a piece of legislation. The feature of His preaching which so impressed those who heard it, that "he taught them as one who had authority, and not as their scribes" (Matt. 7:28), did not invariably characterize His followers, as He intended it to do. He did not train His disciples to be "well-plastered cisterns, never losing a drop"[4] – the ideal set before the pupils of the rabbis – but rather to be His apprentices, sharing His ministry with His own creative freedom. He was not only their teacher, whose lessons were to be memorized and

---

[1] Combining Gen. 1:27 and 2:24. In CD 4:21, Gen. 1:27 is quoted with a similar reference to "the beginning (or foundation) of creation" but as prohibiting bigamy, not divorce.

[2] D. S. Bailey, *The Man-Woman Relation in Christian Thought* (London, 1959), p. 10.

[3] The Greek phrases παρεκτὸς λόγου πορνείας (Matt. 5:32) and μὴ ἐπί πορνείᾳ (Matt. 19:9) could be renderings of the Hebrew phrase 'erwat dābār ("some unseemliness", Deut. 24:1) But as in Deuteronomy, so in Matthew the crucial question is: What do the words mean?

[4] Rabbi Yochanan ben Zakkai's encomium on his pupil Eliezer ben Hyrkanos (*Pirqe Abot* 2:8), but Eliezer was later so intransigent and incapable of adapting his mind to changing conditions that he had to be excommunicated (TB *Baba Meṣia* 59 a, b). See p. 24.

transmitted; He was their Lord and exemplar, to be followed and obeyed.[1]

The question of tradition, then, is central and indeed crucial to the unfolding of the gospel story. At other points Jesus clashed with the sacerdotal and secular authorities in Judaea, but it was here that the cleavage began between Him and what was destined to become "normative Judaism", and it was here that this cleavage became deeper and wider in the next two or three generations between His followers and the synagogue.[2]

[1] Cf. T. W. Manson, *The Teaching of Jesus* (Cambridge, ²1935), pp. 237 ff.
[2] Cf. J. Barr, *Old and New in Interpretation* (London, 1966).

CHAPTER II

APOSTOLIC TRADITION
IN THE NEW TESTAMENT

P AUL, ACCORDING TO ACTS 22:3, WAS EDUCATED IN
Jerusalem at the feet of Gamaliel (the Elder) "according to the strict
manner of the law of our fathers".[1] In his earlier years, he tells the
Galatians, "I advanced in Judaism beyond many of my own age among
my people, so extremely zealous was I for the traditions of my fathers"
(Gal. 1:14). These traditions would include the oral law as handed down
and expounded in the school of Hillel. But with his conversion to Christianity he bade farewell to these traditions and embraced a new principle
of life: for Paul henceforth, in his own words, "to live is Christ"
(Phil. 1:21). That is to say, Torah was displaced from the central place
it had hitherto occupied in his living and thinking: that place was now
occupied by Christ. Paul was not the only convert from Pharisaism to
the way of Christ, but whereas, for many "believers who belonged to
the party of the Pharisees" (Acts 15:5), all that was involved in this new
step was the addition to their existing tenets of belief in Jesus as the
Messiah, Paul's conversion was a radical revolution which brought
with it a complete reorientation of his life. The "law of Moses from
Sinai" gave way to what, in his own words, he "received (*paralambanō*)
from the Lord" (I Cor. 11:23). This new "tradition" stemmed not
from Moses but from Christ. The links in the chain are naturally fewer
and more reliably ascertainable, if only because of the far shorter lapse
of time between the origin of the new "tradition" and Paul's receiving
it.

The Tradition of Christ

When we examine Paul's references to the tradition of Christ, it appears
to have comprised three main elements:
  (a) a summary of the Christian message, expressed as a confession
    of faith, with special emphasis on the death and resurrection of
    Christ;
  (b) various deeds and words of Christ;
  (c) ethical and procedural rules for Christians.[2]

---

[1] See p. 21. On the punctuation of Acts 22:3 and its implications see W. C. van Unnik,
Tarsus or Jerusalem? E. T. (London, 1962), pp. 6 ff.
[2] Cf. R. P. C. Hanson, *Tradition in the Early Church* (London, 1962), pp. 10 ff.

B   29

The Christian Message

(a) The Christian message is the subject-matter of tradition in a passage where Paul tells the Christians of Thessalonica how thankful he is that, "when you received (*paralambanō*) the word of God which you heard from us, you accepted it not as the word of men but as what it really is, the word of God, which is at work in you believers" (I Thess. 2:13). The genuineness of the Thessalonians' acceptance and belief was shown by their readiness to endure persecution for the gospel's sake, as their fellow-believers in Judaea had done.

The outstanding example of the language of tradition in reference to a summary of the message, expressed as a confession of faith, is the first paragraph of I Corinthians 15, where Paul reminds the Christians at Corinth of the gospel which he preached to them when first he came to their city – "which you received (*paralambanō*), in which you stand, by which you are saved, if you hold it fast – unless you believed in vain". This message, common ground to Paul and the Twelve, with James and "all the apostles" – "whether then it was I or they, so we preach and so you believed" (verse 11) – was both "received" and "delivered" by Paul: "for", says he, "I delivered (*paradidōmi*) to you as of first importance what I also received (*paralambanō*), that Christ died for our sins in accordance with the scriptures, that he was buried, that he was raised on the third day in accordance with the scriptures, and that he appeared…" (verses 3–5). There follows a list of resurrection appearances – "to Cephas, then to the twelve . . . to more than five hundred brethren at one time . . . to James, then to all the apostles" (verses 5–7) – all of which Paul had presumably "received" from informants who were in Christ before himself. To these he adds one appearance of the risen Lord which he had not "received" in this sense but experienced directly and personally: "Last of all, as to one untimely born, he appeared also to me" (verse 8). But while he had not "received" this from others, he could and did "deliver" it to others, so that henceforth it was part of the *paradosis*. This, then, is a "tradition" originating with Paul, so far as the chain of human transmission is concerned, although Paul would say that it originated with the risen Lord, revealed to him on the Damascus road.[1]

Even in the summary preceding "Last of all . . . he appeared also to me" it had been thought that Paul makes a contribution of his own to the *paradosis,* where he says that it was "for our sins" that Christ died.[2] This is a note, it is pointed out, which is absent from the early summaries of the apostolic preaching in Acts: "forgiveness of sins" through Christ is proclaimed in them (Acts 2:38; 3:19; 5:31; 10:43) but is not brought into

[1] Cf. G. Widengren, "Tradition and Literature in Early Judaism and in the Early Church", *Numen* 10 (1963), pp. 79 ff.
[2] Cf. Widengren, *ibid.*, p. 79: "This statement clearly is a theological interpretation of the tradition."

close association with His death. On the other hand, a passage like Rom.
4:24 f., "Jesus our Lord, who was delivered to death for our trespasses
and raised for our justification", may be regarded with high probability
as a quotation from a confession not formulated by Paul.[1] The interpretation of the death of Christ in terms of the passion of the Servant in
Isa. 52:13–53:12, whose language is echoed in these words, is quite
certainly pre-Pauline,[2] and there is no conclusive argument for excluding
the phrase "for our sins" from the message that Paul "received", especially
as it is difficult not to recognize Isa. 52:13–53:12 as foremost among the
"scriptures" in accordance with which Christ is said to have died.

One question is raised acutely by Paul's description of the gospel which
he "delivered" to his converts as something which in turn he himself had
"received": how is such a statement to be reconciled with his emphatic
declaration elsewhere that the gospel came to him as a direct revelation,
through no human intermediary? "For I did not receive (*paralambanō*)
it from man", he tells the churches of Galatia, "nor was I taught it, but
it came through a revelation of Jesus Christ" (Gal. 1:12). It might indeed
be argued that when in I Cor. 15:3 he says "I delivered to you . . . what
I also received" he means "what I received by revelation of Jesus Christ" –
after all, tradition must start somewhere, and why not on the Damascus
road? – but this argument is difficult to sustain, because it would imply
that it was by revelation that Paul learned about the resurrection appearances to Peter, James and the others, and few, if any, will go so far as this.

The gospel which Paul received without mediation on the Damascus
road consisted in the revelation not of a fact but of a person – Jesus the
risen Lord. God, he says, "was pleased to reveal his Son to me, in order
that I might preach him among the Gentiles" (Gal. 1:16) – in these words,
incidentally, he shows how closely his conversion and his call to the
Gentile apostolate coincided in time. Others had come to know Jesus as
the risen Lord before Paul did, but it was not from their testimony that
Paul derived this personal knowledge for himself. On the other hand, the
historical events of Holy Week and Easter and the following days were
communicated to him by those who had experienced them at first hand:
in this sense he "received" the gospel from others.

Another reconciliation of the tension between the gospel as revelation
and the gospel as tradition in Paul's experience is propounded by Professor
Oscar Cullmann. In fact, to his mind the problem is an unreal one because
of the utter identification of the earthly Jesus with the exalted Lord in the
thinking of Paul and the other apostles. What was derived from the

---

[1] Cf. A. M. Hunter, *Paul and his Predecessors* (London, ²1961), pp. 30 ff.
[2] The phrase "was delivered up for our trespasses" (Rom. 4:25, in the more literal RV
rendering) could almost be the exact Greek translation of a phrase in the Aramaic Targum of
Isa. 53:5; the verb "deliver up" is used of the Servant in two other places in the Targum of
that chapter (verses 6, 12).

earthly Jesus and was transmitted through the apostles was at the same time continuously validated by the exalted Lord through His Spirit in the apostles, so that revelation and apostolic tradition are but two sides of one coin. Jesus does not figure simply in apostolic tradition as Moses does in rabbinic tradition: as the ever-living Christ He maintains and authenticates the tradition throughout the apostolic age until it ceases to be oral tradition and becomes Holy Scripture. Tradition is thus one way in which the risen Lord imparts His revelation through the Spirit.[1]

So far as Paul's "receiving" the account of resurrection appearances is concerned, we are not left to speculate about an occasion when this might have taken place: he indicates a most appropriate occasion when he tells the Galatians how, three years after his conversion, he went up to Jerusalem to make Peter's acquaintance and during the fifteen days that he stayed with him "saw none of the other apostles except James the Lord's brother" (Gal. 1:18 f.). Since among the resurrection appearances listed in I Cor. 15:5–7 he mentions two only which were granted to individuals, these individuals being Peter and James, the question when and from whom he acquired this information is not difficult to answer.[2]

Deeds and Words of Christ

(b) Paul shows himself familiar with various sayings of Jesus which, in one form or another, have been independently preserved in our gospel tradition. Jesus' ruling on the divorce question,[3] for example, was part of the tradition which the Corinthians received, either at an earlier stage or (at latest) when Paul dealt with this subject in his correspondence with them: "To the married I give charge, not I but the Lord, that the wife should not separate from her husband . . . and that the husband should not divorce his wife" (I Cor. 7:10 f.). To this dominical ruling Paul adds his own gloss (if the wife does separate, "let her remain single or else be reconciled to her husband") and his own exceptive clause, relating to the special missionary situation, not contemplated in the original setting of our Lord's words, in which one party to the marriage has become a Christian and the other treats this conversion as ground for dissolving the marriage tie: "in such a case the brother or sister is not bound" (I Cor. 7:12–16). Even so, he takes care not to represent his own interpretation or exception as a "tradition from the Lord". Again, he appeals to the

---

[1] O. Cullmann, "The Tradition", in *The Early Church* (London, 1956), pp. 66 ff.

[2] For the view that Paul combines two streams of tradition which he "received", one (Galilaean) stemming from Peter and the other (Jerusalem) stemming from James, cf. A. Harnack, *Sitzungsbericht der preussischen Akademie der Wissenschaften, phil.-hist. Klasse* (1922), pp. 62 ff., and B. W. Bacon, *The Apostolic Message* (New York, 1925), pp. 132 ff.; *The Story of Jesus* (London, 1928), pp. 304 ff.

[3] Mark 10:2 ff.; see pp. 26 f.

Lord's authority for laying down the principle that "those who proclaim the gospel should get their living by the gospel" (I Cor. 9:14), paralleled in the gospel tradition in the commissions to the Twelve (Matt. 10:11–13; Luke 9:4) and to the Seventy: "the labourer deserves his wages" (Luke 10:7; cf. I Tim. 5:18).

Eucharistic Origins

Paul's fullest quotation of sayings of Jesus comes in his narrative of the institution of the Eucharist, of which he says, "I received *(paralambanō)* from the Lord *(apo tou kyriou)* what I also delivered *(paradidōmi)* to you" (I Cor. 11:23). It has been argued that the use of the preposition *apo* in the phrase "from the Lord"[1] indicates transmission of the information through one or more intermediaries, whereas *para* with the genitive would have ruled out such mediation. This is doubtful: what *is* important is the use of the terminology of tradition, *paralambanō* and *paradidōmi*.[2] At the same time, Paul makes it plain that the Lord is the ultimate authority for the tradition of which he reminds the Corinthians; here, if anywhere, we find justification for the title of an important article on this subject by Oscar Cullmann: "*Kyrios* as Designation for the Oral Tradition concerning Jesus."[3] Paul did receive direct visions and revelations from the Lord, but these did not take the form of information about incidents which were already known to eyewitnesses who could tell Paul about them. Here too it is difficult to think of a more probable informant than Peter, during the fifteen days that Paul spent with him in Jerusalem in or around A.D. 35.[4]

A comparison of Paul's account of the institution with those in the Synoptic Gospels throws some interesting light on the growth of tradition: the main deeds and words are fixed, but interpretative glosses are added and conflation is practised, just as happens to this day both in churches which have a liturgically prescribed form of words for the communion service and in those where considerable freedom is exercised by the celebrant. The Pauline account bears a close resemblance to the longer text of Luke 22:19 f. (translated in the footnotes of RSV and NEB), but repeats the injunction "Do this in remembrance of me" after the institution

---

[1] Cod. D. reads παρά.

[2] Cf. F. Büchsel, *s.v.* παράδοσις, *TDNT* ii, E.T. (Grand Rapids, 1964), p. 173 with n. 11 (where further references are given).

[3] *SJT* 3 (1950), pp. 180 ff.

[4] In view of the evidence of Gal. 1:18 ff., it is strange that some scholars should maintain that Paul received the traditions to which he refers in I Cor. 11:23 ff.; 15:3 ff., not in Jerusalem but in some centre of Hellenistic Christianity, such as Damascus or Syrian Antioch (so, e.g., W. Heitmüller, "Zum Problem Paulus und Jesus", *ZNW* 13, 1912, pp. 320 ff., especially p. 331; M. Dibelius, *From Tradition to Gospel*, E. T., London, 1934, p. 29). This is not a valid inference from Gal. 1:12.

of the cup as well as that of the bread, and omits the words "which is poured out for you" from the institution of the cup. Whereas the Markan account speaks of "my covenant blood" (Mark 14:24), Paul (with the longer Lukan text) adds "new" before "covenant", thus making explicit what is in any case implicit. The longer Lukan text changes Mark's "for many" (an allusion, probably, to Isa. 53:11 f.) to "for you", assimilating the words over the cup to those over the bread and in both instances directly identifying the communicants as those for whom Jesus' life was given. Matthew, for his part, retains Mark's "for many" but adds the epexegetic phrase "for the remission of sins" (Matt. 26:28).

The later forms of the New Testament text reflect the process of liturgical formulation; thus the AV of I Cor. 11:24 represents a text which prefaced "This is my body" with "Take, eat" (from Matt. 26:26)[1] and amplified "which is for you" to "which is broken for you".[2]

One of the earliest forms of eucharistic service to have come down to us is that in the *Apostolic Tradition* of Hippolytus (early third century), where Paul's account of the institution is incorporated in the prayer of thanksgiving as follows:

> . . . thy beloved Servant Jesus Christ . . . who when he was betrayed *to voluntary suffering that he might abolish death and rend the bonds of the devil and tread down hell and enlighten the righteous and establish the ordinance and demonstrate the resurrection,* taking bread and giving thanks *to thee* said, "Take, eat; this is my body which is broken for you [for the remission of sins]." Likewise also the cup, saying, "This is my blood *which is shed for you:* when you do this [you] do it in remembrance of me."[3]

The opening part of the passage is considerably amplified by the inclusion of the italicized words; the words spoken over the cup are abbreviated.

Or we may compare two later liturgical texts, where similarly the added words are italicized. First, from the Prayer of Consecration in the Roman Missal:

> . . . our Lord Jesus Christ: who the day before he suffered took bread *into his holy and venerable hands,* and *with his eyes lifted up to heaven unto thee, God, his Almighty Father,* giving thanks *to thee,* he *blessed,* broke *and gave it to his disciples,* saying, "Take and eat ye *all of this, for* this is my body." In like manner, after he had supped, taking also *this excellent* chalice *into his holy and venerable hands; also giving thanks to thee, he blessed and gave it to his disciples,* saying, "*Take and drink ye all of this; for* this is the chalice of my blood, of the new *and eternal*

---

[1] "Take, eat" is added in the Byzantine text and by a few other authorities.
[2] The Latin, Coptic and Armenian versions have "is given for you"; this may be as much a matter of idiomatic translation as of assimilation to Luke 22:19 (longer text).
[3] *Apostolic Tradition* 4:4–10; cf. G. Dix (ed.), *The Apostolic Tradition of St Hippolytus* (London, 1937), pp. 7 ff. See p. 126.

testament; *the mystery of faith, which shall be shed for you and for many for the remission of sins.* As often as ye shall do these things, ye shall do them in remembrance of me."

And again, from the corresponding passage in the Book of Common Prayer:

... Our Saviour Jesus Christ ...: who, in the same night that he was betrayed, took Bread; and, when he had given thanks, he brake it, and *gave it to his disciples,* saying, Take, eat, this is my Body which is given for you: Do this in remembrance of me. Likewise after supper he took the Cup; *and, when he had given thanks, he gave it to them,* saying, *Drink ye all of this for* this is my Blood of the New Testament, *which is shed for you and for many for the remission of sins:* Do this, as oft as ye shall drink it, in remembrance of me.[1]

In both these liturgies we note, among other things, the expansion of the Pauline text of the words spoken over the cup by the Matthaean "which is shed for many for the remission of sins", the phrase "for many" being further conflated with the (longer) Lukan "for you".[2]

As for "non-liturgical" communion services, it is quite common to hear Paul's concluding comment, "For as often as you eat this bread and drink the cup, you proclaim the Lord's death until he comes" (I Cor. 11:26), adapted to the style of a dominical utterance: " ... my death until I come". This is not completely inept, because Paul's comment is itself the transposition into a different eschatological idiom of the Lord's words in the Gospels: "I shall not eat it [the Passover] until it is fulfilled in the kingdom of God. ... from now on I shall not drink of the fruit of the vine until the kingdom of God comes" (Luke 22:16, 18).[3] But the text of I Cor. 11:26 is too firmly fixed for its transmission to be affected by such an unofficial adaptation: the adaptation remains oral or, at most, is reflected in hymns, as in Horatius Bonar's lines:

> For the words that tell of home,
> Pointing us beyond the tomb,
> "Do ye this until I come",
>   We give Thee thanks, O Lord.

[1] The *Order for Holy Communion* (Alternative Services: Second Series), authorized for experimental use in the Church of England for not more than four years from July 7, 1967, follows the Book of Common Prayer closely here, but adds "to thee" after each of the two occurrences of "when he had given thanks".

[2] The Book of Common Order of the Church of Scotland (Oxford, 1940) also conflates the texts in its Order for the Lord's Supper, where the minister is directed to say to the communicants: "Take ye, eat ye; this is the body of Christ which is broken for you: do this in remembrance of Him ... This cup is the new covenant in the blood of Christ, which is shed for many unto remission of sins: drink ye all of it."

[3] Cf. Mark 14:25, "I shall not drink again of the fruit of the vine until that day when I drink it new in the kingdom of God".

Nevertheless, we have here a good illustration of the important part played by liturgical practice in the development of tradition.

Ethical Teaching

(c) Paul's account of the institution of the Eucharist comes in the course of his reply to a letter from the Corinthians in a section which begins, "I commend you because you remember me in everything and maintain the traditions even as I have delivered (*paradidōmi*) them to you" (I Cor. 11:2). Presumably they had said in their letter to him, "We remember you in everything and maintain the traditions even as you have delivered them to us." To which he replies in effect: "That's fine; I commend you. But, if all I hear is true, you do not invariably maintain the traditions as I delivered them to you, because with regard to the conduct of women in your church services you deviate from the custom approved by myself and observed by the churches generally (I Cor. 11:16) and at the communion table you behave in a way that denies the whole meaning of that sacred occasion. Shall I commend you in this? No, I will not" (I Cor. 11:17–22).[1]

Here the traditions cover a fairly wide range of ethical and procedural rules, embracing not only liturgical practice but Christian morality and convention.

"As . . . you received (*paralambanō*) Christ Jesus the Lord," the Colossian Christians are exhorted by Paul, "so live in him, rooted and built up in him and established in the faith, just as you were taught . . ." (Col. 2:6 f.). This "tradition of Christ" had regard to doctrine and practice alike: on the side of doctrine, it was calculated to guard them against every "human tradition" (Col. 2:8) and perversion of the gospel like the Colossian heresy which was infiltrating into their midst; on the side of practice, it is spelt out in the ethical directions of Col. 3:5–4:6, grouped under the captions "Put off" (3:5–11), "Put on" (3:12–17), "Be subject" (3:18–4:1), "Watch and pray" (4:2–6). Whether or not the language about "putting off" old vices and "putting on" new virtues was associated with symbolic exchanging of old garments for new at one's baptism, such an ethical catechesis as this, fragments of which are quoted or reflected in various parts of the New Testament, appears to have been current from an early date in the church.[2] This catechesis constituted a *paradosis* of practical teaching such as Paul could safely assume the Roman Christians had learned when, as he says in Rom. 6:17, "you have become obedient from the heart to the standard of teaching to which you were committed"

---

[1] Cf., however, J. C. Hurd, *The Origin of I Corinthians* (London, 1965), pp. 78 ff., 182 ff.

[2] Cf. E. G. Selwyn, *The First Epistle of Peter* (London, 1946), pp. 363 ff.; C. H. Dodd, *Gospel and Law* (Cambridge, 1951), *passim;* G. B. Caird, *The Apostolic Age* (London, 1955), pp. 109 ff.

- or "to the form of teaching which you were delivered" (passive of *paradidōmi*).[1]

To a similar effect the Thessalonian Christians are enjoined (with special reference to sexual morality) "that as you received *(paralambanō)* from us how you ought to live and to please God, just as you are doing, you do so more and more; for you know what instructions we gave you through the Lord Jesus" (I Thess. 4:1 f.).

Another aspect of this ethical catechesis is found in II Thess. 3:6, where the same Thessalonians are told to "keep away from any brother who is living in idleness and not in accord with the tradition which you received *(paralambanō)* from us". In the context this injunction refers to the very practical duty of earning an honest livelihood and not living at the expense of others. In this respect, the apostle goes on, "you yourselves know how you ought to imitate us" (3:7); by example as well as by precept he and his companions gave their converts this direction: "If any one will not work, let him not eat" (3:10).

This appeal to personal example is a note that recurs in the letters of Paul, and is bound up with the tradition of which he speaks. "What you have learned and received *(paralambanō)* and heard and seen in me, do" (Phil. 4:9). Like all authentic Christian tradition, this too derives its authority from the earthly Jesus who is now the heavenly Lord: "Be imitators of me, as I am of Christ" (I Cor. 11:1).[2]

Whereas western Christians tend to set "scripture" and "tradition" over against each other, as though tradition were oral only and not written,[3] there is no reason why tradition should not take written form. If it is apostolic tradition, in due course it takes written form and becomes apostolic scripture. Whether Paul's teaching was given orally or in writing, it equally carried apostolic authority; hence he can encourage the Thessalonian Christians to "stand firm and hold to the traditions which you were taught by us, either by word of mouth or by letter" (II Thess. 2:15).

In the Johannine letters the technical language of apostolic tradition is not used, but the same idea is present in the emphasis on "that which was from the beginning", which is confirmed to a later generation of Christians by the last survivors of the original eyewitnesses, so that believers of more recent date may be established in the true divine fellowship (I John 1:1–3). "If what you heard from the beginning abides in you, then you will abide in the Son and in the Father" (I John 2:24). Any pretended advance on this is really a departure from it, and is therefore to be refused. "Any one who goes ahead and does not abide in the doctrine of Christ does not have God; he who abides in the doctrine has both the Father and

[1] Cf. A. M. Hunter, *Paul and his Predecessors*[2], pp. 52 ff.
[2] Cf. W. P. De Boer, *The Imitation of Paul* (Kampen, 1962).
[3] See pp. 163 ff.

the Son. If any one comes to you and does not bring this doctrine, do not receive him into the house or give him any greeting; for he who greets him shares his wicked work" (II John 9 f.).

Elsewhere in the later New Testament documents the apostolic tradition acquires more definitely fixed lineaments: it is "the faith which was once for all delivered *(paradidōmi,* passive) to the saints" (Jude 3).[1] In the Pastoral Epistles a more concrete word than *paradosis* is used to denote this body of tradition – *parathēkē*, "deposit". Twice Timothy is charged to "guard the deposit" – the "good deposit" which has been entrusted to him (I Tim. 6:20; II Tim. 1:14). Not only must he guard it; he must deliver it to others – a charge which is expressed by the verb *paratithemai,* corresponding to the noun *parathēkē.* As Paul entrusts *(paratithemai)* this charge to Timothy (I Tim. 1:18), so Timothy in his turn must hand on the torch: "what you have heard from me before many witnesses entrust *(paratithemai)* to faithful men who will be able to teach others also" (II Tim. 2:2). Here we have four steps in a teaching succession – (i) Paul, (ii) Timothy, (iii) "faithful men" and (iv) "others also" – and so, towards the end of the New Testament period, provision is made for the maintenance of the apostolic tradition generation by generation.

---

[1] Cf. II Peter 2:21, with its references to those who have left "the way of righteousness" and "the holy commandment delivered to them".

CHAPTER III

TRADITION AND THE GOSPEL

THAT THE GOSPEL – THE GOOD NEWS OF GOD'S SAVING act in Christ – was originally delivered from one to another by word of mouth is so self-evident as hardly to require saying. "It was declared at first by the Lord," says the writer to the Hebrews, "and it was attested to us by those who heard him" (Heb. 2:3). Paul, as we have seen, uses the technical language of tradition to describe its transmission (I Cor. 15:3),[1] and we have graphic pictures of the process in action in the Acts of the Apostles. From Acts and the earlier New Testament epistles we can derive some idea of the content and presentation of the gospel before ever there was a written "Gospel".[2] But it has been a major preoccupation of New Testament students for the past fifty years and more to scrutinize the written Gospels in order to find some evidence not simply of earlier written sources such as their predecessors identified but of layers of oral tradition between the primary event and the extant record.

This preoccupation has left its mark in the titles of many Gospel studies belonging to this period, such as *The History of the Synoptic Tradition* (R. Bultmann),[3] *From Tradition to Gospel* (M. Dibelius),[4] *The Formation of the Gospel Tradition* (V. Taylor),[5] *The Gospel Tradition and its Beginnings* (H. Riesenfeld),[6] *Historical Tradition in the Fourth Gospel* (C. H. Dodd),[7] *Jesus and the Gospel Tradition* (C. K. Barrett),[8] *The Tendencies of the Synoptic Tradition* (E. P. Sanders).[9]

Oral Tradition

It may be relevant to compare the nature and process of tradition in this context with oral tradition as it is understood by Old Testament students. The various elements in early Hebrew tradition are viewed as being originally associated each with a particular time and place. But in the form

---

[1] As also does Luke: "the things which have been accomplished among us . . . *were delivered* (παραδίδωμι) to us by those who from the beginning were eyewitnesses and ministers of the word" (Luke 1:1 f.).

[2] Cf. C. H. Dodd, *The Apostolic Preaching and its Developments* (London, ²1944).

[3] E. T. (Oxford, 1963) of *Die Geschichte der synoptischen Tradition* (Göttingen, ²1931).

[4] E. T. (London, 1934) of *Die Formgeschichte des Evangeliums* (Tübingen, ²1933).

[5] London, 1933.

[6] London, 1957 (see pp. 67 f.).

[7] Cambridge, 1963.

[8] London, 1967.

[9] Cambridge, 1969 (see pp. 72 f.). A more comprehensive study (albeit with primary reference to the OT) is K. Koch, *The Growth of the Biblical Tradition*, E. T. (London, 1969).

in which these traditional elements have been preserved, they have been
dissociated from their original life-settings and been incorporated in one
or another of the literary compositions which make up the Old Testament. Literary criticism concentrates on the end-product, which is the
one fixed datum available to us, but in view of the great increase in historical knowledge of the context of Hebrew and Israelite origins it is
possible for historical criticism to try to reconstruct the original form of
an individual tradition, attaching it to its primary time and place. In
addition, what is called the "traditio-historical" approach, specially
pursued by Scandinavian scholars, endeavours to trace the development
of the tradition, stage by stage, from its primary life-setting to its final
literary presentation.[1]

   This we can understand very well in relation to the narratives of the
patriarchs and the judges, many of which embody *hieroi logoi* associated
with various sanctuaries. We think, for example, of the association of
Abraham with Shechem and Hebron, of Isaac with Beersheba, of Jacob
with Bethel and Shechem, of Gideon with Ophrah.[2] We can understand
it also in the setting of the smaller and larger units of community life in
Israel – the family, the clan, the tribe, the amphictyony (if it is still permitted to use this word)[3] – and in the setting of the principal epochs of
Israel's history: the Exodus, the wilderness wanderings, the settlement,
the monarchy, the Assyrian threat, the Josianic reformation, the exile, the
return, the Maccabaean crisis. We can understand it, too, when we think
of the determinant role of the cult in the transmission of the mighty acts
of God in the deliverance from Egypt and conquest of Canaan.[4] The
recognition of the true life-setting of the successive phases is necessary
to the true interpretation of the material received and delivered by one
generation after another.

Oral Tradition and Eyewitness Testimony

   When we turn to the New Testament, we are faced with a different
situation. The period of the New Testament covers fewer decades than the

[1] Cf. E. Nielsen, *Oral Tradition* (London, 1954); *The Ten Commandments in New Perspective*,
E. T. (London, 1965), pp. x, 94 ff. *et passim*.
[2] Cf. R. Brinker, *The Influence of Sanctuaries in Early Israel* (Manchester, 1946).
[3] The word "amphictyony" is applied in Greek history to a league of city-states which
met periodically at a common sanctuary (e.g. the temple of Apollo at Delphi) to celebrate
a festival and transact business of joint concern. The members were bound to observe certain
principles of inter-state right which had to be observed under protection of the deity even in
time of war. By analogy the term has been applied to the covenant community of the tribes
of Israel with their central sanctuary at Shiloh or elsewhere. "The comparison is helpful,
provided we do not press it too far and try to find all the features of the Greek amphictyonies
in the Israelite federation" (R. de Vaux, *Ancient Israel*, E. T., London, 1961, p. 93).
[4] Cf. G. von Rad, *Old Testament Theology*, E. T., i, ii (Edinburgh, 1962, 1965), where the
attempt is made to find the basis of OT theology in the repeated proclamation of these mighty
works in Israel's worship.

Old Testament period covers centuries. At the end of the first century A.D. a few eyewitnesses of the ministry of Jesus were still alive, and very many more who had known eyewitnesses and heard them describe what they had seen and heard. This makes a difference which is too often overlooked by Gospel form critics.

We know, of course, how tradition can grow within quite a short space of time, to the point where even eyewitnesses "remember" the account given by tradition and not what actually took place before their eyes and ears. Under the Hitler régime in Germany a noble tradition was fostered of the selfless devotion, heroism and martyrdom of one Horst Wessel, from whom the anthem of the Nazi party, the "Horst Wessel hymn", received its name. Many people in Germany, and others elsewhere, did not take the traditional account at face-value, because they had access to other sources of information about Horst Wessel which they regarded, with good reason, as more objective. But one can readily imagine a turn of events which would have led to the suppression of unworthier versions of his life-story and to the exaltation of the party legend to the status of an undisputed *hieros logos*.

Even so, the availability of eyewitness recollection imposes a certain check on the free development of tradition. In a radio address broadcast in 1949, Professor Dodd said that in his younger days he felt the gap of some thirty-five years between the events recorded in the Gospel of Mark and the writing of the Gospel to be "a very serious matter". Later on he suddenly realized that thirty-five years did not seem at all such a long time: he and his contemporaries in 1949 had a vivid memory of the events of the summer of 1914, leading to the outbreak of World War I (just as today many of us have a vivid memory of the events of the 1930s, leading to the outbreak of World War II). "When Mark was writing," he said, "there must have been many people about who were in their prime under Pontius Pilate, and they must have remembered the stirring and tragic events of that time at least as vividly as we remember 1914.[1] If anyone had tried to put over an entirely imaginary or fictitious account of them, there would have been middle-aged or elderly people who would have said (as you or I might say) 'You are wasting your breath: I remember it as if it were yesterday!'"[2]

This commonsense approach to the situation should be kept in mind; for lack of it, some form critics led Vincent Taylor to remark, over thirty years ago, that if they were right, "the disciples must have been translated to heaven immediately after the Resurrection".[3]

[1] Or, bringing the reference up to date, as vividly as people of fifty years old and upward today remember 1939. Some of us remember the course of European history from 1933 to 1945 well enough, without the aid of reference books, to recognize immediately a distorted account of these years.
[2] *About the Gospels* (Cambridge, 1950), pp. 13 ff.
[3] *The Formation of the Gospel Tradition* (London, 1933), p. 41.

Form Criticism

Form criticism is the analytical study of the "forms" assumed by various categories of tradition, especially in its oral, preliterary phase. The German word *Formgeschichte* ("form history") suggests, as the English "form criticism" does not, a study of the *history* of the tradition as revealed by the development of its "forms". While the term *Formgeschichte* does not appear to have been current in the field of Gospel criticism until the publication in 1919 of Martin Dibelius's *Die Formgeschichte des Evangeliums*, the discipline itself was not new. The similar term *Formengeschichte* occurs in the sub-title of Eduard Norden's *Agnostos Theos* (Leipzig, 1912): *Untersuchungen zur Formengeschichte religiöser Rede* ("Inquiries into the *history of the forms* of religious speech"). So far as the Gospels are concerned, some of the most familiar characteristics of the form-critical approach were anticipated at the beginning of this century by Allan Menzies, Professor of Biblical Criticism in the University of St. Andrews, in his book *The Earliest Gospel* (London, 1901). Here we find features which are commonplace in the present-day treatment of the Gospels: emphasis on the lack of continuity in the Markan narrative, the part played by Christian meetings in the growth of the gospel tradition, first in its oral and then in its written phase, an attempt to ascertain the "state of the tradition before Mark wrote", and so forth.

The pioneer of form criticism in the study of the Bible was Hermann Gunkel, who applied it to biblical literature in his *Schöpfung und Chaos in Urzeit und Endzeit* (Göttingen, 1895), a form-critical comparison of Genesis 1 and Revelation 12. Gunkel's most fruitful application of this method (which others had already applied to the heroic traditions of Greece and Northern Europe) was to the Psalter, which he classified according to the types *(Gattungen)* of composition represented in the collection, assigning to each type its life-setting – a life-setting almost invariably to be found in Israel's national worship.[1] It is perhaps no accident that it was Gunkel who awakened in Dibelius an interest in the comparative study of religion.

Part of the business of Gospel form criticism is to classify the component elements in the tradition. One major classification imposes itself at once – the classification into narratives and sayings. Even these two groups of materials cannot be hermetically sealed off from each other, for sayings frequently occur in the context of narratives, and one important "form" consists of a narrative which is told largely for the sake of the epigrammatic saying which constitutes its punch-line. This is the "form"

---

[1] H. Gunkel, *Einleitung in die Psalmen*, ed. J. Begrich (Göttingen, 1933); cf. also S. Mowinckel, *The Psalms in Israel's Worship*, E. T. (Oxford, 1962).

which has been called "paradigm" by Dibelius,[1] "apophthegm" by Bultmann[2] and (more aptly) "pronouncement story" by Vincent Taylor.[3] Examples are the story of Jesus sharing a meal with tax-farmers and other people of ill repute, which drew upon Him the censure of the scribes, concluding with His defence, "Those who are well have no need of a physician, but those who are sick; it was sinners, not the righteous, that I came to call" (Mark 2:15-17),[4] or the incident of the tribute-money, which is recorded on account of His response, "Render to Caesar the things that are Caesar's, and to God the things that are God's" (Mark 12:13-17).[5]

Other narrative forms are miracle stories (in which healing narratives are included)[6] and "stories about Jesus" such as those relating to His baptism, temptation, transfiguration and resurrection.[7] Sometimes these also show features in common with pronouncement stories; thus the healing of the Capernaum paralytic is from one point of view a miracle story but from another it is told for the sake of the statement that "the Son of man has authority on earth to forgive sins" (Mark 2:10), while the point of the temptation narrative lies not in its graphic details but in the threefold rebuttal of the tempter with quotations from Deuteronomy (Matt. 4:4, 7, 10/Luke 4:4, 8, 12).

"Sayings" forms, as distinguished by Bultmann, embrace (i) Wisdom words or *logia*, (ii) prophetic and apocalyptic sayings, (iii) laws and community rules, (iv) sayings introduced by the emphatic pronoun "I" and (v) parables.[8]

These are not the only ways in which the gospel material can be classified: T. W. Manson in *The Teaching of Jesus* classified the sayings according to the various kinds of audience addressed – disciples, Pharisees, the general public[9] – while C. H. Dodd in *History and the Gospel* classified the material in groups according to similarity of subject-matter, each group including distinct "forms" and drawn from various documentary sources.[10] The classification by form is valuable, in Professor Dodd's words, because "it enables us to study our material in fresh groupings, which point to distinct strains of tradition, preserved from various

---

[1] *From Tradition to Gospel*, E. T. (London, 1934), pp. 37 ff.
[2] *The history of the Synoptic Tradition*, E. T. (Oxford, 1963), pp. 11 ff.
[3] *The Formation of the Gospel Tradition*, pp. 30, 63 ff.
[4] See pp. 59 f.
[5] See pp. 62 f.
[6] Cf. Dibelius, *From Tradition to Gospel*, pp. 70 ff., where they are called "tales" (*Novellen* in German); Bultmann, *The History of the Synoptic Tradition*, pp. 209 ff.
[7] Called "legends" by Dibelius (*From Tradition to Gospel*, pp. 104 ff.) and Bultmann (*The History of the Synoptic Tradition*, pp. 244 ff.).
[8] *The History of the Synoptic Tradition*, pp. 69 ff.
[9] *The Teaching of Jesus* (Cambridge, ²1935), pp. 19 ff.: "both as to matter and method the teaching of Jesus is conditioned by the nature of the audience". For an important breakthrough in this direction cf. now J. A. Baird, *Audience Criticism and the Historical Jesus* (Philadelphia, 1969), dedicated appropriately to T. W. Manson, "a man ahead of his time".
[10] *History and the Gospel* (London, 1938), pp. 92 ff. See p. 56, n. 3.

motives, and in some measure through different channels, and to compare these strains of tradition much as we compared Mark and 'Q', in search of convergences and cross-convergences."[1]

Our German colleagues sometimes find fault with British scholars for remaining content with this aspect of form criticism instead of using it as a tool for determining the historicity of the material thus classified.[2] And indeed, if form criticism were merely a matter of classification, we might wonder why so much has been made of it. In a lecture delivered in 1949, but first published (posthumously) in 1962, T. W. Manson expressed himself on this subject in characteristically down-to-earth language. "Strictly," he said, "the term 'form-criticism' should be reserved for the study of the various units of narrative and teaching, which go to make up the Gospels, in respect of their form alone . . . But a paragraph of Mark is not a penny the better or the worse for being labelled 'Apothegm' or 'Pronouncement Story' or 'Paradigm'. In fact if Form-criticism had stuck to its proper business, it would not have made any real stir. We should have taken it as we take the forms of Hebrew poetry or the forms of musical composition."[3]

How then has form criticism departed from its "proper business"? Because, said Manson, it got mixed up with two other things: one was the theory that the narrative of Mark, for the most part, consisted of disconnected units joined together by means of generalizing summaries devoid of any historical value of their own; the other was the doctrine of the life-setting (Sitz im Leben).

In expressing himself thus, Manson was defining form criticism much more narrowly than is commonly done. The theory that Mark's Gospel consisted of disconnected units strung together editorially was adumbrated, as has been said, by Allan Menzies, but it is specially associated with the work of Karl Ludwig Schmidt.[4] Since Schmidt aimed at determining the character of the tradition as it came into Mark's hands, his study is highly relevant to form criticism. So also (perhaps even more so) is the endeavour to establish the life-setting of the component elements in the gospel tradition, since it can shed light on the form which an incident or saying originally took, or on the form in which it was transmitted in the community.

The epoch-making work of K. L. Schmidt on the framework of the gospel story was published in 1919. According to him most of the units in Mark's record, until he reaches the passion narrative, came to him rather like separate bricks, which he joined together with editorial cement,

[1] History and the Gospel, p. 91.
[2] E.g. H. Conzelmann, art. "Jesus Christus", RGG[3] iii (Tübingen, 1959), col. 621; cf. also H. Zahrnt, The Historical Jesus, E. T. (London, 1963), pp. 79 ff.
[3] "The Quest of the Historical Jesus – Continued", Studies in the Gospels and Epistles (Manchester, 1962), pp. 4 ff.
[4] Der Rahmen der Geschichte Jesu (Berlin, 1919).

arranging them according to similarity of topic or their aptness to illustrate some feature of the ministry, since very few of them contained any
indication of time or place by which they could be arranged chronologically. The evangelist smooths the transition from one to another by con-
necting particles such as "again" or his favourite "immediately", or by
short summaries, such as "And he went throughout all Galilee, preaching
in their synagogues and casting out demons" (Mark 1:39). Sometimes
part of his work had been done for him already; for example, the five
"conflict stories" of Mark 2:1–3:6 were probably grouped together
before they came into Mark's hands, perhaps in order to illustrate the
early escalation of controversy between Jesus and the synagogue authorities in Galilee. In a well-known essay, C. H. Dodd argued that the
generalizing summaries isolated by K. L. Schmidt were no invention of
the evangelist but fragments of an outline of the ministry comparable to
fragmentary outlines which can be traced in some of the early kerygmatic
speeches in Acts.[1] Whether this argument can be sustained or not – I
believe it can, despite the critical analysis to which it was subjected in an
essay by D. E. Nineham[2] – it remains true, if a subjective judgement may
be voiced, that the general framework of Mark's gospel suggests a
sequence and development in the story of the ministry too spontaneous
to be artificial and too logical to be accidental. But certainly the work of
Schmidt and others has made it henceforth impossible to treat the individual units fitted into this framework as so chronologically consecutive
and watertight that any material from another source which cannot be
accommodated within the Markan sequence of events must on that
ground alone be regarded as historically suspect.[3]

Life-setting

As for the emphasis on the life-setting of the individual units in the
gospel tradition, we must define more precisely what is meant by their
life-setting. We have to distinguish the original life-setting of narratives
or sayings in the ministry of Jesus from the life-setting in the early church
which influenced the fact and the form of their preservation and repro-
duction.[4] Then we could go on to think of the life-setting in which each

[1] "The Framework of the Gospel Tradition", *Expository Times* 43 (1931–32), pp. 396 ff.,
reprinted in *New Testament Studies* (Manchester, 1953), pp. 1 ff.
[2] "The Order of Events in St Mark's Gospel – An Examination of Dr Dodd's Hypothesis",
Studies in the Gospels: Essays in Memory of R. H. Lightfoot, ed. D. E. Nineham (Oxford, 1958),
pp. 223 ff.
[3] Cf. F. C. Burkitt's argument against the historicity of the raising of Lazarus (John 11) in
The Gospel History and its Transmission (Edinburgh, ²1907), pp. vii ff., 221 ff.
[4] Cf. T. W. Manson, "Is it possible to write a Life of Christ?" *Expository Times* 53 (1941–
42), p. 249: "Of any story or teaching we may ask concerning its 'Sitz im Leben' – is it a
'Sitz im Leben Jesu' or a 'Sitz im Leben der alten Kirche'? It is sometimes overlooked that an
affirmative answer to the latter alternative does *not* automatically carry with it a negative
answer to the former."

of the completed Gospels appeared, not to mention intermediate life-settings which called forth earlier and shorter collections, some of them envisaged as sources drawn upon by our four Evangelists.[1]

This last aspect, especially with regard to the production of the canonical Gospels, is now usually regarded as belonging to the province of "editorial criticism" (*Redaktionsgeschichte*) rather than of form criticism. The distinction between these phases of criticism has been made in other departments of literary study: it is a whole generation, for example, since this approach to Homer was commended by W. J. Woodhouse in *The Composition of Homer's Odyssey* (Oxford, 1930) and C. M. Bowra in *Tradition and Design in the Iliad* (Oxford, 1930). More recently C. K. Barrett has drawn another analogy from the Homeric epics, many of whose peculiar features are due to the crossing of two historical contexts – the Late Bronze Age, in which the fall of Troy and attendant events actually took place, and the Iron Age, in which the tradition was fixed first in oral and then in written form.[2] In the Gospels, of course, the interval is measured in decades and not in centuries, which, as we have seen, makes a substantial difference.

The life-setting on which many (perhaps most) form critics have concentrated in studying the gospel tradition has been the life-setting in the early church. Since the Gospels are all written – self-evidently! – from a post-Easter perspective, they point out, the tradents and Evangelists were more concerned with the "Christ of faith" (the exalted Lord) than with the "Jesus of history", and the context in which the components of the tradition are to be understood is mainly the post-Easter context. Let me in passing stake a claim for the possibility that, in T. W. Manson's words, Jesus "was at least as interesting, *for his own sake,* to people in the first century as he is to historians in the twentieth",[3] and for the thesis (never questioned by some of us, but now being sustained as a novelty by others who were brought up to leave it out of their reckoning) that there is no discontinuity or dichotomy between the church's Lord and the historical Jesus – that, in New Testament language, in one or the other we are alike confronted by "this same Jesus".

But (to go on with tradition and life-setting) "the whole tradition", says Hans Conzelmann, "may be extremely varied in form, but there is an over-riding material unity: in all its forms (confession of faith, narrative about Jesus, words of Jesus) it depicts the Christ of faith."[4] The task of exegesis, as he sees it, is accordingly threefold, as we work back from (a) interpretation of the Gospels in their present form, through (b) interpretation of the tradition which lies behind them, to (c) reconstruction of the proclamation of Jesus.

[1] Cf. C. K. Barrett, *Jesus and the Gospel Tradition* (London, 1967), pp. 12 ff.
[2] *Jesus and the Gospel Tradition*, pp. 3 ff., 14.
[3] *Studies in the Gospels and Epistles*, p. 6.
[4] *An Outline of the Theology of the New Testament*, E. T. (London, 1969), p. 98.

Criteria of Authenticity

These last words recall the title of a work by a very distinguished graduate of my own University of Manchester and a former pupil of T. W. Manson – *Rediscovering the Teaching of Jesus,* by Professor Norman Perrin of Chicago University.[1]

According to Dr. Perrin, the nature of the Synoptic tradition is such that the burden of proof rests on those who would maintain the authenticity of any part of it. He then lays down some criteria of authenticity – primarily (*a*) the criterion of dissimilarity, (*b*) the criterion of coherence and (*c*) the criterion of multiple attestation.

Criterion of Dissimilarity

Of these the first, the criterion of dissimilarity, is most important.[2] It amounts to this: that we can be reasonably sure of the authenticity of any saying (or, for that matter, action)[3] ascribed to Jesus only if it is unparalleled in the early church or in rabbinical tradition. This is being much more stringent than historians usually are with historical figures. If pushed to extremes, it would almost postulate for Jesus the quality of uniqueness assumed in that uninstructed piety which is disturbed when it is suggested that someone else – be it the Teacher of Righteousness or any other person – said or did something similar to what is recorded of Jesus.[4] It is antecedently probable that men and women in the early church were influenced by the teaching of Jesus and repeated it and adapted it to fresh situations; and it is antecedently improbable that Jesus differed at every point from His rabbinical contemporaries. It is, for example, against the considerable area of agreement between Him and the Pharisees that the

---

[1] London, 1967.

[2] Cf. R. Bultmann, *The History of the Synoptic Tradition,* p. 205; E. Käsemann, *Essays on New Testament Themes,* E. T. (London, 1964), p. 37; H. Conzelmann, *RGG*[3] iii, col. 623.

[3] Cf. its application to the miracle stories by R. H. Fuller, *Interpreting the Miracles* (London, 1963), p. 26. In respect of action, it may be added, one feature where the criterion of dissimilarity may have something to say is the absence from the gospel tradition of any miracles of judgement against human beings, like those against Ananias and Sapphira or Elymas the sorcerer (Acts 5:1 ff.; 13:8 ff.), with which may be associated the disciplinary visitations of I Cor. 5:4 f.; 11:30. The nine lepers who (unlike their Samaritan companion) neglected to express due gratitude for their cure (Luke 17:12 ff.) did not on that account get smitten with leprosy all over again, as they would have been in other familiar forms of healing narrative. When on one occasion the disciples suggested the performance of a miracle of judgement according to a precedent set by Elijah, Jesus was shocked that such an idea should have entered their heads (Luke 9:54 f.). The "cursing" of the fig-tree (Mark 11:12 ff.) is not in its origin a miracle of judgement.

[4] Or that uninstructed agnosticism which assumes that Christianity has been dealt a mortal blow if such parallels to the teaching or activity of Jesus can be established. We have had plenty of this sort of obscurantism in recent years in partisan controversy over the Dead Sea Scrolls.

points of cleavage between them stand out so clearly.[1] Rabbinical parallels should be examined with critical scrutiny; where they are not only later than the time of Jesus but later than the composition of the Gospels, it is preposterous on their account alone to deny the authenticity of the version ascribed to Jesus.

Even so, the criterion of dissimilarity is, within limits, a useful instrument. Just as, in a different theological and critical climate, P. W. Schmiedel's nine "pillar-passages" in the Gospels[2] provided a convenient basis for the study of the life and teaching of Jesus because (as he thought) they deviated so much from later Christian tendencies that no one in the post-Easter community was likely to have invented them, so the criterion of dissimilarity commends itself when we compare the issues which the gospel tradition represents as crucial in Jesus' ministry with those which Acts and the epistles represent as crucial in the early church.[3]

For example, sabbath controversies in the Gospels have a more natural life-setting in the ministry of Jesus than in the experience of the church. True, such a dictum as that "the sabbath was made for man, and not man for the sabbath" (Mark 2:28) would be remembered and quoted when necessary, but it stems from a mind which treated the requirements of the law with a sovereign freedom and could distinguish clearly between fundamental principles and temporary applications of these principles. The sabbath does not appear to have constituted a disputed issue in the Palestinian church, perhaps because Christians in first-century Judaea,

---

[1] Cf. P. Winter's conclusion that Jesus "might have been representative of pre-rabbinical Pharisaism not only in his ethical teaching, but also in his eschatology" (On the Trial of Jesus, Berlin, 1961, p. 133), with C. K. Barrett's qualified approval of this assessment (Jesus and the Gospel Tradition, p. 62). That such judgements should commend themselves to scholars who themselves practise form-critical methods indicates how restricted is the validity of the criterion of dissimilarity. Even if these judgements are viewed with some reserve, we may remind ourselves of "the cumulative strength of the arguments adduced by Jewish writers favourable to the authenticity of the discourses in the Fourth Gospel", based especially on the contemporary modes of rabbinical debate which they reflect (I. Abrahams, "Rabbinic Aids to Exegesis", Cambridge Biblical Essays, ed. H. B. Swete, Cambridge, 1909, p. 181; cf. his Studies in Pharisaism and the Gospels i, Cambridge, 1917, p. 12).

[2] Art. "Gospels", Encyclopedia Biblica ii (London, 1901), cols. 1881–1883. The nine passages are (a) about Jesus in general: Mark 10:17 f.; Matt. 12:31 f.; Mark 3:21; Mark 13:32; Mark 15:34 (= Matt. 27:46); (b) about His miracles: Mark 8:12; Mark 6:5 f.; Mark 8:14–21; Matt. 11:5 (= Luke 7:22).

[3] How, in reference to the criterion of dissimilarity, should we decide on the issue raised by S. G. F. Brandon in Jesus and the Zealots (Manchester, 1967) and The Trial of Jesus of Nazareth (London, 1968)? Should sayings which could be interpreted in a near-zealot sense – "I have not come to bring peace, but a sword" (Matt. 10:34), "I came to cast fire upon the earth" (Luke 12:49), "let him who has no sword sell his mantle and buy one" (Luke 22:36) – be rejected because of Zealot parallels? Should injunctions not to resist evil (Matt. 5:39) and to "render to Caesar the things that are Caesar's" (Mark 12:17) be accepted as authentic because they ran counter to contemporary Zealot tendencies? Or (as Professor Brandon himself would argue) in view of the apologetic emphasis of Acts and the positive attitude to the Roman state expressed in Rom. 13:1–7, should the texts which lend themselves to a Zealot interpretation be accepted as "pillar passages" because they are so far out of step with later Christian thought, and the "pacific" passages rejected because they are so completely in line with it? In this area, at any rate, these critical criteria are double-edged weapons.

like Christians in twentieth-century Israel, had little choice but to treat it as a rest-day, not to mention the many observant "zealots for the law"[1] among them who would have sanctified the day on principle. It was more of an issue in the Pauline mission-field, especially where Gentile converts were urged by Judaizing or syncretistic teachers to assume the yoke of the law; hence Paul's criticism of the Galatians for observing "days" (Gal. 4:10) and his admonition to the Colossians: "Let no one pass judgement on you . . . with regard to . . . a sabbath" (Col. 2:16). For himself, the observance or non-observance of the sabbath made no religious difference: "One man esteems one day as better than another, while another man esteems all days alike. Let every one be fully convinced in his own mind" (Rom. 14:5).

This is quite similar to his attitude to circumcision: "in Christ Jesus neither circumcision nor uncircumcision is of any avail, but faith working through love" (Gal. 5:6).[2] Only where circumcision was accepted by Gentile Christians as a religious obligation was the gospel undermined. But, unlike the sabbath-law, circumcision was very much a religious issue in the early church, as Acts and the epistles alike witness. Has this issue left any trace in the Gospels? Do they ascribe to Jesus any pronouncement on circumcision? None.[3]

Or take disputes with regard to marriage and divorce. In view of the debates on this subject in the Palestinian schools, it is not surprising to find our Lord invited to give His ruling.[4] His ruling accords perfectly with the life-setting of the ministry, apart (possibly) from the Matthaean exceptive clauses.[5] The question of marriage and divorce, in a somewhat different form, cropped up in the Pauline mission-field. In so far as the dominical ruling applies to the situations on which his advice was sought by the Corinthian church, Paul quotes it as absolutely binding – "not I but the Lord" (I Cor. 7:10) – but where no such ruling is available he does not invent one; instead, he expresses his own judgement without laying down the law: "I say, not the Lord, . . . I have no command of the Lord, but I give my opinion . . . and I think that I too have the Spirit of God" (I Cor. 7:12, 25, 40). This suggests that rulings arising from the early church situation were not transferred back into the mouth of Jesus so freely as is sometimes argued.[6]

---

[1] Acts 21:20.
[2] Cf. Gal. 6:15; I Cor. 7:19. In line with this attitude is Paul's circumcision of Timothy, as reported in Acts 16:3, which was the regularizing of the social status of one who, as the son of a Jewish mother and brought up in the faith of Israel, was, in Gentile and Jewish eyes alike, a Jew in everything save circumcision.
[3] In the one place in the Gospels where Jesus refers to circumcision He assumes its validity; He does not discuss it (John 7:22 f.; see p. 25).
[4] Mark 10:1–12; see pp. 26 f.
[5] Matt. 5:32; 19:9; see p. 27.
[6] See pp. 32, 64 with n. 2.

The Mission of the Twelve

The Gentile mission, or at least the conditions on which it was to be prosecuted, presented another controversial issue in the early church. While those who opposed it altogether could appeal to the injunction, "Go nowhere among the Gentiles", found only in the Matthaean account of the mission of the Twelve (Matt. 10:5), and those who favoured it could quote the post-resurrection commission, "Go therefore and make disciples of all the nations" (Matt. 28:19),[1] no recorded saying of Jesus bears on the terms on which Gentiles were to be admitted to the community of His disciples. When Peter, in Acts 11:16, defends his action in visiting the house of Cornelius and preaching the gospel to those gathered there, he quotes the post-resurrection logion, "John baptized with water, but you shall be baptized with the Holy Spirit"[2] (cf. Acts 1:5), but there is, of course, no explicit reference to Gentiles here.

It would be difficult to find a life-setting in the early church for the injunction, "enter no town of the Samaritans" (Matt. 10:5) – unless we envisage some opposition by the more conservative party in the Jerusalem church to the evangelization of Samaria by Philip the Hellenist, which in due course received the approval of the apostles (Acts 8:5–25). Indeed, the ban on entering any Samaritan town stand out as an exception in the context of our Lord's ministry, if we consider the more positive references to the Samaritans elsewhere in the Synoptic tradition.[3] As for the Johannine tradition, the Samaritan mission of John 4:30–42 has been thought on the one hand to reflect the Hellenistic mission under Philip,[4] but on the other hand a perfectly natural setting for it has been recognized in the earlier (southern) phase of Jesus' ministry, as a sequel to the activity of John the Baptist and his disciples in the neighbourhood of Shechem (John 3:23):[5] these would then be the "others" into whose labour Jesus' disciples are said to have entered (John 4:38).[6]

The Matthaean account of the mission of the Twelve provides us in other respects with an unusually clear opportunity of distinguishing two or more life-settings. The first paragraph (Matt. 10:5–15), paralleled

---

[1] Cf. Luke 24:47; Acts 1:8. (This commission was given to the Twelve, whose leaders according to Gal. 2:6–9, agreed to concentrate on the evangelization of Jews, not Gentiles.)

[2] Based on John's own declaration: "I have baptized you with water; but he [the Coming One] will baptize you with the Holy Spirit" (Mark 1:8; cf. Matt. 3:11 = Luke 3:16).

[3] Especially in Luke (cf. 10:30 ff.; 17:11 ff.).

[4] Cf. O. Cullmann, "Samaria and the Origins of the Christian Mission", *The Early Church* (London, 1956), pp. 185 ff.

[5] Cf. W. F. Albright, "Recent Discoveries in Palestine and the Gospel of St John", *The Background of the New Testament and its Eschatology*, ed. W. D. Davies and D. Daube (Cambridge, 1954), pp. 153 ff.; *The Archaeology of Palestine* (Harmondsworth, 1960), pp. 244 ff.

[6] Cf. J. A. T. Robinson, "The 'Others' of John 4.38", *Twelve New Testament Studies* (London, 1962), pp. 61 ff.

in part by Mark 6:7-13 and Luke 9:1-5,[1] has its life-setting within the limits of Jesus' Galilaean ministry, of which the mission of the Twelve formed part. But this is followed by a paragraph (verses 16-23) which refers to the conditions of a later period, possibly to the Palestinian and wider Jewish mission of the decades preceding the war of A.D. 66-73, when the missioners would be liable not only to undergo synagogue discipline but to "be dragged before governors and kings . . . to bear testimony before them and the Gentiles" (words which scarcely point to Gentile evangelization in the ordinary sense).[2] This period of activity is to be terminated by the coming of the Son of Man, before the task of evangelizing all "the cities of Israel" has been completely finished[3] – words which, whatever more precise significance they may have, point to a life-setting not later than A.D. 70 for the paragraph which they round off.[4]

In Matt. 10:16-23 there are manifest parallels to passages in Matt. 24:9-14, but those in Matt. 10:16-23 represent an earlier stage of the tradition of these words. For, while Matt. 24:9-14 is dependent on Mark 13:9-13, Matt. 10:16-23 is in some ways more primitive than Mark 13:9-13,[5] and may even be related to one of the sources from which the document underlying Mark 13 was composed about A.D. 40, to encourage Jewish Christians to meet the crisis precipitated in that year by the Emperor Gaius's decree for the erection of his statue in the Jerusalem temple.[6]

Verba Christi

The use of the designation "the Son of Man" in the gospel tradition (Synoptic and Johannine) is an outstanding instance of the usefulness of the criterion of dissimilarity; as is well known, it is found only once in the New Testament outside the Gospels[7] and it does not appear to have

[1] Cf. also the mission of the Seventy (Luke 10:1-20).

[2] Cf. K. Kundsin, "Primitive Christianity in the Light of Gospel Research", E. T. in R. Bultmann and K. Kundsin, Form Criticism, ed. F. C. Grant (New York, ²1962), pp. 107 ff.

[3] Matt. 10:23 – the pivot text for A. Schweitzer, The Quest of the Historical Jesus, E. T. (London, 1910).

[4] Cf. the similar language of Matt. 16:23 (where we have a Vorlage for comparison in Mark 9:1, as we have not in Matt. 10:23).

[5] Cf. B. S. Easton, Christ in the Gospels (New York, 1930), pp. 19 ff.

[6] The view is taken here that the dominical logia of Mark 13:5-37 were collected and published around A.D. 40, because the crisis which they foretold was thought to have been inaugurated by Gaius's decree, and that this publication was later incorporated in the Gospel of Mark. It does not follow that the interpretation of these logia as a prophecy of the events of A.D. 40 corresponds to their original intention. On the interpretation of the passage cf. G. R. Beasley-Murray, Jesus and the Future (London, 1954); A Commentary on Mark Thirteen (London, 1957).

[7] Acts 7:56 (the reading "Son of God" in P⁷⁴, 491, 614, is scarcely to be preferred, despite its advocacy by G. D. Kilpatrick, Theologische Zeitschrift 21, 1965, p. 209). See my This is That (Exeter, 1969), pp. 26 ff.; the corporate aspect of the Son of Man underlines the continuity of Jesus both with the old Israel and with the new.

been current in the early church. On the other hand, the title "Son of David" became one of the most regular designations for Jesus from the earliest days of the church, but no claim to Davidic descent is present in His recorded teaching. He does not appear to have repudiated the title when it was given to Him, as by Bartimaeus of Jericho,[1] but on the only occasion when He is recorded as raising the subject Himself, He suggests that Messiah is David's Lord rather than David's son.[2]

Evidently among the Jews of His day, and equally among His followers after His death and resurrection, Messiahship and Davidic sonship were synonymous. And in view of the regular application to Jesus of the title Messiah or Christ by Christians, both early and late, to the point where it became practically an alternative personal name for Him, it is the more striking that in the Gospels He does not use it of Himself.[3] When Peter, at Caesarea Philippi, says "You are the Christ", Jesus immediately charges him and the other disciples to maintain strict silence about it (Mark 8:29 f.) and if, at His trial, He answers the high priest's question "Are you the Christ?" with "I am", He proceeds at once to define the sense in which He admits Messiahship – a sense in which the claim to David's throne plays no part.[4] This reticence on His part forms such a contrast to the claims made for Him by His followers that, to judge by the criterion of dissimilarity, the "messianic secret"[5] in the Gospel of Mark may well be recognized as reflecting the historical state of affairs. True, according to the apostolic preaching, it is the risen and exalted Jesus whom God has made "both Lord[6] and Christ" (Acts 2:36), but even when Jesus referred to coming vindication and glory, as in His reply to the high priest, He spoke of the Son of Man, not the Messiah.

The emphatic "*I* say to you", whether preceded or not by the single (or double) "Amen", has every appearance of being a characteristic expression of Jesus which was preserved (but not imitated) in the early church. Language like this, especially as it appears in the antitheses of the Sermon on the Mount – "it was said . . . but *I* say" (Matt. 5:21 ff.) – implies a

---

[1] Mark 10:47 f. Peculiar to the First Gospel is the use of the title by the Canaanite woman (Matt. 15:22) and by the crowds at the entry into Jerusalem (Matt. 21:9).

[2] Mark 12:35 ff., in a discussion on the significance of Ps. 110:1.

[3] In the Samaritan context of John 4:25 f., the reference is most probably to the coming *Taheb*, conceived of by the Samaritans as the prophet like Moses (Deut. 18:15 ff.), not as the son of David. Even in the Fourth Gospel, from which the motif of messianic secrecy is generally absent, the Jews of Jerusalem have to say to Jesus less than four months before His passion, "How long will you keep us in suspense? If you are the Christ, tell us plainly" (John 10:24).

[4] Mark 14:62 (see my *This is That*, p. 81).

[5] Cf. W. Wrede, *Das Messiasgeheimnis in den Evangelien* (Göttingen, ²1913). It is understood that an (overdue) English translation by J. C. G. Greig is being prepared.

[6] We may further note how rarely the designation "Lord" (κύριος) is given to Jesus in the Gospels (when it is given Him by the Evangelists, especially Luke, it is from the post-Easter perspective), although it was so regularly used of Him in the early church. See my "Jesus is Lord" in *Soli Deo Gloria*, ed. J. McD. Richards (Richmond, Va., 1968), pp. 23 ff.

claim to be on a level with Moses if not indeed superior to him. Jesus was popularly called rabbi, and those of greater insight acknowledged that He was a prophet, but the authority expressed in these words is greater than that of any rabbi or prophet. The "Amen" bespeaks an immediate and unreserved assurance of divine utterance, and on men's response to this divine utterance through the lips of Jesus depends their judgement at the end-time.[1]

The mode of addressing God as *Abba,* which according to Paul is a sure sign of the reception of His Spirit (Rom. 8:15 f.; Gal. 4:6), is indeed a usage attested in early Christianity, but nevertheless its Aramaic origin and unparalleled employment in reference to God carry us back to the usage of Jesus Himself. The use of "our Father" (*'abinu*) or even "my Father" (*'abi*) in reference to God was familiar in personal and synagogue usage among the Jews, but Jesus both addressed God and apparently spoke of Him by the form *Abba,* which was the affectionate word used in the family circle (as distinct from the slightly more formal terms used in synagogue), and taught His disciples to do the same. But if, as all the evidence indicates, "*Abba* as an address to God is *ipsissima vox*, an authentic and original utterance of Jesus," then, says Joachim Jeremias, "we are behind the Kerygma."[2] We have got back to the heart of Jesus' teaching about God, and nothing else in His teaching was so decisive as this.

Behind the simple "Father" with which the Lord's Prayer, in its Lukan form, opens (the Matthaean form with the introductory "Our Father" is more liturgical), we are most probably to recognize this distinctive *Abba.* Not only the introductory word, but the whole of the prayer, goes back to the period of the ministry. It is echoed here and there in the epistles, but is antecedent to them; it was transmitted orally in the community of the disciples as well as in written form in the Gospels of Matthew and Luke. Even today there is no text of Scripture so well known as this, but it is usually learned, not by memorizing the written words but by constantly hearing and repeating the spoken words. When people find an unfamiliar version of the prayer, in a new translation of the New Testament, for example, they will say, "Surely they could have left the Lord's Prayer alone" – and yet if they were to look up the wording of the Lord's Prayer even in the most familiar Bible version they would probably discover that neither in Matthew nor in Luke is the wording identical with what they have learned by tradition.[3]

The Lord's Prayer presents us with a brief compendium of Jesus'

---

[1] Cf. E. Käsemann, *Essays on New Testament Themes,* pp. 37 ff.

[2] *The Central Message of the New Testament* (London, 1965), p. 30.

[3] For example, the familiar Prayer Book version of the Lord's Prayer (with or without the concluding doxology) is not identical with the text of Matt. 6:9–13 or Luke 11:2–4 in any English version of the Bible. The form that has been popularized in Presbyterianism, through its incorporation in the Westminster Shorter Catechism, is that of Matt. 6:9–13 in AV (KJV).

teaching about God and His children, or about God and His kingdom (which amounts in practice to the same thing). In it the followers of Jesus are taught to pray for the coming of God's kingdom – the accomplishment of His purpose in the world – and to ask Him for their daily bread, the forgiveness of their sins and preservation from the trial which their faith cannot survive. To use this prayer intelligently would demand familiarity with their Master's teaching on all these matters.[1]

In particular, the petition for the coming of God's kingdom implies acquaintance with what Jesus had to say about this kingdom, already present within the limitations of His ministry but destined to be unleashed "with power"[2] when the Son of Man, the recipient (with his people) of the divine sovereignty, was vindicated after "suffering many things and being treated with contempt" (Mark 9:12; Luke 17:25).

This teaching was regularly conveyed to Jesus' hearers in the form of parables. Parallels to His use of parables have been identified in rabbinical tradition and elsewhere, but in the most characteristic parables of the Gospels there is such a distinctive note that the criterion of dissimilarity points to them as further samples of the authentic words of Jesus.[3] Certainly there is nothing comparable to them in the Acts and epistles. No doubt, as they were handed down in the church, they acquired interpretative and other accretions which form-critical analysis enables us to recognize for what they are. Moreover, the preservation in different strata of variant forms of one and the same parable helps us to discern the original form more clearly. Professor Jeremias, in particular, has also shown how, with the aid of form criticism, it is possible to remove a later Hellenistic layer which has overlain an earlier Palestinian layer, and so to move back from a setting in the life of the early church to a setting in the life of Jesus.[4] Even this procedure, however, must be followed with caution, if only because first-century Palestine was part of the world of Hellenistic culture, while Hellenists were included in the Jerusalem church from its early days, if not indeed among the disciples of Jesus during His ministry.

Criterion of Coherence

The criterion of coherence comes into play when once a body of sayings or incidents has been authenticated by the criterion of dissimilarity. Once we have established a firm core of *ipsissima verba* or *ipsissima facta* in the Gospels, we can go on to identify units which are "coherent" or consistent with these. In an attempt to lay down "a positive criterion of

[1] Cf. J. Jeremias, "The Lord's Prayer in Modern Research", *Expository Times* 71 (1959–60), pp. 141 ff.

[2] Mark 9:1.

[3] Cf. N. Perrin, *Rediscovering the Teaching of Jesus* (London, 1967), pp. 77 ff.; his exegesis of the Parables of the Kingdom is of special value.

[4] Cf. J. Jeremias, *The Parables of Jesus*, E. T. (London, ²1963).

canonicity", C. E. Carlston has staked a claim for the genuineness of those units which not only reflect the conditions of the ministry rather than those of the post-Easter situation but also fit reasonably well into Jesus' eschatologically based demand for repentance.[1] The criterion of coherence can be extended beyond the canonical Gospels to sayings or actions attributed to Jesus in uncanonical writings: if they are congruent with sayings and actions which can be established as authentic, then there is some point in going on to examine in greater detail the evidence for recognizing them as historical.

Multiple Attestation

The principle of "multiple attestation" applies to gospel criticism the biblical injunction "that every word may be confirmed by the evidence of two or three witnesses" (Matt. 18:16).[2] It means that the case for recognizing a saying or incident as primitive, if not authentically located in the ministry of Jesus, is strengthened if it is attested in two or more independent lines of transmission.

In the first decade of this century F. C. Burkitt listed thirty-one sayings which he believed could be with great confidence attributed to Jesus Himself because they appeared both in the Gospel of Mark and in the non-Markan material common to the other two Synoptic Gospels (the material conveniently labelled Q).[3]

One simple example of this multiple attestation is a saying already referred to, where Jesus says that the Son of Man must "suffer many things" and combines this affirmation with a reference to the rejected stone of Psalm 118:22, the Greek word for "rejected" varying from one place to another. Thus, in the Gospel of Mark, Jesus warns the disciples that "the Son of man must suffer many things, and be rejected (apodokimasthēnai) by the elders and the chief priests and scribes" (8:31) and says that it is "written of the Son of man, that he should suffer many things and be treated with contempt (exoudenēthē)", while in Luke 17:25 (a passage which, whether it be labelled Q or L, is clearly non-Markan) He says that before the manifestation of the Son of Man, "he must suffer many things and be rejected (apodokimasthēnai) by this generation".

In all these passages the phrase "suffer many things" (polla pathein) is constant; as for the "rejecting" or "treating with contempt", it is expressed in two of them (Mark 8:31; Luke 17:25) by the verb used of the rejected stone in the Septuagint of Psalm 118:22, while the verb in Mark 9:12 is perhaps influenced by the use of a similar verb in several Greek versions as the equivalent of "despised" in Isa. 53:3. We have twofold attestation

---

[1] "A Positive Criterion of Authenticity?" *Biblical Research* 7 (1962), pp. 33 ff.
[2] Echoing Deut. 19:15 (cf. II Cor. 13:1).
[3] *The Gospel History and its Transmission*, pp. 147 ff.

at least for our Lord's reference to the Son of Man's suffering and rejection as something that must necessarily be undergone: the "must" of the three passages implies, what one of them (Mark 9:12) states expressly, the necessity that prophetic scripture should be fulfilled, and no prophetic scripture suggests itself more readily than the fourth Servant Song (Isa. 52:13–53:12).[1]

Another form of multiple attestation was presented over a generation ago by Sir Edwyn Hoskyns and Dr. F. N. Davey in a chapter of their exciting book *The Riddle of the New Testament,* in which they compared miracles, parables and aphorisms and concluded that widely diverse forms are equally permeated with the messianic idea.[2] A few years later Professor Dodd classified the gospel material in groups according to similarity of subject-matter, each group including a variety of "forms" and representing a variety of sources, and reached the same conclusion. "Whether or not Jesus explicitly made, or admitted, His claim, it is not doubtful that from the beginning the tradition affirmed that He lived, taught, worked, suffered and died as Messiah. We can find no alternative tradition, excavate as we will in the successive strata of the Gospels."[3]

More recently Professor Dodd has argued for yet another kind of multiple attestation, in his investigation of the historical tradition in the Fourth Gospel and comparison of it with various strands of Synoptic tradition. He has unearthed parables in the Johannine material not unlike those with which the Synoptic Gospels have made us familiar, and has shown how, beneath the diversity of dialogue form as between the Synoptists and John, there is at times a community of theme which suggests that in this respect the Synoptic and Johannine traditions alike go back to an earlier "unformed" tradition. Moreover, he envisages the probability that more of this "unformed" tradition of Jesus' teaching lies behind Johannine dialogues which have no parallels in the Synoptic tradition, though they can be integrated with it. The recognition of such material calls for delicate and experienced judgement, but the quest is far from hopeless.[4]

Not only in such detailed "forms", but in the general outline of the ministry, the points of coincidence between the Synoptic and Johannine traditions are of great importance, especially if the Fourth Gospel is essentially independent of any of the Synoptic Gospels (as I believe it is).[5] In addition to their agreement in associating the beginning of Jesus'

[1] See *This is That,* pp. 96 ff.
[2] *The Riddle of the New Testament* (London, 1931), pp. 162 ff.
[3] *History and the Gospel,* p. 103. See p. 43, n. 10; p. 44, n. 1.
[4] *Historical Tradition in the Fourth Gospel* (Cambridge, 1963), pp. 315 ff.
[5] Cf. P. Gardner-Smith, *St. John and the Synoptic Gospels* (Cambridge, 1938); J. A. T. Robinson, "The New Look on the Fourth Gospel", *Twelve New Testament Studies,* pp. 94 ff.; A. J. B. Higgins, *The Historicity of the Fourth Gospel* (London, 1960); A. M. Hunter, *According to John* (London, 1968).

public life with John the Baptist and in the main outlines of the passion narrative at the end of His public life,[1] special attention should be devoted to their agreement in treating the feeding of the multitude and Peter's confession which followed it as outstanding incidents in a complex of events which constituted a critical turning-point in the ministry.[2]

The Ring of Truth

Further considerations in "rediscovering the teaching of Jesus" are that the reconstruction and interpretation of His teaching should do justice to its historical context – the context of Palestinian Judaism in the first decades of Judaea's existence as a Roman province administered by imperial prefects, while Herod Antipas was still tetrarch of Galilee; that it should do justice to the more specific circumstances and situation of the ministry and to the nature both of our existing documents and of such sources as can be discerned behind them. Such critical sifting of the minutiae of the gospel tradition is, for the scholar, indispensable. But when this painstaking work has been accomplished and the core of the tradition authenticated as securely as possible, he will do well to stand back among the rank and file of Gospel readers and, listening with them to the witness of the Evangelists, join in acknowledging that this witness has the "ring of truth".[3]

[1] Cf. C. H. Dodd, *The Apostolic Preaching and its Developments²*, pp. 69 ff.
[2] Compare Mark 6:34-52; 8:14-21, 27-33 with John 6:5-71.
[3] Cf. J. B. Phillips, *Ring of Truth: A Translator's Testimony* (London, 1967).

CHAPTER IV

THE SETTING OF THE GOSPEL TRADITION

WHEN WE CONSIDER THE CIRCUMSTANCES IN WHICH THE gospel tradition was preserved and handed down, it is best to think of all the aspects of the church's life and work. There has been a tendency at times to concentrate on one aspect, as though it provided *the* determinant factor – preaching, controversy, worship or instruction.

Preaching

Martin Dibelius, for example, in his pioneer contributions to form-critical study,[1] attached high importance to preaching; his approach, indeed, has been summed up in the words: "In the beginning was the Sermon".[2] The units in the gospel tradition on which he laid special emphasis were those which he called "paradigms" (from Greek *paradeigma*, "example") because they served as illustrations in the preaching. From the reference in Luke 1:2 to "those who from the beginning were eyewitnesses and ministers of the word" he drew this conclusion:

> The first stories of Jesus came from the circle of witnesses who afterwards themselves became preachers. Then there followed other preachers, who had not been eye-witnesses. These again passed on the stories in their sermons.[3]

The reference in Luke 1:2 thus points to a "close connection between the preaching and the formation of the Gospel tradition"[4] which, Dibelius believed, could be established on more general grounds. As he envisaged the primitive community – unsophisticated and unliterary, feeling no obligation to hand down a record to posterity, since the present world was about to pass away – it had no interest in biography or chronological presentation.

> What was needed was rather a knowledge of what Jesus had said and done and suffered. The peculiarly fragmentary form of our tradition was determined by the style of preaching.[5]

Without subscribing to all the details of Dibelius's portrayal of the

---

[1] Especially *Die Formgeschichte des Evangeliums* (Tübingen, [1]1919, [2]1933, [3]1959), E. T. of 2nd edition by B. L. Woolf, *From Tradition to Gospel* (London, 1934).
[2] E. Fascher, *Die formgeschichtliche Methode* (Giessen, 1924), p. 54.
[3] *Gospel Criticism and Christology* (London, 1935), p. 31.
[4] *Ibid.*
[5] *Gospel Criticism and Christology*, p. 29.

58

primitive Christian community, there is much in what he says that commands ready agreement. The first half of Acts bears witness to the part played by public preaching in early Christian witness.[1] For example, when Peter is reported as reminding the crowd in Jerusalem on the first Christian Pentecost of "Jesus of Nazareth, a man attested to you by God with mighty works and wonders and signs which God did through him in your midst, as you yourselves know" (Acts 2:22), it is natural to think of this as a summary which, in an actual sermon, would be amplified by the inclusion of some typical "mighty works and wonders and signs" performed by Jesus. Similarly, when the same speaker in the house of Cornelius at Caesarea is said to have described Jesus as one who "went about doing good and healing all that were oppressed by the devil" (Acts 10:38), some instances of this activity of His would have driven the message home. Peter's account in the house of Cornelius, "beginning from Galilee after the baptism which John preached" and going on to Jesus' resurrection from the dead and commission to His disciples, could well be regarded as the kind of skeleton which the Gospel of Mark clothes with the flesh and sinews of narrative detail.[2]

Controversy

Rudolf Bultmann draws our attention to the controversies in which the early Christians were engaged as a formative factor in the growth of the gospel tradition.[3] Several of the units which Dibelius called "paradigms" and which Bultmann himself prefers to call "apophthegms"[4] have the nature of controversial dialogues (Streitgespräche). Something is said or done by Jesus or His disciples to which others (most commonly "scribes") take exception: their objections are silenced by an authoritative word from Jesus. The best-known of these dialogues are the five recorded one after another in Mark 2:1–3:6, in a group which perhaps already existed as such when it came into Mark's hands.[5] Jesus assures a paralytic that his sins are forgiven; the scribes' objection that the forgiveness of sins is God's exclusive prerogative is answered by the pronouncement: "The Son of man has authority on earth to forgive sins" (Mark 2:10). Jesus and the disciples share a meal with tax-farmers and several others whose way of life stamped them as "sinners" in the eyes of the religious leaders; to the inevitable criticisms of His doing so He replies: "Those who are well have

---

[1] Cf. M. Dibelius, From Tradition to Gospel, pp. 17 ff. Dibelius himself treats the speeches in Acts as containing fragments of tradition but as being substantially composed by Luke (Studies in the Acts of the Apostles, E. T. London, 1956, pp. 138 ff.); contrast the more realistic assessment by C. H. Dodd, The Apostolic Preaching and its Developments (London, ²1944), pp. 17 ff.; History and the Gospel (London, 1938), pp. 72 f.

[2] Cf. C. H. Dodd, The Apostolic Preaching and its Developments, pp. 27 f.

[3] The History of the Synoptic Tradition, E. T. (Oxford, 1963), pp. 39 ff.

[4] The History of the Synoptic Tradition, pp. 11 ff.

[5] See p. 45.

no need of a physician, but those who are sick; I came not to call the righteous, but sinners" (Mark 2:17).[1] Jesus' disciples do not fast like those of John the Baptist and the Pharisees; when their failure to conform to this pious practice is questioned, the explanation is given: "Can the wedding guests fast while the bridegroom is with them? As long as they have the bridegroom with them, they cannot fast" (Mark 2:19). When Jesus' disciples break the sabbath law, as traditionally interpreted, by plucking ears of grain and rubbing them to extract the kernel on their way through the fields, the ensuing censure is countered with the dictum: "The sabbath was made for man, not man for the sabbath; so the Son of man is lord even of the sabbath" (Mark 2:28). When Jesus Himself cures a man's paralysed arm in the synagogue on another sabbath, He defends His action with the unanswered question: "Is it lawful on the sabbath to do good or to do harm, to save life or to kill?" (Mark 3:4).[2]

It is widely held that such controversial dialogues were preserved and recorded because similar conflicts arose between members of the early Palestinian church and their theological opponents among the Pharisees and other Jews; that the shaping of the tradition was dictated by the needs of the church and that this part of the tradition was the response to this particular need. But there are features in these dialogues which bespeak the sovereign freedom of our Lord's mind rather than the more prudential outlook of the early church. The apostles and their associates did pronounce the forgiveness of sins in Jesus' name, but they did not call Him the Son of Man as they did so, and their doing so at all is more easily understood if they knew that He in fact had claimed "authority on earth to forgive sins."[3] Nor would they have consorted with those who were stigmatized by the Jewish establishment as disreputable sinners – in so far as they consorted with such people at all – but for their Master's example. The community rule of Matt. 18:17, directing that the contumacious brother be treated "as a Gentile and a tax collector", was more congenial to many Palestinian Christians than the memory of Jesus' personal example.[4] The really crucial problem of table-fellowship in the early church concerned table-fellowship with Gentiles, not with tax-farmers

---

[1] Dibelius thinks that the original *logion* was "Those who are well have no need of a physician, but those who are sick". "But the tradition enshrined in the preaching obtains from this saying 'a doctrine' – that Jesus has come to call sinners and not the righteous – and this teaching is placed in the mouth of Jesus Himself" (*From Tradition to Gospel*, p. 64). There is no good reason for this hypothesis. On the other hand, the phrase "to repentance", which appears after "sinners" in the Byzantine text of Mark 2:17 (cf. Luke 5:32) has all the appearance of an epexegetic addition.

[2] See pp. 25 f., 48 f.

[3] Cf. Luke 24:47; Acts 10:43; Col. 1:14; I John 2:12.

[4] It is worth considering with care how in fact Jesus Himself treated Gentiles and tax collectors.

and their kind, and no precedent is recorded as laid down by Jesus on this subject, whether in precept or in practice.[1]

As for the pronouncement about fasting, the Christians of the apostolic age did fast, so far as our evidence goes, and it is improbable that our Lord's defence of His disciples for *not* fasting arose out of the necessities of the situation in the early church.[2] True, they may not have observed the same fasts as the Pharisees did, although it is uncertain how early Wednesday and Friday were selected as the two fast-days of the Christian week instead of Monday and Thursday.[3] True, they may have paid careful attention to the directions of Matt. 6:16–18 and kept the knowledge of their fasting to themselves. But the defence of the disciples in Mark 2:19 is a defence of them for not fasting at all, and any embarrassment felt by the early church arose from the inconsistency of their practice with the implications of their Lord's defence, not with contemporary Jewish custom. Hence the question which they had to answer was not "Why do you not fast?" but "Why do you fast, since your Master exempted you from this duty?" To this question the answer is provided in the supplementary pronouncement of Mark 2:20, "The days will come, when the bridegroom is taken away from them and then they will fast in that day." It is the supplementary pronouncement that fits the life-setting of the early church; the substantive pronouncement can have no other life-setting than the ministry of Jesus. "By just such an example we may recognize the good quality of the tradition, and its conservative character."[4] It is a helpful instance of the "criterion of dissimilarity".[5]

As for the sabbath controversies of Mark 2:23–3:6, they may or may not have had relevance to the life of the Palestinian church. We have no evidence of any controversy between it and its Jewish opponents on this score. Where the sabbath does emerge as a controversial issue in the apostolic church is when attempts are made to impose it on Gentile Christians. Among them the observance of "days, and months, and seasons, and years" as a religious obligation is strongly deprecated by Paul (Gal. 4:10): "let no one pass judgement on you . . . with regard to a festival or a new moon or a sabbath", he tells the Colossians (Col. 2:16), while he assures the Roman Christians (a mixed Jewish and Gentile community) that the observance or non-observance of special days, like the eating or refusal of certain kinds of food, is a matter for the individual

---

We may indeed discern a principle relevant to this situation in Mark 7:14–23, but it was certainly not discerned by the disciples at the time.

[2] It is instructive to observe the tendency in later authorities for the text of the Gospels and Acts to add fasting to prayer where it is absent from earlier authorities (cf. Mark 9:29; Acts 10:30).

[3] Our earliest evidence is *Didachē* 8:1. Cf. A. Jaubert, *La date de la Cène* (Paris, 1957), pp. 60 ff. See p. 120, n. 6.

[4] M. Dibelius, *From Tradition to Gospel*, p. 66. The supplementary pronouncement, he says, "is a typical Paradigm ending".

[5] See p. 47.

conscience, in which the claims of Christian liberty must be balanced by the claims of Christian charity (Rom. 14:5 f.). But in the Jerusalem church, it appears, the policy in this as in a number of other respects was to "observe the customs" (Acts 21:21). An interesting question arises about the life-setting of "Western" addition to Luke's version of the walk through the grainfields, where Jesus, seeing a man working on the sabbath, says to him, "Man, if indeed you know what you are doing, you are blessed; but if not, you are accursed, and a transgressor of the law" (Luke 6:5b D). The form of the pericope suggests a Palestinian origin; we may relate it to a more liberal interpretation of the sabbath law in which a violation of its letter was permissible, and even praiseworthy, if it were based on principle, but condemned if it were nothing but a deliberate or careless flouting of convention.[1]

The suggestion has been made that, before the collection of controversial dialogues in Mark 2:1–3:6 reached the Evangelist, it formed the first part of a larger collection, the second part of which he separated from what preceded it and placed in the context of Holy Week.[2] Some colour is lent to this suggestion by the fact that the first collection of five dialogues ends with a coalition of Pharisees and Herodians against Jesus (Mark 3:6), while the second collection begins with such a coalition (Mark 12:13). But the controversial dialogues in Mark 12:13 ff. have a different form from those in Mark 2:1 ff.; in the later group the controversy is initiated by Jesus' opponents and not stimulated by anything said or done by Jesus or His disciples. The two questions in the later group, that raised by the Pharisees and Herodians regarding tribute to Caesar and that raised by the Sadducees on the subject of resurrection, are completely in keeping with the setting of Jesus' ministry, although they would be recalled repeatedly when these questions were raised in the church, and especially in the Palestinian church, in the generation preceding the Jewish revolt of A.D. 66.

The tribute question must have become increasingly acute with the growth in Zealot sentiment during these years, and the patriotism of Palestinian Christians would tend to be tested more and more by the answer given to the question: "Is it lawful to pay taxes to Caesar, or not?"[3] It was all very well for Paul, writing to Roman Christians in A.D. 57, to exhort them to pay "taxes to whom taxes are due" (Rom. 13:7), but Roman Christians, whether Gentile or Jewish, were not liable to be put on the spot by their fellow-countrymen in this respect as their Palestinian brethren were. Yet the answer to the question, "Give

---

[1] Cf. J. Jeremias, *Unknown Sayings of Jesus*, E. T. (London, ²1964), pp. 61 ff.; he argues for the authenticity of the pericope (as a saying of Jesus, not as part of the original text of Luke).

[2] Cf. B. S. Easton, *Christ in the Gospels* (New York, 1930), p. 35. The life-setting of the earlier group of dialogues is Galilaean, that of the latter Judaean.

[3] That the tribute to Caesar was supremely offensive to Zealot sentiment is clear from Josephus (*BJ* ii. 118; *Ant.* xviii. 4 ff.)– if, indeed, the "fourth philosophy" founded by Judas the Galilaean is to be identified with the party of the Zealots.

back[1] to Caesar the things that are Caesar's, and to God the things that are God's" (Mark 12:17), is more likely to have been pronounced by Jesus and remembered by the primitive community than to have been devised within the community.

But tribute to Caesar was not the only form of tax which was calculated to raise a conscientious issue among the Jewish followers of Jesus. There was also the temple tax, the half-shekel contributed annually by every male Jew between the ages of twenty and fifty towards the maintenance of the Jerusalem temple.[2] One pericope in the gospel tradition is concerned with this tax: that recorded only in Matt. 17:24-27, where the collectors of the half-shekel ask Peter in Capernaum if his "teacher" pays the tax, and are told that he does.

> And when he came home, Jesus spoke to him first, saying, "What do you think, Simon? From whom do kings of the earth take toll or tribute? From their sons or from others? And when he said, "From others", Jesus said to him, "Then the sons are free. However, not to give offence to them . . ."

and then follow the directions about finding a stater in a fish's mouth which would pay the tax for Peter and his Master together.[3] The story was not recorded for the sake of the coin in the fish's mouth, but for the sake of those Jewish Christians in the interval between the ministry of Jesus and the end of the temple order. Should they continue to pay the half-shekel or not? The answer implied in the story was that they were no longer under a divinely imposed obligation to pay it – with the advent of the kingdom of God "something greater than the temple is here" (Matt. 12:6) and they are "the sons of the kingdom" (Matt. 13:38) – but out of consideration for their fellow-Jews, who would be scandalized if they refused to pay, it would be a courteous gesture on their part to continue to do so.

The life-setting of this piece of tradition, so far as its relevance to the early church is concerned, cannot be later than A.D. 70. After that date the temple tax was diverted by the Emperor Vespasian to the upkeep of the temple of Jupiter on the Capitoline hill in Rome.[4] The payment of the *fiscus Iudaicus* in this new situation would be a matter of conscience for Jewish Christians, as for all pious Jews, but on this problem neither the

---

[1] "Give back" seems to be the appropriate rendering of *apodidōmi* in this context. "The coin bears Caesar's name; let him have it back." Some Jews were so conscientious that they would not handle or even look at a coin bearing the imperial image, for fear of breaking the first and second commandments of the Decalogue; and the implication may be that such a coin was fit only to be returned to the pagans who issued it.

[2] Cf. Ex. 30:13 f. For fifty as the upper age-limit see Josephus, *Ant.* iii. 196; it was either raised or abolished by Vespasian.

[3] The stater or tetradrachm belonged to the Tyrian coinage which was prescribed for the payment of this impost. It was more or less equivalent in value to a shekel.

[4] Josephus, *BJ* vii. 218; see my *New Testament History* (London, 1969), pp. 369 f.

incident of the stater nor any other element in the gospel tradition provided clear guidance.

Worship

We have already considered ways in which the gospel tradition was
preserved and shaped by the requirements of the church's worship. If
we reflect on the realities and probabilities of the situation in which the
primitive community found itself, we may come to the conclusion that
several features of the tradition must have stabilized themselves in the
course of its regular meetings. Had Jesus not appeared to them "alive
after his passion", had they been left with a sense of disillusionment and
betrayal, it is conceivable that they might have wished to forget their
association with Him as completely as possible – although the analogy of
others who have had this kind of experience does not encourage us to
think so. As it was, the knowledge that their Master had conquered
death and was now reigning at God's right hand was all-determinant in
their living and thinking. But the awareness of Jesus as the exalted Lord,
manifesting His presence among them by the Spirit, would not have
diminished the eagerness with which memories of their association with
Him were shared on the many occasions when "those who feared the
Lord" gathered together and "spoke with one another" (Mal. 3:16).
"Hidden memories came to the surface; new meanings were seen in
clearly remembered scenes and words."[1] The first days spent in His
company at the beginning of the ministry and the last days in Jerusalem
would stand out with special vividness in the memory of those who were
there, and would be described by them to those who were not there.
The first anniversary of the trial and crucifixion would stimulate their
memories and occasion the re-telling of the events of Holy Week, as is
the manner of first anniversaries. There is nothing at all surprising in the
fact that the passion narrative is the earliest element in the gospel tradition
to assume coherent continuity.

The role of prophets in the formation of the tradition has been greatly
exaggerated. We have simply no concrete evidence to indicate that prophets in church meetings uttered words in the name of the exalted Lord
which were preserved in the tradition as sayings of Jesus "in the days
of his flesh".[2] From the few details of prophetic utterances that have

---

[1] W. K. L. Clarke, *New Testament Problems* (London, 1929), p. 27; the whole essay, "The
Formgeschichtlich Method" (pp. 18–30), from which the quotation is taken, is a fresh and valuable approach to this subject.

[2] See F. Neugebauer, "Geistsprüche und Jesuslogien", *ZNW* 53 (1963), pp. 218 ff., for a
critical scrutiny of Bultmann's arguments to this effect (*The History of the Synoptic Tradition*
pp. 108 ff.). Bultmann (p. 127) cites Rev. 16:15 as a case in point, but apart from the question-
able validity of arguing from the apocalyptic genre to a quite different one, this *logion* has
claims to be regarded as a quotation from the earthly Jesus, in view of its parallels elsewhere

been recorded in the New Testament, they seem to have been pedestrian in character, relating to *ad hoc* situations like the famine in the days of Claudius and Paul's arrest at Jerusalem[1] – not the sort of thing that was likely to be ascribed to Jesus.

The New Testament prophets had little in common with the great prophets of Old Testament times apart from their designation; their utterances did not manifest exceptional insight into "the council of the LORD"[2] and had little of the salt of immortality about them. But Jesus was widely recognized as a great prophet,[3] and the form in which much of His teaching is cast by the Evangelists is marked by the same kind of rhythm and parallelism as we find in the oracles of the Hebrew prophets of earlier days.[4] This is relevant to another aspect of our present study.

Instruction

Under preaching Dibelius included instruction or teaching[5] – not inappropriately, for there is no precise line of demarcation between preaching and teaching, between *kērygma* and *didachē*. Yet a distinction has to be made between the proclaiming of the way of salvation to men and women (whether Jews or Gentiles) outside the believing community and the instruction of those within. In the Pauline letters a special place in the church's ministry is given to teachers, as distinct from apostles, prophets and evangelists.[6] These teachers, for the most part, had no first-hand acquaintance with the saving events; they had themselves to be taught before they could teach others. As the Gentile mission expanded and the number of churches multiplied, something in the nature of teacher-training courses, in however rudimentary a form, became neces-

---

[1] Cf. Acts 11:28; 20:23; 21:4, 11. Paul makes the prophetic gift subordinate to the apostolic (I Cor. 12:28).

[2] Jer. 23:18, 22.

[3] Mark 6:15; 8:28; Luke 7:16; 24;19.

[4] Cf. C. F. Burney, *The Poetry of our Lord* (Oxford, 1925). Cf. also C. H. Dodd: "since Jesus appeared to His contemporaries as a prophet, and prophets were accustomed to give oracles in verse, it is credible that we have here something approaching His *ipsissima verba*" (*History and the Gospel*, London, 1938, pp. 89 f.). The putative "sayings" collection from which the "Q" material in Matthew and Luke is drawn has been envisaged, with great probability, as similar in structure to the books of the OT prophets, which present the prophet's oracles in a minimum of narrative framework and never include an account of the prophet's death: we might think of the collection as "The Book of the Prophet Jesus".

[5] *Gospel Criticism and Christology*, p. 29.

[6] I Cor. 12:28; Eph. 4:11.

---

in the NT (Luke 12:39; I Thess. 5:2, 4). Literary compositions like the letters to the seven churches (Rev. 2:1–3:22) are not on the same footing as prophetic utterances at meetings of the church. Bultmann (p. 128) also quotes as relevant in this regard the words of Christ in *Ode of Solomon* 42:6, "I have risen and stand by them, and speak through their mouth"; but this has no special reference to prophets, but to believers in general, who speak in their Lord's name (cf. Luke 21:15).

sary, in order that "the commandments of the Lord" might be learned systematically and imparted to others.[1] It is in this kind of setting that we may envisage the compiling of the Sayings-collection usually held to underlie the non-Markan material common to Matthew and Luke. The beginning of the Gentile mission at Antioch would provide the occasion for such a compilation, and there is nothing in the "Q" tradition that demands a date later than A.D. 50. Nor would it be surprising if, about the same time, a parallel body of teaching material was compiled in Jerusalem, for the corresponding requirements of the mission to the "circumcision". It is many years since T. W. Manson pointed out the parallels in the sequence of the "Q" material, as arranged by Luke, and of the "M" materials, as arranged by Matthew.[2]

The important role of instruction in the forming and transmitting of the gospel tradition has been studied in recent years by some distinguished Swedish scholars.

In 1954 Krister Stendahl (now Professor of New Testament in Harvard Divinity School) published his doctoral dissertation on *The School of St. Matthew*,[3] in which he argued that a school was the most natural life-setting for the Gospel of Matthew. Some years earlier G. D. Kilpatrick had emphasized the influence of the liturgical practice of the day on the production of this Gospel;[4] Dr. Stendahl examined this thesis and found it wanting, for in his view "the systematizing work, the adaptation towards casuistry instead of broad statements of principles, the reflection on the position of the church leaders and their duties, and many other similar features, all point to a milieu of study and instruction."[5] A parallel to the Matthaean life-setting is found in the Qumran community: in particular, resemblance is traced between Matthew's "formula quotations" from the Old Testament and the *pesher* interpretation of Old Testament texts in the Qumran commentaries.[6] In a new preface to the second edition of his work in 1968 Professor Stendahl indicates that, in his judgement, "the primary justification for this study was – and is even more now – its analysis of the OT text in the gospel" of Matthew.[7] No doubt he is right, but there are convergent lines of argument suggesting that Matthew's record is a teaching manual, compiled by "a scribe . . . trained for the kingdom of heaven" who, like a householder, "brings

---

[1] Cf. B. S. Easton, *Christ in the Gospels*, p. 51.

[2] *The Sayings of Jesus* (London, 1949), pp. 22 f. (originally published as Part II of *The Mission and Message of Jesus*, by H. D. A. Major, T. W. Manson and C. J. Wright, London, 1937, pp. 314 f.).

[3] Lund, [1]1954, [2]1968.

[4] *The Origins of the Gospel according to St. Matthew* (Oxford, 1946).

[5] *The School of St. Matthew*, p. 29.

[6] *The School of St. Matthew*, pp. 183 ff.

[7] P. i. See also R. H. Gundry, *The Use of the Old Testament in St. Matthew's Gospel* (Leiden, 1967); Gundry criticizes Stendahl's thesis (pp. 155 ff.) and is himself criticized by Stendahl in *Biblica* (forthcoming).

out of his treasure what is new and what is old" (Matt. 13:52) and who in addition may deliberately have cast the teaching of Jesus into the form of a new Torah, in which, as in the old Torah, instruction and narrative are interwoven.[1] The community in which this work took shape, as Professor Stendahl pictures it, "grew out of Hellenistic Judaism" and existed in conscious opposition to the synagogue, but

> had learned to make the transition to an increasing gentile constituency with-out suffering much tension or problem in that process . . . In such a setting traditions could be preserved and elaborated in a style which in other com-munities had become suspect or outdated. On the basis of such traditions and in such a milieu Matthew brings his gospel to completion. That he once was a Jew cannot be doubted. That he had had Jewish training in Palestine prior to the War is probable. That he belongs to a Hellenistic community is obvious. That this community includes gentiles is sure. What does this make the gospel? A witness to a far smoother transition from Judaism to Christianity than we usually suppose . . . Matthew is comprehensive by circumstance, and that makes it a rich and wise book.[2]

So much for the formative power of instruction at this later stage in the growth of the gospel tradition; what about its earlier stages? In the first edition of his book Professor Stendahl envisaged the possibility of "an unbroken line from the School of Jesus via the 'teaching of the apostles'" through the teaching of Paul, Mark, John and their associates to the school of Matthew.[3] Later he speaks of this suggestion as a rather careless playing with the idea;[4] if the formula quotations represent the characteristic emphasis of the Matthaean school, indeed "the crown of its scholarship",[5] there is no evidence that they were a feature of the teaching of Jesus.

But other Swedish scholars have found in the teaching of Jesus the determinant factor in fixing the gospel tradition at its outset – notably Harald Riesenfeld and Birger Gerhardsson. In 1957 Professor Riesenfeld delivered to the Four Gospels Congress at Oxford an address on *The Gospel Tradition and its Beginnings,* described in its sub-title as "a study in the limits of 'Formgeschichte'".[6] In this he maintained that what Jesus delivered to the apostles was a "holy word", embracing His deeds as well as His sayings. So important was it in His eyes that this "holy word" should be transmitted intact that special persons – the Twelve – were

---

[1] Cf. T. W. Manson, *Ethics and the Gospel* (London, 1960), pp. 45 ff.; W. D. Davies, *The Setting of the Sermon on the Mount* (Cambridge, 1964), pp. 187 ff. *et passim.*
[2] *The School of St. Matthew*², pp. xiii f.
[3] *The School of St. Matthew,* p. 34.
[4] *The School of St. Matthew*², p. x.
[5] *The School of St. Matthew,* p. 34.
[6] Published as a separate pamphlet (London, 1957), also in the Proceedings of the Congress, *Studia Evangelica* i = *TU* 73 (Berlin, 1959), pp. 43 ff., reprinted in *The Gospels Reconsidered* Oxford, 1960), pp. 131 ff.

selected to bear this responsibility. The original life-setting of the gospel tradition should be sought neither in missionary preaching nor in the communal instruction of the primitive church but in Jesus' teaching of the Twelve. It was memorized by them and recited (with exposition) to their converts. But (and here is the major obstacle to the full acceptance of Professor Riesenfeld's thesis) "the reason why the words and deeds of Jesus were probably never quoted verbally in the missionary preaching and only on rare occasions in the community instruction" was this:

> The tradition which was recited was holy and hence, in contrast to present-day practice, was not readily mentioned by word of mouth. Mission preaching, indeed, pointed and led to it. The instruction in the community presupposed it and linked itself up with it. But in its verbal form and in its *Sitz im Leben* in the community it was *sui generis*.[1]

The fixation of this tradition – first the sayings and then the deeds of Jesus – in a written text meant among other things a relaxing of its original exclusiveness, especially when Luke incorporated it in a literary and apologetic framework intended for a wider public.

With many of the points made by Professor Riesenfeld it is easy to express cordial agreement – e.g. with his insistence, on the basis of the New Testament evidence, that the gospel tradition originated with Jesus Himself and not with the post-Easter church, with his recognition of the determinant role of the apostles and eyewitnesses as the first links in the chain of tradition, and with his appeal to prophetic and rabbinic analogies. The prophetic analogy is specially apt. But whereas Isaiah committed his oracles to his disciples with instructions to seal them up until the day of their fulfilment and only then to publish them,[2] no such instructions were given by Jesus when He delivered His teaching to the Twelve. The conception of the original tradition as a *disciplina arcani*, to be recited until it was memorized in catechetical classes but not to be repeated in general church meetings, let alone in addressing outsiders, is so antecedently improbable in the light of the New Testament record that positive and explicit evidence of the strongest kind would be necessary to establish it.[3]

Four years after the publication of Professor Riesenfeld's monograph there appeared a *magnum opus* by Birger Gerhardsson, entitled *Memory and*

---

[1] *The Gospel Tradition and its Beginnings* (London, 1957), p. 23.

[2] Isa. 8:16.

[3] It may well be that in the rabbinical schools "the oral tradition was esoteric, and this not in the sense that it was treasured as a dark secret, but that is was not entrusted to everyone nor was it at everyone's disposal to use as he wished" (*The Gospel Tradition and its Beginnings*, p. 18); but it is precarious to argue from this situation to that of early Christianity. The "secrecy" element in the Gospel tradition, concerning "matters which in Jesus' lifetime were intended for a more esoteric and narrower circle of disciples" (p. 25), had quite a different motivation, and was not intended to survive His death and resurrection – nor did it.

Manuscript: Oral Tradition and Written Transmission in Rabbinic Judaism and Early Christianity.[1] Rather more than half of this book is devoted to a study of the transmission of the written and oral Torah in Judaism; this is followed by an interpretation of the delivery of the gospel tradition in early Christianity on the rabbinical analogy. In this interpretation the controlling function of the apostles is stressed, as "those who from the beginning were eyewitnesses and ministers of the word" (Luke 1:2), together with the normative role of Jerusalem, in the spirit of the ancient oracle: "out of Zion shall go forth the law, and the word of the LORD from Jerusalem" (Isa. 2:3//Mic. 4:2). For this last thesis some support is provided even from the writings of Paul. Despite his independence of Jerusalem, Paul found it expedient at an early stage in the Gentile mission to go up to Jerusalem to set before the leaders of the church there "the gospel which I preach among the Gentiles, lest somehow I should be running or had run in vain" (Gal. 2:2). This is a remarkable admission that, apart from the fellowship and approval of Jerusalem, the execution of the apostolic commission, which he had received not from the Jerusalem leaders but directly from the exalted Christ, would be abortive. Again, while Paul began to exercise his apostolic ministry in Damascus and Arabia (Gal. 1:17), he later describes it in retrospect as exercised "from Jerusalem and as far round as Illyricum" (Rom. 15:19), as though the gospel could not be conceived of except as "beginning from Jerusalem" (Luke 24:47). But even Luke, with his special emphasis on Jerusalem, shifts the centre of interest from Jerusalem as his narrative proceeds, and makes it clear, for example, that the Gentile mission was begun spontaneously, in independence of Jerusalem and the apostles. We can hardly go so far as to say with Professor Gerhardsson that the "*collegium* of the Apostles . . . in Jerusalem"[2] constituted "the highest doctrinal court" to which Paul presented his gospel for approval.[3] Paul's concern was for the effectiveness of his missionary service, not for the maintenance of the Jerusalem leaders' authority: he esteemed those leaders as being (like himself) witnesses to the risen Christ, but what he thought of attempts to impose their authority over himself or his converts is evident from his references to the "superlative apostles" in II Cor. 11:5; 12:11.

But these are peripheral matters in relation to Professor Gerhardsson's central thesis, and we may readily agree with him that Jesus' disciples would preserve His teaching as faithfully as the disciples of the rabbis preserved theirs. He has, indeed, been criticized for assuming that the memorizing techniques of the rabbinical schools in the Tannaitic period (*c.* A.D. 70–200) were in vogue at the beginning of the first century,

---

[1] Lund, 1961.
[2] *Memory and Manuscript*, p. 279.
[3] *Memory and Manuscript*, p. 276.

whereas but few of the *ipsissima verba* of teachers of this earlier period have survived; he has been criticized also for failing to take into account the diversified character of Jewish religious teaching before A.D. 70 by contrast with the "normative" Judaism imposed from the Tannaitic period onwards.[1] Some of these criticisms are exaggerated, and Professor Gerhardsson found no difficulty in answering his more extreme critics in a smaller work published in 1964, *Tradition and Transmission in Early Christianity,* in which at the same time he repeats some of his earlier material in a form less liable to be misunderstood.

Undoubtedly he has given us a major study in the principles of oral transmission in the Jewish schools. The question remains whether this presents the best analogy to the transmission of the gospel material. We have already mentioned T. W. Manson's suggestion that Jesus regarded His disciples as "apprentices" rather than "pupils" in the sense of the rabbinical schools.[2] It is evident, too, from a comparative study of His teaching as preserved in the various Gospels and gospel strata that it had not been fixed in such a way as to exclude the degree of variation which confronts us in our texts. It is true that His sayings have been preserved with less variation than their narrative context (as appears, e.g. from a comparison of the incident of the centurion's servant in Matt. 8:5–13 with the parallel in Luke 7:2–10), but even so the variation is greater than would have been expected had He required the Twelve to memorize His teaching and deliver it *verbatim* as a *hieros logos.*

Jesus was popularly given the designation "Rabbi", but even those who referred to Him thus recognized that He was a rabbi with a difference. There was a quite distinctive note of creative authority about His words, such as is missing even from the Old Testament prophets. They said "Thus says the LORD"; He said "*I* say to you". A closer parallel is provided by the Qumran Teacher of Righteousness, as Professor Gerhardsson hints: "Jesus was regarded as the eschatological mediator of revelation, *the 'only' teacher* in the most qualified meaning of the word."[3] But He was more than that: the Teacher of Righteousness was not a messianic personage but the preparer of the way for the messianic age, whereas

---

[1] Some of the critical reviews of *Memory and Manuscript* are in their own right important contributions to this subject; cf. W. D. Davies, "Reflections on a Scandinavian Approach to 'The Gospel Tradition'", *Neotestamentica et Patristica* = Supplement to *NovT* 6 (Leiden, 1962), pp. 14 ff., reprinted in *The Setting of the Sermon on the Mount,* pp. 464 ff.; J. A. Fitzmyer, *Theological Studies* 23 (1962), pp. 442 ff.; G. Widengren, "Tradition and literature in Early Judaism and in the Early Church", *Numen* 10 (1963), pp. 42 ff.; M. Smith, "A Comparison of Early Christian and Early Rabbinic Tradition", *JBL* 82 (1963), pp. 169 ff.; C. K. Barrett, *JTS* n.s. 14 (1963), pp. 445 ff.; R. Benoit, *Revue Biblique* 70 (1963), pp. 269 ff.; P. Winter, *Anglican Theological Review* 45 (1963), pp. 416 ff.

[2] See pp. 27 f.

[3] *Tradition and Transmission in Early Christianity* (Lund ,1964), p. 41. His designation of Jesus as "the only' teacher" (cf. Matt. 23:8–10) is comparable to the designation of the Teacher of Righteousness as the *mōreh ha-yāḥid,* the 'unique teacher', in CD 20:1, 14.

Jesus was acknowledged by His followers as the Messiah of Israel, not only "the eschatological mediator of revelation" but also "the eschatological saviour".[1] He was *sui generis,* and the sovereign freedom with which He taught was delivered, along with the content of His teaching, to His disciples. That this freedom should not clash with the spirit of His own teaching was safeguarded not so much by painstaking memorizing (although this played its part in the handing down of the gospel tradition) as by the gift of the Spirit. No account of the transmission of His message is adequate if it fails to reckon with the role of the Spirit to which the bearers of the tradition themselves bear witness.

It is, perhaps, the principal merit of the works of Professors Riesenfeld and Gerhardsson that they point us unambiguously to the ministry of Jesus as the original life-setting of the gospel tradition, while all the activities of the early church – preaching, controversy, worship and instruction – provided settings for its preservation, shaping and transmission.

[1] *Ibid.*

APPENDIX TO CHAPTER IV

Criteria for Late and Early Dating

In *The Tendencies of the Synoptic Tradition* (Cambridge, 1969), E. P. Sanders examines some of the chief criteria which are used to determine the relative earliness or lateness of material in the Synoptic tradition. These criteria have been applied to various stages in the transmission of the material: they are used by source critics and textual critics as well as by form critics; indeed, they are applicable not only to the canonical Gospels but to the apocryphal Gospels too. Thus those form critics who endeavour to establish the earliest form of some unit of tradition by discovering and applying the laws of oral transmission find their counterpart in those eclectic textual critics who endeavour to establish the earliest text of some variously attested passage by reference to the particular style of the author and the general tendencies of scribes. Again, the hypothesis that increased use of personal names is a mark of lateness or that the presence of Semitisms is a mark of primitiveness can be illustrated from a comparison of the apocryphal with the canonical Gospels as well as within the canon itself. But neither of these hypotheses is a secure basis in itself, as appears when we reflect that Mark is the only evangelist who refers to the blind man of Jericho by his name Bartimaeus, or that Luke is capable of constructing Semitisms of his own where his fellow-Synoptists have none (cf. Luke 20:11, 12, with Matt. 21:36 and Mark 12:4, 5).

The criteria which Professor Sanders singles out for special study are (i) increasing length, (ii) increasing detail and (iii) diminishing Semitism – each commonly considered as a feature of the progressing tradition. In addition, he pays more cursory attention to (iv) direct discourse and (v) conflation. Each criterion is examined in the light of evidence (*a*) from the post-canonical tradition and (*b*) from the Synoptic tradition. The firm conclusion is reached that *"dogmatic statements that a certain characteristic proves a certain passage to be earlier than another are never justified"* (p. 272). For, as is shown in detail, "on all counts the tradition developed in opposite directions. It became both longer and shorter, both more and less detailed, and both more and less Semitic" (p. 272). While the tendency to replace indirect discourse by direct is uniform in the post-canonical tradition examined, it is not uniform in the Synoptic Gospels.

The equivocal evidence of these criteria has implications for the Synoptic problem (both for Markan priority and for the two-document hypothesis) and for the pre-canonical tradition. Can the tendencies which mark the transition from the canonical to the post-canonical phase be assumed for the transition from the pre-canonical to the canonical phase? Not with any measure of dogmatism, yet Dr. Sanders suggests that this approach may be set beside the approach from folk-tradition (as in the German school), from rabbinical tradition (as in the Scandinavian school) and from the evidence of the early New Testament epistles (as in the English school); none of these approaches is adequate in itself; each makes a contribution.

The two positive conclusions which Dr. Sanders permits himself are generalizations: the tradition moved from the more formal to the less formal and from the less popular to the more popular. But he insists in a final sentence – and rightly so – that his negative conclusions are at least as important as the positive ones.

CHAPTER V

TRADITION AND INTERPRETATION

TRADITION IS USUALLY RECEIVED AND DELIVERED IN ORAL form before it is crystallized in writing, even if (as we have found with some phases of New Testament tradition) the written crystallization follows the oral stage within no great interval. But there is one form of oral tradition which presupposes the existence of a written text: that is the tradition which is concerned with the proper interpretation of sacred scriptures. This form of tradition appears in the earliest age of Christianity, the sacred scriptures with whose interpretation it is concerned being the Hebrew Bible (or its Greek translation), known to Christians as the Old Testament.

A Common Bible?

The church shared these sacred scriptures with the synagogue, but the main lines of Christian and Jewish interpretative tradition were too far apart for this joint heritage to constitute a firm bond between them. The possession of a common Bible does not guarantee religious unity: very much depends on the way in which this common Bible is read and understood. Divergent interpretations tend to produce religious divisions. In the New Testament period this tendency is prominent where, for example, the divergent traditions have to do with the observance of the law and religious practice in general – especially where those who embrace one line of interpretation band themselves together in local fellowships, like the Pharisees, or in covenant-communities, like the men of Qumran. It is in complete accordance with this general pattern that the first really serious external threat to the life of the Christian church should be bound up with the charge that Stephen understood Christianity to involve changing "the customs which Moses delivered *(paradidōmi)* to us" (Acts 6:13 f.) and that the first internal threat to the unity of the church should be posed by sharply divergent views on the necessity for Gentile converts to be "circumcised according to the custom of Moses" and so undertake an obligation to keep the Jewish law (Acts 15:1-5).

As against those who took the latter line, including "believers who belonged to the party of the Pharisees" (Acts 15:5), the narrative of Acts represents Paul and the Jerusalem leaders as sharing substantially the same tradition.[1] But a hint is given of another tradition, perhaps as far to the 'left' as the Pharisaic believers were to the 'right', represented by Apollos

[1] Acts 15:6 ff.; 21:17 ff.

of Alexandria, who was an expert in biblical exegesis, well versed in the story of Jesus, so that he could argue powerfully from the Old Testament that Jesus was the Messiah – yet his understanding of the Way deviated so much from the tradition which Acts presents as the main stream that by the standard of the latter it was positively defective (Acts 18:24–28).[1]

Interpretative Tradition at Qumran

For the readiest Jewish analogy to the distinctive Christian method of Old Testament interpretation we have to look not at rabbinical jurisprudence but at the literature of the Qumran community.

The Qumran community read for the most part the same sacred scriptures, so far as we can judge, as many of their fellow-Jews; but they read them through spectacles of quite a different sort and therefore understood them quite differently. This is true not only (as we have seen above) of Law, but even more so of their interpretation of the Prophets and Psalms, and of prophetic oracles and canticles found here and there in other Old Testament books. It is here that we find the really distinctive "tradition" by which the scriptures were understood at Qumran. This "tradition", by the testimony of the Qumran texts themselves, was established by the Teacher of Righteousness, whom God raised up to lead the faithful remnant "in the way of his heart, and to make known to the last generations what he was about to do to the last generation – the congregation of deceivers" (CD 1:11 f.). This man taught his followers how to interpret the prophetic writings, and enabled them to see their own duty and prospects written clearly there. To the prophets much had been revealed, but not everything. One thing in particular had been withheld from them – the *time* at which their oracles would be fulfilled – and the withholding of this meant that their oracles remained mysteries even to the prophets themselves, not to speak of their readers. But when the time of their fulfilment was at last revealed, the mystery was a mystery no longer: with this further revelation its solution was imparted. The man chosen by God to be the recipient of this further revelation was the Teacher of Righteousness. Of the oracle of Habakkuk, for example, the Qumran commentator on that prophet says: "God commanded Habakkuk to write the things that were coming on the last generation, but the fulfilment of the epoch he did not make known to him. And as for the expression, 'that he may run who reads it', its interpretation concerns the Teacher of Righteousness, to whom God made known all the mysteries of the words of his servants the prophets" (1 Qp Hab. 7:1–5, on Hab. 2:1 f.).

[1] It is tempting to speculate on the source or channel of Apollos's knowledge of the story of Jesus; evidently the Jerusalem community was not the only centre in Palestine from which the gospel was transmitted.

There are, of course, exceptions to the rule that the prophets were not told when their predictions would be fulfilled. We may recall passages in Isaiah, Jeremiah and Ezekiel where periods of between forty and seventy years from the prophet's time are prescribed for the accomplishment of certain events, such as Jeremiah's fixing of seventy years as the epoch of the desolations of Jerusalem (Jer. 25:11 f.; 29:10).[1] But the "epoch" which the Qumran interpreters had in mind was that which marked the end of the current age. In this respect they had only one canonical predecessor, Daniel. When Daniel reinterprets Jeremiah's seventy years as seventy sevens of years, the terminus of the period is not now a return from exile but the inauguration of the age to come, with the putting of an end to sin and the bringing in of everlasting righteousness (Dan. 9:2, 24–27). Josephus remarks that Daniel alone among the prophets of old was able to state the *time* of the fulfilment of his oracles;[2] in Qumran terminology, which is in essence that of the book of Daniel, his visions embrace both the mystery and its interpretation. Indeed, there is probably a closer relation between Daniel and the Teacher of Righteousness than can be established thus far by detailed evidence; it is somewhat surprising that, so far as I know, no one has thought of identifying the two.[3]

At any rate, instructed by the Teacher of Righteousness and the men who learned from him their principles of biblical exegesis, the members of the Qumran community found the sacred scriptures an open book. The interpretative "tradition" which they "received" – a "tradition" which to their minds was as fully the product of divine revelation as were the written oracles themselves – embodied a few simple principles:

(i) God revealed his purpose to the prophets, but the relevance of his purpose could not be understood until the *time* of its fulfilment was revealed to the Teacher of Righteousness.

(ii) All the words of the prophets referred to the time of the end.

(iii) The time of the end is at hand.

It was in the eschatological situation which the rise of the Teacher of Righteousness showed to be imminent that the interpretative context of any oracle was sought; the text was atomized, regardless of the original context, so as to fit here or there into the eschatological situation. Variant readings were selected so as best to serve the interpreter's purpose. Where a relation could not otherwise be established between the text and the eschatological situation, allegorization was employed.[4]

The men of Qumran, properly instructed in these principles, had no

---

[1] Cf. also Isa. 7:8; 23:15 ff; Ezek. 29:11 ff.

[2] *Ant.* x. 267.

[3] Cf. F. F. Bruce, "The Book of Daniel and the Qumran Community", *Neotestamentica et Semitica*, ed. E. E. Ellis and Max Wilcox (Edinburgh, 1969), pp. 221 ff.

[4] Cf. K. Elliger, *Studien zum Habakuk-Kommentar vom Toten Meer* (Tübingen, 1953); O. Betz, *Offenbarung und Schriftforschung in der Qumransekte* (Tübingen, 1960); F. F. Bruce, *Biblical Exegesis in the Qumran Texts* (London, 1960).

difficulty in understanding passages like Psalm 37:12, "the wicked watches the righteous and seeks to slay him",[1] or Hab. 1:4, "the wicked surrounds the righteous".[2] Language like this pointed unmistakably to the attacks made on the Teacher of Righteousness by his inveterate enemy, the Wicked Priest. References to the overthrow of Israel's enemies – the "sons of Sheth" in Balaam's oracles (Num. 24:17),[3] the Assyrians in Isaiah (Isa. 10:4 ff.;[4] 31:8),[5] the Chaldaeans in Habakkuk (Hab. 1:6 ff.),[6] Gog in Ezekiel (Ezek. 38:1 ff.)[7] and Daniel's last "king of the north" (Dan. 11:36 ff.)[8] – were understood not of nations contemporary with these prophets but of the last Gentile oppressors of the people of God, the *Kittim* of the commentaries and of the War scroll, who would come to their end, with none to help them (Dan. 11:45).

Again, references to the building of a wall or a city were understood of the building either of the righteous community or of some rival enterprise, political or religious, according as the building was spoken of in terms of approval, promising success, or in terms of reprobation, portending destruction. "Samaria" in Micah 1:5 is interpreted of the "spouter of falsehood, who led the simple astray" (perhaps some early leader of the group that developed into the party of the Pharisees), while "Jerusalem" is related to "the Teacher of Righteousness, who expounded the law to his council, to all who voluntarily pledged themselves to join the elect of God" (1 Qp Mic., fragments 8–10). The builders of the unstable wall in Ezek. 13:10 ff. are similarly the "spouter of falsehood" and his associates (CD 4:19; 8:12 f.); on the other hand, the "wall" of Micah 7:11 is the fence (the rule of life) which keeps the righteous community insulated from the contamination of evil (CD 4:12).[9]

The members of the righteous community are not only the builders of the well-founded wall; they are also the diggers of the well of Num. 21:17 f.: "'the nobles of the people' are those who have come to dig the well with the staves which the lawgiver appointed for them to walk withal during the whole epoch of wickedness" (CD 6:3 ff.).

And so on. When once the basic principles of the interpretative tradition are grasped, the sacred text becomes luminous.

Old Testament Interpretation in the Primitive Church

We turn now to the parallel situation in the early church.

[1] Cf. 4Qp Ps^a, col. 4, lines 7 ff.
[2] Cf. 1 Qp Hab 1:12 f.
[3] Quoted in CD 7:20; 1 QM 11:6; 4Q *Testimonia* 13.
[4] Cf. 4Qp Isa^a, *passim*.
[5] Quoted in 1 QM 11:11 f.
[6] Cf. 1 Qp Hab 2:11 ff.
[7] Cf. 1 QM 11:16.
[8] Cf. 1 QM 1:1 ff.
[9] Cf. the descriptions of scribes or members of the Sanhedrin as builders in TB *Shabbat* 114a; *Berakot* 64a, etc. (also Acts 4:11, "you builders" in a critical sense).

That the Old Testament prophecies were "mysteries" whose inter-pretation was concealed from the prophets themselves is a theme as common among the early Christians as it was at Qumran. The prophets, according to one New Testament writer, foretold the advent of the Christian salvation, but they did not grasp the full purport of their own predictions; they "searched and inquired diligently" in order to discover who was the person and what the time pointed to by the Spirit of messianic prophecy within them when bearing witness in advance to "the sufferings of the Messiah and the glories that were to follow" (I Pet. 1:10 f.). But the writer and his readers had no need to search and inquire diligently; they knew that the person was Jesus and the time was now. "This is that which was spoken through the prophet" – Peter's message on the day of Pentecost (Acts 2:16)[1] – is writ large over the New Testament writings; it is plainly affirmed in the gospel tradition itself. Jesus congratulates his disciples because they see and hear things to which prophets and righteous men had looked forward with longing expectation, but which they did not live to witness (Matt. 13:16 f.//Luke 10:23 f.).

Occasionally the very word "mystery", in the sense which it bears in Daniel and the Qumran texts, is used in this regard. "To you", says Jesus to His disciples, "has been given the secret (mystery) of the kingdom of God, but for those outside everything is in parables, so that they may indeed see but not perceive, and may indeed hear but not understand . . ." (Mark 4:11 f.).[2] One aspect of the gospel – the manner and purpose of its communication to the Gentile world – is treated in the Pauline letters as a mystery "which was not made known to the sons of men in other generations as it has now been revealed to Christ's holy apostles and prophets in the Spirit" (Eph. 3:4 f.).[3] That the Gentiles would place their hope on the Davidic Messiah and rejoice in Israel's God was foretold in the Old Testament, as Paul emphasizes in a catena of quotations in Rom. 15:9–12, but the implications of this hope were not appreciated until the time of its fulfilment.

This interpretative tradition pervades all the strata of the New Testament. We find it in the Synoptic records and in the Fourth Gospel, in Paul and Peter, in the Epistle to the Hebrews and the Revelation to John. The various writers have their distinctive hermeneutical principles and methods, it is true. Matthew records how this or that incident in the life of Jesus "took place in order that it might be fulfilled which was spoken through the prophet" (Matt. 1:23, etc.).[4] Paul sees the temporary and partial setting aside of Israel as clearly foretold in the Law, the Prophets

---

[1] Introducing the quotation from Joel 2:28 ff. about the eschatological outpouring of the Spirit.
[2] Quoting Isa. 6:9 f.
[3] Cf. Col. 1:26 f.; Rom. 16:25f.
[4] Cf. R. H. Gundry, *The Use of the Old Testament in St. Matthew's Gospel* (Leiden, 1967).

and the Psalms, as he finds the ingathering of the Gentiles adumbrated there (Rom. 9-11, *passim;* II Cor. 3:14 f.). John the Evangelist portrays Jesus as the fulfiller of a number of Old Testament motifs, such as the word, the glory and the tabernacle of Yahweh,[1] the bread of life,[2] the water of life,[3] the light of life;[4] while the Apocalypse, in Austin Farrer's words, is "a rebirth of images" from the Old Testament and other ancient lore[5] – some of them remarkably recalcitrant to a Christian purpose, yet all pressed into service to depict the triumph of Christ.[6] But, however variously the interpretative tradition be treated by the different New Testament writers, the core of the tradition is common property: the central subject of the Old Testament writings is Jesus; He is the one to whom they all bear witness.

The analogy of Qumran would lead us to the conclusion which is in any case the plain testimony of the gospel record: that the main lines of this tradition were laid down by Jesus Himself, whose "treatment of the Old Testament", it has been well said, "is based on two things: a profound understanding of the essential teaching of the Hebrew Scriptures and a sure judgement of his own contemporary situation."[7] The insistence that "so it is written" is too deeply imbedded in all the gospel strata to be reasonably suspected of being altogether an accretion, due to reflection in the post-Easter church on the events of the ministry and passion of Jesus. Even more impressive than the influence of the fourth Isaianic Servant Song (Isa. 52:13–53:12) in this regard is the way in which the visions and oracles of Zech. 9–14 have entered into the Evangelists' passion narratives, and this, I believe, stems from Jesus' own initiative – from His deliberate choice of "a colt, the foal of an ass" (Zech. 9:9)[8] as a mount when He rode into Jerusalem on Psalm Sunday, and His reference, an

---

[1] All three motifs are combined in John 1:14.

[2] John 6:35 (cf. Ps. 78:24 f.).

[3] John 4:10 ff.; 7:37 f. (cf. Ps. 78:15 f., 20; 105:41; Ezek. 47:1 ff.; Zech. 14:8; Rev. 22:1, 17).

[4] John 8:12 (cf. Ps. 56:13; 1 QS 3:7). These motifs, of course, were widespread in antiquity beyond the Old Testament. Cf. R. A. Henderson, *The Gospel of Fulfilment* (London, 1936); J. G. H. Hoffmann, "Le quatrième Evangile", *La Revue Réformée* 3 (1952), pp. 1 ff.; and pre-eminently C. H. Dodd, *The Interpretation of the Fourth Gospel* (Cambridge, 1953).

[5] A. M. Farrer, *A Rebirth of Images* (London, 1949). The motif of the heavenly book, familiar in other settings (cf. G. Widengren, *The Ascension of the Apostle and the Heavenly Book*, Uppsala, 1950), has its New Testament representation not surprisingly in the Apocalypse. This work is introduced by the words, "the apocalypse of Jesus Christ which God gave to him" (Rev. 1:1), and we actually see God giving it to him in Rev. 5:7, in the form of the seven-sealed scroll of destiny. The fulfilment of the divine purpose written down there in advance (cf. the "book of truth" in Dan. 10:21) is launched by the unsealing of the scroll and divulging of its contents. Yet the rich pre-history of the Apocalypse is plain to read even on its surface.

[6] E.g. the use of Isa. 63:1 ff. in Rev. 19:11 ff.

[7] T. W. Manson, "The Old Testament in the Teaching of Jesus", *BJRL* 34 (1951–52), p. 332. We are thus provided, he goes on, with "the standard and pattern for our own exegesis of the Old Testament and the New".

[8] Quoted in Matt. 21:5; John 12:15; cf. Mark 11:1 ff.; Luke 19:29 ff.

hour or two before His arrest, to the words of Zech. 13:7, "Smite the shepherd and scatter the sheep" (Mark 14:27).[1]

This reference to Zech. 9–14 illustrates a feature of New Testament interpretation of the Old Testament which to a large degree distinguishes it from that found in the Qumran texts. The New Testament interpretation of a few words or sentences from the Old Testament which are actually quoted very often implies the context in which these words or sentences occur. In addition to Zech. 9–14 we may think of such contexts as Isa. 40–66 and Psalm 69. Various New Testament writers will quote different words or sentences from the same context in a manner which suggests that the complete context had received a Christian interpretation before these writers quoted from it. It has been pointed out, for example, that from Psalm 69:9 ("zeal for thy house has consumed me, and the insults of those who insult thee have fallen on me") the former part is applied to Christ in John 2:17 and the latter part in Rom. 15:3. While no one is likely to maintain that the one writer has influenced the other, "it would be too much of a coincidence if the two writers independently happened to cite the two halves of a single verse, unless they were both aware that at least this whole verse, if not any more of the Psalm, formed part of a scheme of scriptural passages generally held to be especially significant".[2] This implies something more substantial in the way of primitive Christian exegesis of the Old Testament than a catena of isolated proof-texts or *testimonia* such as has sometimes been envisaged.[3]

Alongside this contextual element in the Christian interpretative tradition there is another, which (unlike the former) does have an analogue at Qumran (as also in rabbinical literature). This is the bringing together of widely separated scriptures which have a significant term in common and giving them a unitive exegesis. One of the most prominent examples of this in the New Testament is the widespread evidence for an integrated messianic interpretation of various "stone" passages in the Old Testament – the stone which the builders rejected in Psalm 118:22, the stone in Nebuchadnezzar's dream which pulverized the great image (Dan. 2:34 f.), the tested corner stone of sure foundation in Isa. 28:16 and the rock of refuge amid the flood waters in Isa. 8:14 which proves a stone of stumbling to those who refuse to take refuge upon it.[4] Again, we find the "one like a son of man" of Dan. 7:13 brought into close relation with the

---

[1] Cf. my *This is That* (Exeter, 1969), pp. 101 ff.

[2] C. H. Dodd, *The Old Testament in the New* (London, 1952), p. 8; cf. his *According to the Scriptures* (London, 1952), p. 57 ("it is more than probable that both writers were guided by a tradition in which this psalm was already referred to Christ"). Cf. further quotations from Ps. 69 in John 15:25; Acts 1:20, and allusions in the passion narratives of Matt. 27:34, 48; Mark 15:36; Luke 23:36; John 19:28.

[3] Cf. J. R. Harris, *Testimonies* i, ii (Cambridge, 1916, 1920). The subject is also treated by B. Lindars, *New Testament Apologetic* (London, 1961).

[4] Cf. Luke 20:17 f.; Acts 4:11 f.; Rom. 9:33; I Peter 2:6–8 (*This is That*, pp. 65 f.).

"son of man" of Psalm 8:4 beneath whose feet all things have been placed and possibly also with the "son of man" of Psalm 80:17 whom God makes strong for Himself;[1] or we find the deliverance from death of God's "holy one" in Psalm 16:10 linked in Acts 13:34 f. with the promise of the "holy things" securely promised to David in Isa. 55:3, so as to provide a joint *testimonium* of the resurrection of Christ.[2]

It is not surprising that the Psalter as well as the Prophets should be expounded thus. As for those royal psalms which were commonly acknowledged in the first century A.D. as 'messianic', it was natural that early Christians should recognize their fulfilment in Jesus. The divine oracle of Psalm 2:7, "Thou art my Son, today I have begotten thee", was spontaneously understood of Him; its opening clause formed part of the utterance with which the heavenly voice addressed Him at His baptism (Mark 1:11); indeed, according to the Western text of Luke 3:22, the heavenly voice simply quoted the ancient oracle. But if Jesus was the one addressed in the oracle, it was not difficult to fit the rest of the psalm into His story. Hence in Acts 4:24–28 the apostles pray:

> Sovereign Lord, who didst make the heaven and the earth and the sea and everything in them, who by the mouth of our father David, thy servant, didst say by the Holy Spirit,
>
>> "Why did the Gentiles rage,
>> and the people imagine vain things?
>> The kings of the earth set themselves in array,
>> and the rulers were gathered together,
>> against the Lord and against his Anointed" –
>
> for truly in this city there were gathered together against thy holy servant Jesus, whom thou didst anoint, both Herod and Pontius Pilate, with the Gentiles and the peoples of Israel, to do whatever thy hand and thy plan had predestined to take place.[3]

There are also several psalms in which a righteous sufferer voices his complaint to God; there were equally naturally interpreted of Jesus, especially Psalm 22, whose language has been woven into the passion narratives of the Gospels, especially Matthew's and John's. Had not Jesus confirmed this interpretation of Psalm 22 by making its opening cry His own in the bitterness of dereliction on the cross?[4]

But if the righteous sufferer was recognized as Jesus, the persecutors

---

[1] Cf. Heb. 2:5–9; I Cor. 15:25–27; Eph. 1:22; I Peter 3:22.

[2] Cf. *This is That*, pp. 69 ff.

[3] A variation on this exegesis is given by Tertullian, *On the Resurrection of the Flesh* 20. Cf. the quotations from (or allusions to) Ps. 2 in Heb. 1:5; 5:5; Rev. 2:26 f., etc.; and the similar appeal to Ps. 110 in Mark 12:35 ff.; 14:62; Acts 2:34 f.; Rom. 8:34; Eph. 1:20; Heb. 1:13; 5:6, etc.; I Peter 3:22, etc.

[4] Ps. 22:1, quoted in Mark 15:34//Matt. 27:46; cf. the extended application of this psalm in Heb. 2:12 and (probably) 5:7.

of the righteous sufferer were identified with Jesus' enemies,[1] and with none more freely than with Judas Iscariot.[2] Here again the cue appears to have been given by Jesus Himself; we need not doubt that at the Last Supper He used the words of Psalm 41:9, "he who ate of my bread has lifted his heel against me", to indicate to his companions that He knew there was a traitor in the camp (John 13:18). It was no difficult matter to find other passages in the Psalter which could be similarly applied to Judas; Peter's quotation in this connexion of Psalms 69:25 ("Let his habitation become desolate, and let there be none to live in it") and 109:8 ("His office let another take") is a case in point (Acts 1:20).

Post-Apostolic Development

With such dominical and apostolic precedent, the Christian church was able so to read the Old Testament writings that they supplied not only an increasing store of christological *testimonia* but additional factual evidence about New Testament events.[3] This tendency we find well established in Justin Martyr, who is capable of finding a passion *testimonium* in the Septuagint version of Jer. 11:19, "Come, let us put wood in his bread" (RSV "Let us destroy the tree with its fruit") – the "wood" being the cross and the "bread" the body of Jesus.[4] We find it again in the *Testimonia* ascribed to Cyprian where, in addition to Jer. 11:19, predictions of the crucifixion are discerned in a variety of Old Testament texts, including Psalm 141:2 ("Let the lifting up of my hands be as an evening sacrifice") and Isa. 65:2 ("I spread out my hands all the day to a rebellious people").[5]

The same tendency was carried to excess in the Middle Ages. The passion narrative in particular was embellished by the liberal importation of Old Testament language and motifs, sometimes divorced from their original context to fit this new one. Here, for example, is the mother of Jesus speaking in the thirteenth-century Pseudo-Anselmian *Dialogue with the Blessed Virgin Mary*:

> When they came to the shameful "place of a skull", where dogs and other carrion were cast forth, they stripped my only son Jesus totally of his garments, and I fainted; yet I took the veil from my head and wound it around his loins. After this they set down the cross on the ground, and stretched him upon it, and first they drove in one nail so hard that then his blood could not flow out,

---

[1] Cf. the quotation and application of Ps. 2:1 f. in Acts 4:25 ff. (p. 81 above).

[2] Cf. John 17:12 ("none of them [the disciples] is lost but the son of perdition, that the scripture might be fulfilled") and Matt. 27:9 f., where Zech. 11:12 f. is used as a Judas *testimonium* (*This is That*, pp. 108 ff.).

[3] This methodology is not extinct; I have heard it argued from the context of Ps. 109:8 (applied to Judas in Acts 1:20) that Judas was a married man with a family (cf. Ps. 109:9).

[4] Justin, *Dialogue with Trypho*, 72.

[5] Cyprian, *Testimonia* ii. 20.

so completely was the wound filled. Next they took ropes and pulled the other arm of my son Jesus, and drove the second nail into it. Then they pulled his feet with ropes, and drove in a very sharp nail, and he was so stretched out that all his bones and members were exposed, so that the saying in the psalm was fulfilled, "They numbered all my bones" [Psalm 22:17].[1]

Further striking examples are provided in the fourteenth-century German mystical treatise now called *Christ's Sufferings seen in a Vision,* where the restrained accounts of the Evangelists are freely eked out with detail from the prophets.[2] Thus, when Christ was arrested in the garden,

he was dragged off with violent, wild, raving mad passion, with heavy blows of armed fists and hands on his neck and between his shoulders and on his back and head and cheeks and throat and breast . . . They pulled the hair from his head so that his locks lay strewn on the ground. Some dragged him by the hair, others by the beard . . .[3]

This expansion has drawn imaginatively on the words of the third Isaianic Servant Song: "I gave my back to the smiters and my cheeks to those who pulled out the beard . . ." (Isa. 50:6). Similarly, when Pilate brought Jesus forth and said "Behold, your King" (John 19:12), "his appearance was so marred, beyond human semblance" after the scourging and crowning with thorns that they turned their faces from him and shouted, "Take him out of our sight . . ."[4] – a palpable borrowing from the fourth Servant Song (Isa. 52:14; 53:3).

Or we may take the fifteenth-century poem *Quia amore langueo,* which breathes the air of Bernard's exposition of the Song of Songs and treats the words of Cant. 1:5, "I am sick with love" (or "I suffer pain for love's sake") as a passion theme:

> Upon this hill I found a tree,
> Under a tree a man sitting;
> From head to foot wounded was he,
> His hearte blood I saw bleeding;
> A seemly man to be a king,
> A gracious face to look unto –
> I asked why he had paining:
> "Quia amore langueo".[5]

Even today this tendency is strong enough in much traditional Christian

[1] *Dialogus S. Anselmi cum B.V. Maria,* ch. 10 (Migne, *PL* 159, col. 271 f.).
[2] *Christi Leiden in einer Vision geschaut,* ed. R. Priebsch (Heidelberg, 1936); ed. F. P. Pickering (Manchester, 1952). Cf. F. P. Pickering, *Literatur und darstellende Kunst im Mittelalter* (Berlin, 1966), especially the section on "Christi Kreuzigung" (pp. 146 ff.).
[3] *Christi Leiden . . .,* ed. Priebsch, p. 32; ed. Pickering, pp. 65 ff.
[4] *Christi Leiden . . .,* ed. Priebsch, pp. 39 ff.; ed. Pickering, p. 72.
[5] Quoted by G. L. Prestige, *Fathers and Heretics* (London, 1954), p. 195 ("its whole contents", says Prestige, "are permeated with the spirit and language of Bernard's exposition of the Song of Songs"). Chapter I of Prestige's book, entitled "Tradition: or, The Scriptural Basis of Theology", is germane to our general theme.

piety to cause some uneasiness when it is found that a modern version of the Old Testament adopts readings or renderings which do not lend themselves so easily to this kind of application as older versions have done. For example, the words of Psalm 22:16, "they pierced my hands and my feet", have been read by thousands as a most precise prophecy of the crucifixion of Jesus, although they are not quoted as a *testimonium* in the New Testament. There is, however, enough uncertainty about the meaning of the Hebrew to make room for other translations (like Moffatt's "my hands and feet are all disfigured"), which are viewed with disquiet and suspicion on quite other grounds than concern for Hebrew lexicography and textual criticism.[1]

Christ in the Old Testament

One important phase of the early Christian interpretative tradition is the tracing of a recurrent pattern in the story of God's dealing with his people. For instance, New Testament writers view the history of Israel in the Old Testament, with special emphasis on the course of events from Egypt to Canaan, as recapitulated either in the personal experience of the Messiah or in the corporate experience of the church.[2]

There is again the interpretative principle which Professor A. T. Hanson calls the "real presence" of Christ in Old Testament history.[3] I do not see so much of it in the New Testament as he does, but it cannot be denied that more than one New Testament writer thought of Jesus in person, before His incarnation, as delivering the Israelites from Egypt and leading them through the wilderness into the promised land.[4] This principle appears fully developed in the second century, not least in Justin's *Apology*[5] and *Dialogue with Trypho*.[6] Justin criticizes the Jewish

---

[1] Cf. the Jerusalem Bible ("they tie me hand and foot", following Jerome) and NEB ("they have hacked off my hands and my feet"). We may think of the sense of loss when the publication of the RV in 1885 revealed that the "plant of renown" (Ezek. 34:29, AV) and the "desire of all nations" (Hag. 2:7, AV) had disappeared from the English Bible, and the agitation in 1952 when the RSV jettisoned "Kiss the Son" from Psalm 2:12 and put "young woman" in place of "virgin" in the text of Isa. 7:14.

[2] Cf. J. R. Harris, "Jesus and the Exodus" *Testimonies* ii (Cambridge, 1920), pp. 51 ff.; E. Käsemann, *Das wandernde Gottesvolk* (Göttingen, 1938); H. Sahlin, "The New Exodus of Salvation according to S. Paul", in A. Fridrichsen *et al., The Root of the Vine* (London, 1953), pp. 81 ff.; R. P. C. Hanson, *Allegory and Event* (London, 1965); J. Daniélou, *From Shadow to Reality*, E. T. (London 1960); S. H. Hooke, *Alpha and Omege* (London, 1961), *passim*; R. E. Nixon, *The Exodus in the New Testament* (London 1963); D. Daube, *The Exodus Pattern in the Bible* (London, 1963); H. H. Rowley, "The Authority of the Bible", *From Moses to Qumran* (London, 1963) pp. 3 ff.; F. F. Bruce, *This is That*, pp. 23, 32 ff. The Exodus pattern has been used already in the history of Israel as a mode of portraying the return from the Babylonian exile, especially in Isa. 40–55.

[3] A. T. Hanson, *Jesus Christ in the Old Testament* (London, 1965), p. 7 *et passim*.

[4] E.g. I Cor. 10:4; Jude 5 (cf. *This is That*, pp. 34 ff.).

[5] *First Apology* 63.

[6] *Dialogue* 59 f.

belief that the one who said to Moses in the bush, "I am the God of Abraham and the God of Isaac and the God of Jacob" (Ex. 3:6), was "the Father and Creator of the universe".[1] No, says Justin, they are wrong, as the spirit of prophecy says, "Israel does not know me, my people have not understood me" (Isa. 1:3);[2] it was the Son of God who spoke those words. For it was "the angel of the Lord" that appeared to Moses in the burning bush (Ex. 3:2), and it is the Son of God, says Justin, "who is called both angel and apostle".[3] Justin was perfectly well acquainted with the Synoptic controversy in which these words from Ex. 3:6 are quoted by Jesus Himself with unambiguous reference to "the Father and Creator of the universe" (Mark 12:26 and parallels);[4] but that could not outweigh his settled interpretative principle that where "the angel of the Lord" appears in the Old Testament narrative – especially in passages where the phrase alternates with "God" or "the Lord" – the pre-incarnate Christ is indicated. In fact, Trypho's exegesis of Ex. 3:6 is more in line with that of Jesus than Justin's is: "This is not what we understand from the words quoted", says Trypho in reply to Justin, "but we understand that, while it was an *angel* that appeared in a flame of fire, it was *God* who spoke to Moses".[5] Justin and Trypho read substantially the same Bible, apart from some textual variations of an interesting character,[6] but in another sense they read different Bibles, because their respective "traditions" were so different.

By the same process Justin argues that it was Christ who announced the birth of Isaac to Abraham and Sarah (Gen. 18:9 ff.),[7] who overthrew the cities of the plain (Gen. 19:1 ff.),[8] who spoke to Jacob in his dreams at Bethel (Gen. 28:10 ff.; 35:6 ff.) and Paddan-aram (Gen. 31:10 ff.) and wrestled with him at Peniel (Gen. 32:22 ff.),[9] who appeared to Joshua as captain of the Lord's host (Josh. 5:13 ff.)[10] and so forth. This line of interpretation has passed into traditional Christian theology; in its main features, however, it is post-apostolic and goes far beyond the limited use made of it in the New Testament.

Quite apart from the differences between the Septuagint and Masssoretic

---

[1] *First Apology* 63:11; *Dialogue* 60:2, 3.
[2] *First Apology* 63:12.
[3] *First Apology* 63:5.
[4] Justin quotes Luke 20:35 f. (parallel to Mark 12:25) in *Dialogue* 81:4.
[5] *Dialogue* 60:1.
[6] While Justin knew and recognized as authoritative several of the books of what later came to be called the New Testament, his Bible did not include a New Testament as the later Christian Bible did (see p. 139). Where his biblical text and Trypho's diverged, as in the famous question of the insertion or omission of ἀπὸ τοῦ ξύλου in Ps. 96:10 (LXX 95:10), Trypho's was the more accurate (*Dialogue* 41; 73).
[7] *Dialogue* 56:6 ff.
[8] *Dialogue* 56:19 ff.
[9] *Dialogue* 58.
[10] *Dialogue* 62:4 f.

texts, Jews and Christians could no longer be said to read the same scriptures in a material sense, in view of the divergent "traditions" by which they understood them. The accepted Christian tradition became more sharply anti-Judaic, and the Jewish tradition in turn became increasingly careful to exclude those renderings or interpretations, previously quite acceptable, which now proved to lend themselves all too readily to Christian use.[1] So, despite the common heritage of the sacred scriptures, the two opposed traditions hardened. Only in more recent times, with the acceptance on both sides of the principle of grammatico-historical exegesis, have their hard outlines softened, so that today Jews and Christians of varying traditions can collaborate happily in joint Bible study, translation and interpretation. No doubt they will still differ when it comes to discerning a *sensus plenior* in the text, but the *sensus plenior* will at least be based on a common foundation of primary exegesis.[2]

---

[1] We may instance the Jewish rejection of the Septuagint (cf. *Sopherim* 1:8 f.) or the shocked surprise of Aqiba's hearers when he appeared still to accept the messianic identification of the "one like a son of man" in Dan. 7:13 (TB *Hagigah 14a, Sanhedrin 36b*).

[2] In the Christian tradition, for example, the *sensus plenior* includes much Christological exposition of the Old Testament, together with the wealth of association that has passed into communal consciousness through the experience and use of the Bible over many generations by the church and its individual members (cf. the kind of light that is shed on the Psalter by such a work as R. E. Prothero's *The Psalms in Human Life*, London, 1903). But the validity and acceptance of all such *sensus plenior* must be subject to the one original sense.

CHAPTER VI

EXTRA-CANONICAL TRADITION

WHAT WE HAVE CALLED THE GOSPEL TRADITION – THE body of tradition ultimately incorporated in our four canonical Gospels – does not exhaust the church's tradition about Jesus. The fourth Evangelist informs his readers that, in addition to the "signs" which he has selected for narration and exposition, "Jesus did many other signs in the presence of the disciples, which are not written in this book" (John 20:30), and, according to a note appended to his Gospel, "there are also many other things which Jesus did; were every one of them to be written, I suppose that the world itself could not contain the books that would be written" (John 21:25).

Agrapha

But in fact hardly any tradition of what Jesus *did*, whether "signs" or otherwise, has been preserved outside the four Gospels.[1] What we have in such a second-century document as the *Infancy Gospel of Thomas*[2] is not tradition, but imaginative fiction. It is otherwise with what Jesus *said*. A considerable number of His utterances (genuine or alleged) may be found in early Christian literature. These utterances are commonly called *agrapha*, "unwritten" sayings – not a very apt designation, for all that it means is that they are not written in the canonical Gospels. They are written elsewhere; otherwise we should know nothing of them, for they have not been preserved to our day by oral tradition. One of these sayings occurs in the New Testament, in Acts 20:35, where Paul, addressing the elders of the Ephesian church, recalls "the words of the Lord Jesus, how he said, 'It is more blessed to give than to receive'." If we had not the Synoptic narratives of the institution of the Eucharist, then Paul's account of it in I Cor. 11:23–25 would have ranked as a most valuable *agraphon*.

Again, some Gospel manuscripts contain sayings of Jesus which, on grounds of textual criticism, cannot be regarded as belonging to the original text. One of these comes immediately after the saying about "a ransom for many" in Matt. 20:28:

[1] The *pericope adulterae* has been preserved by being attached to one of the canonical Gospels – in John 7:53–8:11 or, in family 13, after Luke 21:38. Cf. also the incident of sowing seed on the Jordan in Papyrus Egerton 2 (E. T. in *New Testament Apocrypha*, ed. R. McL. Wilson, i, London, 1963, p. 97).

[2] E. T. by A. J. B. Higgins in *New Testament Apocrypha*, ed. R. McL. Wilson, i, pp. 388 ff.

But do you seek to increase from smallness, and from the greater to become
less . . .[1]

Another, much better known, is the addition to the controversial sabbath
incidents in Luke 6:1–11 found in Codex Bezae (the principal witness to
the Western text of the Gospels and Acts) between verses 5 and 6.[2] These
sayings are not *ad hoc* inventions, but fragments of floating tradition which
scribes or editors have preserved from oblivion by inserting them in appropriate contexts of the canonical record.

Of *logia* preserved in those uncanonical Gospels which have not completely lost touch with the church's tradition, more particularly the *Gospel
according to the Hebrews*,[3] some are independent sayings in general keeping
with canonical sayings like

Never be joyful except when you look on your brother in love.[4]

Some are expansions of canonical sayings, like Jesus' reply to the rich
young man who claimed to have kept the commandments:

How can you say "I have kept the law and the prophets"? For it is written in
the law, "You shall love your neighbour as yourself", and see, many of your
brothers, sons of Abraham, are clad in rags, dying of hunger, and your house
is full of many good things, and nothing at all goes forth from it to them.[5]

Yet others have an apologetic motive, like Jesus' answer to the suggestion
of His mother and brothers that they should all go and be baptized by
John:

What sin have I committed that I should go and be baptized by him? – unless
this thing I have said just now is itself [a sin of] ignorance.[6]

(That Jesus should receive John's "baptism of repentance for the remission
of sins" was something which called for explanation.)

These last two extracts from the *Gospel according to the Hebrews* illustrate the tendency of sayings to be embellished rhetorically or theologically as they were passed on from one to another. A notable example of
such embellishment is provided by the Oxyrhynchus papyrus 840 (first
published in 1907), where Jesus, rebuked by a Pharisaic high priest for
entering the temple precincts (probably the Court of Israel) with His
disciples without having bathed (a requirement which the critic had
scrupulously fulfilled), says:

---

[1] In Cod. D and a few other Western witnesses.
[2] See p. 62 for the *logion*.
[3] Cf. *New Testament Apocrypha* i, pp. 158 ff.
[4] Quoted by Jerome, *Commentary on Eph.* 5:4, from "the Hebrew Gospel".
[5] Quoted by Origen, *Commentary on Matt.* 19:16 ff. (Latin translation), from "a certain
Gospel which is called 'According to the Hebrews'".
[6] Quoted by Jerome, *Against Pelagius* iii. 2, from "the Gospel according to the Hebrews,
which is written in the Chaldaean and Syriac language, but in Hebrew letters, and is used by
the Nazarenes to the present day."

Alas for you blind men who do not see! You have washed in this water which pours forth, in which dogs and pigs have wallowed night and day, and you have washed and scrubbed your outer skin, which harlots and flute-girls also anoint and wash and scrub and beautify to arouse human desire, while inwardly they are filled with scorpions and all unrighteousness. But I and my disciples, whom you declare not to have bathed, have bathed ourselves in the living . . . water which comes down from [heaven].[1]

This saying, which has certain affinities with the *Gospel according to the Hebrews,* cannot be regarded as an authentic utterance of Jesus, although its main emphasis – the superior importance of inward cleansing over that which is external – forms the theme of a number of canonical sayings.

Before the discovery of this papyrus other Greek papyri from Oxyrhynchus had excited great interest because of new sayings of Jesus which they contained. They were Papyrus 1, published in 1897, and Papyri 654 and 655, discovered in 1903.[2] Between them these three papyri, dating from the third century A.D., contained fifteen or sixteen sayings of Jesus, most of which were previously unknown, though a few had reasonably close affinities to sayings in the Synoptic Gospels, and others were paralleled by quotations in early Christian writers.

Their publication made a deep impression. Since the fragments plainly came from a compilation of sayings of Jesus, each introduced by the formula "Jesus said", it was assumed by some people that this compilation was a translation of the work ascribed by Papias to Matthew, who "compiled the *logia* in the Hebrew speech, and everyone translated them as best he could".[3] They were referred to and discussed as the "Oxyrhynchus Logia".[4] Their influence was manifested in poetry and hymnody, notably in Francis Thompson's "The Kingdom of God".[5]

The Gospel according to Thomas

The character of the sayings contained in these three papyri was made plain with the publication in 1959 of the Coptic text of the *Gospel according*

[1] Cf. *New Testament Apocrypha* i, pp. 92 ff. As good a case as can be made for the authenticity of this incident is made by J. Jeremias, *Unknown Sayings of Jesus*, E. T. (London, ²1964), pp. 47 ff., but unsuccessfully. (It is one of 21 *agrapha* which, in Jeremias's opinion, have a serious claim to consideration as genuine utterances of Jesus.)

[2] E. T. in *New Testament Apocrypha* i, pp. 98 ff. (Papyrus 654), 104 ff. (Papyrus 1), 110 ff. (Papyrus 655). Cf. R. A. Kraft, "Oxyrhynchus Papyrus 655 Reconsidered", *HTR* 54 (1961), pp. 253 ff.

[3] Quoted by Eusebius, *Hist. Eccl.* iii. 39. 16. See p. 109.

[4] A natural inference, e.g., from the title of ΛΟΓΙΑ ΙΗCΟΥ (*Sayings of our Lord*), ed. B. P. Grenfell and A. S. Hunt (Oxford, 1897).

[5] The poem beginning "O world invisible, we view thee" (see p. 94). Cf. the hymn "Those who love and those who labour" by G. D. in *Songs of Praise* (enlarged edition), No. 669.

to *Thomas*,[1] one of the forty-nine documents contained in thirteen leather-bound papyrus codices which were discovered by peasants in 1945 in a large jar in a fourth-century Christian tomb at the foot of Jebel et-Tarif in Upper Egypt – the so-called Nag Hammadi papyri.[2]

This *Gospel according to Thomas* is a compilation of 114 sayings of Jesus, translated into Coptic from Greek. The mid-second-century Greek original is plainly the document represented fragmentarily in the Oxyrhynchus papyri. The Coptic version indeed represents a different (more gnosticized) recension of the work from that represented by the Oxyrhynchus papyri, but the essential identity of the two is beyond reasonable doubt.

The *Gospel according to Thomas* begins with words already known in a fragmentary form from the opening lines of Oxyrhynchus papyrus 654:

> These are the secret words which Jesus the Living One spoke and Didymus Judas Thomas[3] wrote down. And he said: "Whosoever finds the interpretation of these sayings shall never taste death."[4] Jesus said: "Let not him who seeks desist until he finds. When he finds he will be troubled; when he is troubled he will marvel, and he will reign over the universe."

The latter saying is quoted by Clement of Alexandria as coming from the *Gospel according to the Hebrews*.[5] The description of Jesus in the opening sentence as the "Living One" probably means the "Risen One"; it is a common motif in Gnostic documents to represent the esoteric teaching which they contain as delivered by Jesus to the disciples in the course of His post-resurrection appearances.[6] But no use is made of this motif in

---

[1] *The Gospel according to Thomas* (Coptic text with English translation), ed. A. Guillaumont, H.-Ch. Puech, G. Quispel, W. Till and Yassah 'Abd al Masih (Leiden and London, 1959); E. T. also in R. M. Grant and D. N. Freedman, *The Secret Sayings of Jesus* (London, 1960), and *New Testament Apocrypha* i, pp. 511 ff. The manuscript bears the colophon, "The Gospel according to Thomas". Three important studies of this compilation are R. McL. Wilson, *Studies in the Gospel of Thomas* (London, 1960); B. Gärtner, *The Theology of the Gospel of Thomas* (London, 1961); H. Montefiore and H. E. W. Turner, *Thomas and the Evangelists* (London, 1962).

[2] Cf. W. C. van Unnik, *Newly Discovered Gnostic Writings*, E. T. (London, 1960); J. Doresse, *The Secret Books of the Egyptian Gnostics*, E. T. (London, 1960).

[3] Didymus (Greek) and Thomas (Aramaic) both mean "twin". The name Judas Thomas suggests a Syrian origin; in the Old Syriac Gospels "Judas not Iscariot" of John 14.22 is identified with Thomas.

[4] A Johannine expression (cf. John 8:51 f.), recurring elsewhere in the *Gospel of Thomas*.

[5] *Stromata* ii. 45.5; v. 96.3.

[6] Cf. the *Apocryphon of John*, one of the Nag Hammadi texts known earlier from the Berlin Coptic Papyrus 8502, on the basis of which its *editio princeps* was published by W. Till in *TU* 60 (Berlin, 1955). E. T. in *Gnosticism: An Anthology*, ed. R. M. Grant (London, 1961), pp. 69 ff.; cf. *New Testament Apocrypha* i, pp. 314 ff. It records a revelation purporting to have been made to the Apostle John by the glorified Christ, beginning thus:

> One day, when John the brother of James (these are the two sons of Zebedee) had come up to the temple, a Pharisee named Arimanaios came up to him and said: "Where is your Master whom you used to follow?" He said to him: "He has gone back to the place from which He came." The Pharisee replied: "This Nazarene deluded you and led you astray; He closed your hearts and took you away from the traditions of your fathers."

the *Gospel of Thomas*: it is not the sayings themselves that are secret, but their interpretation; and that was evidently an interpretation in line with the principles of a particular Gnostic school.

This emerges more clearly from a curious variant of the Caesarea Philippi incident which is related in the *Gospel of Thomas* (Saying 13):

> Jesus said to his disciples: "Compare me and tell me who I am like." Simon Peter said to him: "You are like a holy angel." Matthew said to him: "You are like a wise man and a philosopher." Thomas said to him: "Master, my face is quite unable to grasp who you are like, that I may express it." Jesus said: "I am not your Master, for you have been drinking; you are intoxicated with the bubbling spring which belongs to me and which I have spread abroad." Then he took him and drew him aside, and spoke three words to him. When Thomas came back to his companions, they asked him: "What did Jesus say to you?" Thomas answered: "If I tell you one of the words which he spoke to me, you will take stones and throw them at me, and a fire will come out of the stones and burn you up!"

One of the Gnostic sects, the Naassenes, believed stones to be animate beings, and held that the existence of the world depended on three secret words – *Caulacau, Saulasau, Zeesar*.[1] These words certainly convey an impression of mystery, until one realizes that they are simply corruptions of the Hebrew phrases in Isaiah 28:10, 13, translated "line upon line", "precept upon precept", and "there a little"! And it is probably more than a mere coincidence that Hippolytus refers to a *Gospel of Thomas* which he says was used by the Naassenes.[2]

The literary genre to which the *Gospel of Thomas* belongs is quite a

---

[1] Hippolytus, *Refutation of Heresies* v. 3. The Naassenes were so-called from Heb. *nāḥāsh*, "serpent", because they venerated the serpent of Gen. 3:1 ff. as the communicator of knowledge to men. It is probably the same people who were called Ophites, from ὄφις, the Greek word for "serpent".

[2] *Refutation* v. 2. Hippolytus quotes a passage from the *Gospel of Thomas* which is paralleled in Saying 4 of our Coptic version and in Oxyrhynchus Papryus 654, but is either quoted very freely or taken from yet another recension.

> When I heard that [says John], I came away from the sanctuary to a desolate spot, and with great sorrow of heart I thought: "How then was the Redeemer appointed and why was He sent into the world by His Father who sent Him? And who *is* His Father? And what is the nature of that aeon to which we shall go? He said to us: 'This aeon has taken on the form of that aeon which shall never pass away.' But He did not teach us about that aeon, of what nature it is." Straightway as I thought that, heaven opened, the whole creation was radiant with an unearthly light, and the whole world was shaken. I was afraid and fell to the ground.

Then John tells how the exalted Christ appeared to him in the role of the Gnostic Redeemer, and promised to be with John and his fellow-disciples always. This promise reminds one of Matt. 28:19 f., but the trinitarian language of the canonical Gospel is replaced by the formula: "I am the Father, I am the Mother [probably the Holy Spirit], I am the Son." John goes on to describe how the Christ gave him an account of the origin of the world, of man and of evil, based on a Gnosticizing interpretation of Genesis 1-6, and of the ultimate destiny of souls.

Unlike the canonical Apocalypse of John, which records a revelation by the risen Christ of "things which must shortly come to pass", this apocryphon is more interested in "that which was from the beginning".

familiar one; the best-known contemporary example is probably the anthologized *Thoughts of Mao Tse-tung*.[1]

Memorable words of great men are frequently remembered in their own right, without being related to a firm context. We can see this happening in the case of one of our great contemporaries, Sir Winston Churchill. Some sayings are attributed to him in oral tradition whose authenticity is doubtful at best, and of those that may be accepted as genuine many are not securely attached to a historical setting. But from this oral tradition one fact emerges with clarity: Sir Winston Churchill was the kind of man to whom such pithy sayings are credibly assigned; no one would assign a typical Churchillism to his wartime colleague Earl Attlee!

Another example comes to mind. For a couple of generations and more many pulpits in the Church of Scotland have been occupied by men who studied under Principal James Denney. One thing above all characterizes Denney's men; they can never stop quoting him. Great numbers of Denney's pointed sayings have thus passed into common circulation; but it is difficult, if not impossible, to give chapter and verse for them all. They have a quality which makes their authenticity unmistakable, even if Denney himself never put them on paper. Being preserved in oral tradition, they have no doubt been subjected to those influences to which form critics draw our attention, and they may have had attached to them some anonymous sayings which are sufficiently like the sort of thing that Denney said to deceive all but Denny's own students. When once Denney's last student has gone the way of all flesh, it will be very difficult for anyone who is challenged to demonstrate the authenticity of any particular one of Denny's *agrapha;* yet there is a self-consistency about the bulk of them which will continue to serve as a general guarantee.

Similarly, when we find sayings attributed to Jesus which are not recorded in our primary sources, but are sufficiently in keeping with those canonical sayings which are firmly established as authentic, we may accord them a high rating of probability. When, on the other hand, we find sayings attributed to Him (as sometimes we do in the *Gospel of Thomas* and related writings) which are wildly out of character, we need not hesitate to regard them as spurious and to look to other sources than the apostolic tradition for their motivation.

We can make a convenient classification of the principal sayings on the following lines:

1. Sayings with Canonical Parallels.
2. Canonical Sayings Amplified or Conflated.

[1] These *Thoughts* may even be giving rise to a Logos doctrine: according to a report by a visitor to the People's Republic of China in 1967, some Red Guards, when asked what had brought the universe into being, replied "The thought of Mao Tse-tung."

3. New Sayings.
4. Beatitudes.
5. Parables.
6. Sayings on Fasting, Circumcision and Marriage.
7. Sayings on John the Baptist and James the Just.

1. *Sayings with Canonical Parallels*

Saying 10 in the *Gospel of Thomas* is practically identical with Luke 12:49:

> Jesus said: "I have cast fire on the world, and see, I am watching over it until it sets it aflame!"

Saying 16 is closely related to this, and has a canonical parallel in Matthew 10:34–36 and Luke 12:51–53:

> Jesus said: "Verily, people think that I have come to send peace on the world. But they do not know that I have come to send on earth dissensions, fire, sword and war. Verily, if there are five in a house, they will find themselves ranged three against two and two against three – father against son and son against father – and they will rise up in isolation."

"They will rise up in isolation" means that they will isolate themselves from their families, severing all family ties.[1]

Those sayings which have canonical parallels do not help us to establish the original text of those parallels, apart possibly from one or two exceptional places. But from the way in which the canonical sayings are modified or amplified in the *Gospel of Thomas* we can gather something of the outlook of the compilers of the anthology. Thus the saying in Luke 17:21, "the kingdom of God is within you", probably meant in its original context that the divine kingdom was present in the midst of Jesus' contemporaries by virtue of His ministry among them. But the saying is given a curious twist in the *Gospel of Thomas* (No. 3a):

> If those who entice you say to you, "See, the kingdom is in heaven!" – then the birds of heaven will be there before you. If they say to you, "It is in the sea!" – then the fishes will be there before you. But the kingdom is within you – and without as well.

This is one of the sayings which were already known from one of the Oxyrhynchus papyri (654), although there are verbal differences between the two recensions. It was on the Oxyrhynchus form of the saying that Francis Thompson based his lines:

[1] Cf. Saying 49 (p. 98).

D

> Does the fish soar to find the ocean,
> The eagle plunge to find the air –
> That we ask of the stars in motion
> If they have rumour of thee there?

Papyrus 654, as has been said, represents the beginning of the Greek text of this compilation, in which this saying is one of a group dealing with the question of seeking and finding. This saying follows immediately on the opening words of the compilation, quoted above. The group of sayings represents a recasting of Jesus' injunction "Seek, and ye shall find" (Matt. 7:7; Luke 11:9) together with His words about seeking the kingdom (Matt. 6:33; Luke 12:31), and to this recast version of His words the saying about the presence of the kingdom is attached.

Here is another saying about the kingdom (No. 113):

> His disciples said to him: "When will the kingdom come?" "It will not come when it is expected. They will not say 'See, here it is!' or 'See, there it is!' – but the kingdom of the Father is spread abroad on the earth and men do not see it".[1]

In all these the kingdom is no longer to be understood within the life-setting of Jesus' historic ministry; it has been given a universal reference and the sayings are reproduced as general truths.

One saying (No. 39) is immediately recognizable as a variant of Luke 11:52 (cf. Matt. 23:13):

> Jesus said: "The Pharisees and the scribes have taken the keys of knowledge and hidden them; they have neither entered in themselves nor allowed those who wished to enter in to do so."[2]

"Knowledge" is no doubt given the more technical sense of saving *gnosis*.[3] A commentator might well sum up these words by saying that Jesus condemns the "dog-in-the-manger" attitude of the scribes (referring to one of Aesop's fables). It is remarkable that another saying in the *Gospel of Thomas* (No. 102) uses the picture of the dog in the manger in this very way:

> Jesus said: "Woe to them, the Pharisees, because they are like a dog lying on a pile of fodder, who will not eat it of himself and will not allow it to be eaten by anyone else."

---

[1] This saying apparently goes back to the same original as Saying 3a (Luke 17:20 f.; see p. 93); cf. the beginning of Saying 37 (p. 103).

[2] The saying continues: "But as for you, be prudent as serpents and harmless as doves" (cf. Matt. 10:16); Naassenes or Ophites may have seen special significance in the reference to serpents.

[3] Cf. Saying 3b: "When you know yourselves, then you will be known, and you will know that you are the children of the living Father . . ."

2. Canonical Sayings Amplified or Conflated

No. 31 runs:

> Jesus said: "A prophet is not welcomed in his own town, and a physician works no cure on those who know him."

The saying about a prophet appears in all four canonical Gospels (Matt. 13:57; Mark 6:6; Luke 4:24; John 4:44); the Synoptic writers quote it with reference to Nazareth, the Fourth Evangelist with reference to Judaea. But it is probably from Luke's version, or a version akin to Luke's, that it found its way in this form into the *Gospel of Thomas,* for it is only in Luke that it stands in close association with a saying about a physician.[1]

Saying 25 is at first blush in line with those canonical sayings of Jesus which enjoin brotherly love:

> Jesus said: "Love your brother as your own soul; guard him like the apple of your eye."

But in the *Gospel of Thomas* it is quite likely that "brother" is understood in the sense of "fellow-Gnostic".

In No. 47 we have quite an elaborate conflation of originally independent sayings:

> Jesus said: "No man can mount two horses or draw two bows at once. And no servant can serve two masters, otherwise he will honour the one and be roughly treated by the other. No man ever drinks old wine and desires the same instant to drink new wine; new wine is not poured into old skins, lest they burst, nor is old wine poured into new skins, lest it spoils. And no one sews an old patch on to a new garment, for a rent would be made."

Here the saying about the impossibility of serving two masters (Matt. 6:24; Luke 16:13) is amplified by two illustrations from life, and followed by sayings contrasting the old order and the new, sufficiently similar to Mark 2:21 f. and its parallels – Matthew 9:16 f. and Luke 5:36–39, especially the Lukan parallel – but with curious differences whose secondary character is plain. The pouring of old wine into new skins is not envisaged in the canonical sayings, still less the pointless patching of a new garment with an old piece of cloth. These divergences from the canonical wording are no doubt deliberate: the true Gnostic will not allow his new doctrine to be encumbered with relics from the past.

Another addition to a canonical saying appears in No. 100:

[1] Cf. Luke 4:23, "Physician, heal yourself."

Jesus was shown a gold coin and was told: "Caesar's people are demanding the taxes from us." He said to them: "Give Caesar what is Caesar's; give God what is God's; and give me what is mine!"

For once, the historical setting of the saying is tolerably well preserved – except that in the original form it was not a *gold* coin that He was shown, but a (silver) denarius (Mark 12:15 and parallels). But the added words "and give me what is mine" blunt the point of the incident, so far as its historical meaning is concerned. They do, however, make a new point. It has been noted that this is the only place in the *Gospel of Thomas* where "God" is mentioned. Here probably it is the Old Testament God, the demiurge, that is intended, so that we have an ascending order of dignity: Caesar, God and Jesus. Jesus is viewed as the Gnostic Revealer and Redeemer, and the true Gnostic will make it his chief concern to follow the requirements of saving *gnosis* and so give Jesus His due. He whom Jesus reveals is called "the Father", not "God".

3. *New Sayings*

Some of the sayings have no proper canonical counterpart. Such is No. 77:

Jesus said: "I am the Light which shines upon all. I am the All; All has gone forth from me and All has come back to me. Split the wood, and I am there; lift the stone and you will find me there!"

The first words of this saying, of course, remind us of various passages in the Fourth Gospel, where Jesus is presented as the Light of the world, coming into the world to provide light for every man (John 1:9; 3:19; 8:12; 9:5). But it is not the Incarnate Word who speaks here in the *Gospel of Thomas* but something much more like the pantheistic Logos of Stoicism. The final sentence of the saying has been known since the discovery of Oxyrhynchus papyrus 1 in 1897; it has sometimes been treated as a variant of the words of Jesus in Matthew 18:20 ("For where two or three are gathered together in my name, there am I in the midst of them"); but in reality it means something quite different.

Jesus said: "He who is near me is near the fire, and he who is far from me is far from the kingdom."

This saying (No. 82) was known to Origen, who expressed some doubt about its authenticity: "I have read somewhere that our Saviour said – and I wonder whether some one has falsely assumed our Saviour's role, or recalled the words from memory, or if in fact it is true that He said so – 'He who is near me is near the fire, and he who is far from me is far from the kingdom'."[1] If the fire is to be understood in the same sense as in

[1] *Homilies on Jeremiah*, 20; Didymus of Alexandria (on Ps. 78:8) quotes it from Origen.

Saying 10, then this is another saying about the contention that is the sequel to taking sides with Jesus. But the fire here may be more particularly the fiery trial by which the faith of true disciples must be tested. Joachim Jeremias is disposed to accept this as a genuine saying: those who decide to follow Jesus must be prepared to pass through the fire, but it is only through the fire that they can attain the kingdom.[1] If it is a genuine saying, however, its original meaning need not be identical with the meaning which it had for the compiler and readers of the *Gospel of Thomas*.

Another saying (No. 42) in which Jesus says to His disciples,

Be like those who pass over,

has a parallel in an unexpected place. On a gateway of the mosque erected in 1601 in Fatehpur-Sikri, south of Delhi, by the Mogul Akbar, these words are inscribed:

Jesus, on whom be peace, said: "This world is a bridge. Pass over it, but do not build your dwelling there."

Akbar evidently derived this saying from Muslim tradition: it is ascribed to Jesus quite clearly in Arabic literature.[2]

The principle that the eater assimilates what he eats, taken along with the idea of gradation in the scale of being, leads to a saying like this (No. 7):

Jesus said: "Happy is the lion whom the man eats, so that the lion becomes man; but woe to the man whom the lion eats, so that the man becomes lion!"[3]

A man descends in the scale of value by being assimilated to the lion that devours him; but a lion would be ennobled by being eaten by a man. For some Gnostic schools, indeed, being devoured by a wild beast would mean being confined more securely than ever in a prison-house of flesh. (This is a very different attitude from that with which Ignatius faced the prospect of being devoured by wild beasts.)

4. Beatitudes

The saying last quoted is a combined beatitude and woe. Quite a number of beatitudes occur in the *Gospel of Thomas*, several of them being echoes of those in the Sermon on the Mount. Such, for example, are No. 54:

---

[1] *Unknown Sayings of Jesus*[2], pp. 66 ff.

[2] Cf. J. Jeremias, *Unknown Sayings of Jesus*[2], pp. 111 ff.

[3] Cf. W. C. Till, "New Sayings of Jesus in the Recently Discovered Coptic 'Gospel of Thomas'", *BJRL* 41 (1958–59), p. 457. The same principle is expressed at the beginning of Saying 11b: "Today you eat dead things and make them alive . . ." – and even more simply in Walter de la Mare's short poem, "Little Miss T – ".

Jesus said:"Happy are the poor, for yours is the kingdom of heaven";

No. 68:

Jesus said: "Happy will you be when you are hated and persecuted; but they will find no room in this place till they have driven you forth!";

and No. 69:

Jesus said: "Happy are those who have been persecuted in heart. It is they who have come to know the Father. Happy are they who are famished, because they will be filled and satisfied."

Others are new, like No. 49:

Jesus said: "Happy are the solitary and the chosen ones, for you will find the kingdom. Because you have come forth from it, you will return there again."

The "solitary" are probably those who have disowned family ties, like those described in Saying 16, who "rise up in isolation", after contention has broken out in their family circle.[1] The kingdom is evidently the upper world of light, from which the souls of men have come and to which they may return if they are liberated by *gnosis* from their material environment.

A previous existence in the upper world of light is probably implied also in No. 19a:

Jesus said: "Happy is he who existed before he came to birth."

In an orthodox sense this might refer to Jesus Himself, but a wider reference is more likely in the context of the *Gospel of Thomas*.

Here is a conflation of two quite independent beatitudes, which have an accidental verbal contact which lends itself to a very different interpretation from that which both had in the canonical tradition (No. 79):

In the crowd a woman said to him: "Happy the womb that gave you birth and the breasts that suckled you!" He said to her: "Happy are those who have heard the Father's word and keep it. Verily, the days will come when you will say: 'Happy the womb that never gave birth and the breasts that never suckled children!'"

The first part of this saying, found in Luke 11:27, originally implies that there is something more wonderful than being the mother of Jesus – namely, doing the will of God. But here this saying is linked to the follow-

[1] See p. 93. Cf. No. 75: "Many stand outside at the door, but it is only the solitary who will enter the bridal chamber." This saying, with its companion-piece No. 74, "there are many round the opening but no one in the well" – quoted by Celsus from the Ophite *Heavenly Dialogue* (Origen, *Against Celsus*, viii. 15 f.) – is reminiscent of the canonical "Many are called, but few are chosen" (Matt. 22:14), and also of the Greek mystery-saying: "The wandbearers are many, but the initiates are few" (Plato, *Phaedo* 69c).

ing one in such a way as to suggest that the bearing of children is contrary to the Father's will, and that those who renounce marriage and family life are to be congratulated. This, of course, completely dehistoricizes the second part of the saying, where Jesus in Luke 23:29 is not laying down a permanent principle, but telling the weeping women on the Via Dolorosa that, when the impending distress overtakes Jerusalem, childless women will have something to be thankful for.

5. Parables

Several of the parables familiar to us from the canonical Gospels reappear in this collection, such as the parables of the sower (No. 9), the rich fool (No. 63) and the great feast (No. 64). But there is no exact New Testament parallel to No. 8:

> Then he said: "Man is like a wise fisherman who cast his net into the sea. He brought it up out of the sea full of little fishes, in the midst of which this wise fisherman found a large, excellent fish. He threw all the little fishes back into the sea; without hesitation he chose the big fish. He that has ears to hear, let him hear!"

This parable is only superficially like the New Testament parable of the dragnet (Matt. 13:47 ff.); so far as its lesson is concerned, it bears a closer resemblance to the New Testament parables of the hidden treasure and the costly pearl (Matt. 13:44–46). The big fish is the true knowledge.[1]

The parables of the treasure (No. 109) and the pearl (No. 76) both appear in the Gospel of Thomas, along with several others which begin with some such words as "The kingdom is like . . ."; these include the parables of the mustard-seed (No. 20), the tares (No. 57), the leaven (No. 96), and the sheep that went astray (No. 107). But the kingdom in these parables, as understood by the community to which we owe the Gospel of Thomas, is not the kingdom of the Synoptic Gospels; it is that spiritual realm to which the Gnostic is admitted by his cultivation of gnosis. Sometimes the original form of the parable has to be modified in order to make it bear this new significance. Contrast, for example, the Synoptic parable of the stray sheep with Saying 107 in the Gospel of Thomas:

> Jesus said: "The kingdom is like a shepherd who had a hundred sheep. One of them, the biggest, wandered away. He left the ninety-nine others and sought this single sheep until he found it. After taking this trouble, he said to the sheep: 'I love you more than the ninety-nine others!'"

Here the shepherd takes extra trouble over the hundredth sheep because it is the biggest one, and more valuable than all the others – probably

---

[1] For a parallel to the Markan parable of the seed growing secretly cf. Saying 21c: "Let there be among you a man of understanding: when the fruit ripened he came quickly, sickle in hand, and reaped it."

representing the Gnostic in contrast to the many who make up the rank and file of the faithful.[1]

The parable of the costly pearl is conflated with another saying of Jesus, about laying up treasure in heaven (Matt. 6:19 ff.; cf. Luke 12:33 f.). When the merchant has sold all his load to buy the one pearl, the admonition is added:

> Do you also seek for his [the Father's] imperishable treasure, which abides, where the moth does not enter and eat it up nor does the worm destroy it.

The parable of the hidden treasure has an uncanonical ending: when the buyer of the field had acquired the treasure, then (we are told):

> he began to lend money at interest to whomsoever he would.

This addition is probably not drawn from Matt. 25:27 or Luke 19:23, where the unprofitable servant is told that he might at least have allowed his master's money to accumulate interest if he was unable or unwilling to trade with it more remuneratively.

Here are two uncanonical parables of the kingdom. First comes No. 97:

> Jesus said: "The kingdom of the Father is like a woman carrying a jar full of meal and walking along a long road. The handle of the jar broke, and the meal poured out behind her on the road without her knowing it or being able to do anything about it. When she reached home, she set down the jar and found that it was empty."

This may be a warning against self-confidence, against thinking that one possesses the saving knowledge when in fact one has lost it.

No. 98 points a different kind of moral:

> The kingdom of the Father is like a man who wishes to kill a magnate. In his own house he unsheathes his sword and thrusts it into the wall to make sure that his hand will be steady; then he kills his victim.

The lesson of this odd parable, which may have had its original life-setting among the Zealots or *sicarii*, seems to be much the same as that of the parables of Luke 14:28-32; anyone who embarks upon a costly enterprise must first make sure that he has the resources to carry it out. The magnate who is attacked in the parable may further be identified with the strong man whose house is invaded and whose goods are plundered in Matt. 12:29 and Luke 11:21,[2] the strong man being understood as the

---

[1] Cf. the parable of the big fish in Saying 8 (p. 99).

[2] This canonical *logion* is paralleled in Saying 35: "It is not possible for anyone to enter the strong man's house and take him (? it) by force unless he binds his hands; then he will ransack his house."

demiurge or ruler of the material order. It is unlikely that the wall into which the sword is first thrust should be allegorized.

6. Sayings on Fasting, Circumcision and Marriage

There are sayings about fasting and circumcision which reflect a thoroughly emancipated and non-ascetic attitude towards these institutions. In such matters there were considerable differences of outlook among Gnostic sects. In the *Gospel of Thomas* fasting and related religious practices can be performed in a purely external manner which is positively sinful. So Saying 14 insists:

> Jesus said to them: "When you fast, you will bring sin upon yourselves; when you pray, you will be condemned; when you give alms, you will injure your spirit. When you enter any land and go through the countryside, when you are entertained, eat what is set before you and heal the sick in those places. For nothing that enters into your mouth will defile you, but what comes out of your mouth, that is what will defile you."

The opening words about fasting, prayer and almsgiving represent a summarized reworking of Matthew 6:1–18, and they have had appended to them passages from the commission to the seventy (Luke 10:8 f.) and Jesus' teaching about the source of real defilement (Mark 7:14 f.).

Here is another saying on the subject (No. 104):

> They said: "Come, let us pray and fast today." Jesus said: "What sin have I committed, or what omission am I guilty of? When the bridegroom comes forth from the bridal chamber, one never fasts or prays then."[1]

The introduction of the bridegroom into a context where fasting is under discussion is reminiscent of Mark 2:19 f.; but the form which Jesus' reply takes is similar to the account in the *Gospel according to the Hebrews* of Jesus' rejoinder to His family's suggestion that they should go and be baptized by John.[2]

True fasting, however, is inculcated, as in Saying 27:

> If you do not fast in relation to the world, you will not find the kingdom. If you do not make the sabbath the (true) sabbath, you will not see the Father.

And the character of this true fasting and related religious observances is indicated in No. 6:[3]

---

[1] The "mystery of the bridal chamber" was a sacramental theme in Valentinian Gnosticism: it figures prominently in the *Gospel of Philip* (another Nag Hammadi text); cf. R. McL. Wilson, *The Gospel of Philip* (London, 1962), pp. 118 ff.

[2] See p. 88.

[3] Partially preserved in Oxyrhynchus Papyrus 654.

His disciples questioned him; they said: "Do you wish us to fast? How shall we pray and give alms, and what shall we feed upon?" Jesus said: "Tell no falsehood and do not [to others] what is hateful to yourselves; for all these things are manifest in the sight of heaven. Nothing hidden will fail to be revealed and nothing concealed will fail to be published abroad."[1]

With this transformation of religious obligations into ethical injunctions we may compare the process revealed in the Western text of Acts 15:20, 29, where the terms of the Apostolic Decree have been ethicized and amplified by the addition of the Golden Rule (in its negative form, as here).[2]

As for circumcision, it has no value unless it is spiritualized. According to Saying 53:

His disciples said to him: "Is circumcision useful or not?" He said to them: "If it were useful, men's mothers would have borne them to their fathers circumcised already. But it is the true circumcision in the spirit that is profitable."

A modern reader will find the references to women and to marriage out of keeping with the general tenor of the canonical Gospels. Sexual life and the propagation of children are discouraged, as we have seen in Saying 79.[3] The ideal state is to be as free from sexual self-consciousness as little children are.[4] There are several sayings to this effect which are obviously related to words ascribed to Jesus in the *Gospel according to the Egyptians,* another work of Naassene affinities. In the *Gospel according to the Egyptians* this attitude is summed up in the statement: "I came to destroy the works of the female."[5] This statement is not reproduced in the *Gospel of Thomas,* but others from the same source and to the same effect are found. Thus Saying 22 contains the words:

Jesus said to them: "When you make the two one[6] ... and when you make the male and the female one, so that the male is no longer male and the female no longer female ... then you will enter the kingdom."[7]

[1] With the last sentence in this saying cf. Mark 4:22//Luke 8:17; also Matt. 10:26; Luke 12:2.

[2] Cf. Tobit 4:15, "What you hate, do not do to any one"; Hillel in TB *Shabbat* 31a: "What is hateful to you, do not do it to your fellow: this is the whole law; everything else is commentary."

[3] See p. 98.

[4] So the canonical *logion* about becoming like little children (Matt. 18:3) is interpreted in part of Saying 22: "These children who are being suckled are like those who enter the kingdom..." (cf. also Saying 37, p. 103).

[5] Quoted by Clement of Alexandria, *Stromata* iii. 9. This saying is practically the text of Robert Graves' *King Jesus* (London, 1946). Cf. also *Gospel of Philip* 71: "When Eve was in Adam there was no death; but when she was separated from him death came into being. If she be reabsorbed in him again, death will cease to exist."

[6] Cf. the opening words of Saying 106: "When you make the two one, you will become sons of man..."

[7] In the *Gospel according to the Egyptians* words like these are spoken by Jesus to Salome (Clement of Alexandria, *Stromata* iii. 13). They could represent a Gnostic interpretation of the words of Paul in Gal. 3:28: "there can be no male and female."

And Saying 37 runs thus:

> His disciples said to him: "When will you appear to us? When shall we see you?"[1] Jesus said: "When you disrobe yourselves without being ashamed, when you take off your garments and lay them at your feet as small children do, and trample on them, then you will become the sons of the Living One, and you will have no fear."[2]

Just as the primal sin in Eden was followed by sexual awareness and a sense of fear and shame at the consciousness of being naked, so the restoration of original innocence will be marked by a loss of sexual awareness (and indeed of sexual distinction) and an absence of any sense of embarrassment at appearing unclothed.

Women, one gathers, cannot attain to the higher life. This is the implication of Saying 114:

> Simon Peter said to them: "Let Mary depart from our midst, because women are not worthy of the life [that is life indeed]." Jesus said: "See, I will so clothe her that I may make her a man, in order that she also may become a living spirit like you men. For every woman who becomes a man will enter into the kingdom of heaven."

In spite of her faithfulness as a disciple, even Mary Magdalene can enter the kingdom only by being changed into a man (perhaps in a future phase of existence). We may infer that women, because of their function in conception and childbirth, were judged incapable of ever achieving complete liberation from material entanglements.

7. Sayings on John the Baptist and James the Just

Other Gospel personages who are mentioned by name in the *Gospel of Thomas* are John the Baptist and James the Just. Saying 46 recasts a well-known canonical reference to John (Matt. 11:11; Luke 7:28):

> Jesus said: "From Adam to John the Baptist, among those who have been born of women none is greater than John the Baptist. But lest your eyes [should be blinded] I have said: 'He among you who is least will come to know the kingdom, and will be more exalted than John.'"

But in the present context the meaning of the words is that the true Gnostic is more exalted than even the greatest of men excluded from the privileged circle. Another canonical saying about John (Matt. 11:7 f.; Luke 7:24 f.) is reproduced in Saying 78, but the reference to John is omitted:

[1] Perhaps a rewording of the question of Mark 13:4 and parallels (Luke 21:7 and more especially Matt. 24:3). Cf. Saying 113 (p. 94).
[2] This saying survives in a fragmentary form in Oxyrhynchus Papyrus 655. The passage from the *Gospel according to the Egyptians* quoted on p. 102 above includes a reference to "trampling on the garment of shame".

Jesus said: "Why did you go out to the open country? Was it to see a reed shaken by the wind, or to see a man dressed in fine apparel? [No; such persons are found in the houses of] your kings and magnates, those who are so dressed; but they do not know the truth."

Here the contrast is not between the well-to-do and John, but between the well-to-do and those who know the truth (that is, the Gnostics).

We know the answer which the disciples received from Jesus in the canonical Gospels when they asked who was greatest in the kingdom of heaven.[1] A different answer is given in Saying 12 in the *Gospel of Thomas*:

The disciples said to Jesus: "We know that you are going to leave us: who will be greatest over us?" Jesus said to them: "In the place where you go, you will betake yourselves to James the Just, on whose behalf heaven and earth alike were made."

This idea evidently goes back to that wing of the Church of Jerusalem which regarded James as high priest and representative of the new Israel.[2] According to Hippolytus the Naassenes claimed to derive their doctrines from James.[3]

The *Gospel of Thomas* presents us with the product of an oral tradition of the sayings of Jesus within a circle whose basic presuppositions differ considerably from those of apostolic Christianity. The relationship of the sayings which it contains to the Synoptic and Johannine traditions is a complicated question. Some of the sayings bear a close resemblance to parallels in the Gospels of Matthew and Luke – not only to their common material but to elements peculiar to one or the other, especially Luke. Thus all the parables in Matt. 13 have parallels in the *Gospel of Thomas,* including those which are not paralleled in other canonical Gospels, like the parables of the tares, the dragnet, the hidden treasure and the pearl of great price. Again, Saying 79, for example, which brings together two originally unrelated utterances about motherhood, has canonical counterparts only in Luke's Gospel. We probably should think of the compilation as drawing in part on the canonical Gospels, in part on the oral tradition behind or parallel to these Gospels, and in part on tradition unrepresented in them – the whole taking colour from the increasingly gnosticizing tendency of the community in which the compilation took shape.

We must bear in mind, too, that the *Gospel of Thomas* has an inner development of its own. The Oxyrhynchus fragments suggest that different recensions of the collection were current, and one would like to

---

[1] Matt. 18:1 ff.; cf. Mark 9:34; Luke 9:46; 22:24 ff.
[2] But no reflection of this state of affairs is discernible in the canonical Gospels, not even in the "M" stratum of Matthew. The implications of this for the life-setting of the Gospel tradition should not be overlooked.
[3] *Refutation* v. 2.

have a second-century Greek text of the collection as complete as the fourth-century Coptic translation which is now available. Then perhaps we could speak with greater confidence about the relation of the work to the canonical Gospels.

At one point is has been suggested that a passage in the *Gospel of Thomas* goes back to an independent version of Jesus' Aramaic wording: that is in the parable of the sower (No. 9) where the *Gospel of Thomas* says that some seed fell *on* the road, not *by* the road, as the Greek Gospels (and the Coptic versions of the Greek Gospels) say. It has frequently been pointed out that the Aramaic preposition was no doubt '*al,* which can mean either "on" or "by" according to the context, and that *epi* would have been a preferable Greek rendering of it in this context to *para*. The Coptic preposition used in Saying 9 corresponds in sense to Greek *epi* rather than to the canonical *para*.

This suggestion of contact with a line of tradition derived independently from an early Aramaic life-setting is not more than a possibility: the choice of Coptic preposition may have been due to editorial initiative. We do not know which preposition was used in the Greek text of the compilation. But the suggestion has been taken along with the reference to James the Just in Saying 12 as evidence for a Jewish-Christian setting for the orginal compilation. Over against this, however, the attitude to circumcision expressed in Saying 53 is more in accordance with the Pauline outlook than with that of James and his circle. We probably have to think of sayings drawn rather indiscriminately from a variety of environments.

Even a compilation of dominical sayings which could all without exception be established as authentic would not necessarily give us a true picture of Jesus or deserve to be called a gospel. The Sayings Source which has commonly been discerned behind the Q material in Matthew and Luke should not be described as a gospel, if only because it appears to have lacked a passion narrative. Not only is a passion narrative equally (and inevitably) lacking in the *Gospel of Thomas;* it does not even contain sayings of Jesus in which His passion is mentioned. But it is only in the context of His active ministry, which was crowned by His passion, that His sayings can be properly appreciated. The events of His life, death and resurrection constitute the basis of the gospel; the sayings bring out the meaning of the events.

But in the *Gospel of Thomas* the sayings are divorced from their context in the ministry; they are detached even from a life-setting in the early church.[1] Such life-setting as they now have is that of a circle of

---

[1] It is arguable that the *Gospel of Thomas* indicates a process in the gospel tradition in which the memory of the historical life-setting for sayings of Jesus was progressively lost – by contrast with the view that the sayings came originally to the canonical Evangelists detached from contexts in Jesus' life. The conclusion is possible that "Thomas once and for all disproves the theory that the Evangelist had no more to work upon than 'a heap of unstrung pearls'" (R. McL. Wilson, *Studies in the Gospel of Thomas*, p. 86).

gnosticizing Christians, whose presuppositions go far to impose a new meaning even on the most indubitably genuine elements in the compilation. Thanks to the principles on which the sayings have been selected, together with their dehistoricization and new interpretative environment, they no longer present a Jesus who came to serve others and to give His life a ransom for many, a Jesus who personally embodies the law of love which He taught His followers. The religion of the *Gospel of Thomas*, as of Gnosticism in general, is an affair of the individual. Unlike the Bible, the *Gospel of Thomas* sets forth the ideal of the "solitary" believer. When the Jesus of the *Gospel of Thomas* speaks of His mission in the world, this is what He says (Saying 28):

> I stood in the midst of the world and I manifested myself in the flesh to these. I found them all intoxicated; I found none thirsty among them. And my soul was grieved for the children of men, because they are blind in heart and do not see; because they have come into the world empty, they still seek to go out of the world empty. But may someone come and set them right! Then, when they have slept themselves sober, they will repent.

These words express a real concern for the blindness and ignorance of men, but on the whole it is the concern of one who has come to show them the true way rather than of one who has come to lay down his own life that true life may be theirs. What the Jesus of the *Gospel of Thomas* has come to give is secret knowledge, as Saying 17 once more makes plain:

> Jesus said: "I will give you what eye never saw, what ear never heard, what hand never touched, and what never entered the heart of man."

This reminds us at once of the words quoted by Paul from some unknown source in I Cor. 2:9 (although Paul says nothing about "what hand never touched"). The *Gospel of Thomas* is not the only work to ascribe them to Jesus; they are so ascribed in other second-century apocrypha.[1] But in the present context they may well have formed part of a Naassene formula of initiation, referring to the secret knowledge imparted to the initiates under oath. And this underlines an essential difference between New Testament Christianity and Gnosticism. In the context where Paul quotes words similar to these he does indeed speak of the hidden wisdom which the Corinthian Christians are incapable of receiving, but the reason for their incapacity is their spiritual immaturity. And this spiritual immaturity has more to do with ethics than with intellect; the Corinthians' deficiency was not in *gnōsis* but in *agapē*. To mature Christians this wisdom is freely imparted, not to a select minority, but to all.

---

[1] E.g. *Acts of Peter* 39; *New Testament Apocrypha*, ed. R. McL. Wilson, ii (London, 1965), pp. 320 ff.

So, too, the First Epistle of John opens with a declaration that the writer is about to share with his readers everything that he and his companions had experienced of the Word of Life. It has indeed been held that, when he emphasizes this experience in terms of that "which we have heard, which we have seen with our eyes, which we have looked upon and touched with our hands" (I John 1:1), he is deliberately opposing a gnosticizing claim to impart "what eye never saw, what ear never heard, what hand never touched . . ."[1] This may well be so. But over and above this emphasis, he insists that the true knowledge is accessible to all his readers without distinction – children, young men and fathers – instead of being confined to a spiritual élite, as the other party taught: "You, no less than they," he says, "are among the initiated; this is the gift of the Holy One, and by it you all have knowledge" (I John 2:20, NEB). This initiation which admits them to the true knowledge is the anointing of the Spirit by which they are all bound together with God in the fellowship of that love whose perfect revelation is the self-sacrifice of Christ. "It is by this that we know what love is: that Christ laid down his life for us. And we in our turn are bound to lay down our lives for our brothers" (I John 3:16, NEB). It is the loss of this note of self-sacrificing love that chiefly distinguishes the general tendency of the *Gospel of Thomas* from the earlier gospel tradition.

[1] A. Ehrhardt, *The Framework of the New Testament Stories* (Manchester, 1964), pp. 29 ff.

CHAPTER VII

TRADITION IN THE EARLY CATHOLIC CHURCH

THE APPEAL TO "THAT WHICH WAS FROM THE BEGINNING", "that which we have seen and heard",[1] which finds expression in the Letters of John, at the end of the first Christian century, continued to be voiced after the last and longest-lived eyewitnesses of the saving events had died. We have glanced at the practice, found especially in some Gnostic works, of claiming to reproduce teaching given secretly by Jesus to the disciples, preferably during the interval between His resurrection and ascension.[2] This period, forty days in duration according to Acts 1:3, might be quite substantially extended, as in *Pistis Sophia*, a product of the Valentinian school, which purports to record revelations imparted to the disciples over a period of eleven years following the resurrection.

Papias

But in contrast to this ascription of later teaching to Jesus, there is ample evidence of more historically-minded Christian students in the second century who made it their business to ascertain what the eyewitnesses had told others. If the eyewitnesses themselves were no longer accessible, their younger associates could be consulted. One who made a special point of consulting them was Papias, bishop of Hierapolis in Phrygia[3] around A.D. 130, and he was not alone in this. He was perhaps about thirty years old at the end of the first century (as we know his contemporary Polycarp to have been)[4] and his procedure is described in one of the surviving fragments of his five-volume *Exegesis of the Dominical Oracles*.[5] In the preface to this work[6] he wrote:

---

[1] I John 1:1, 3 (cf. pp. 37, 107).

[2] See p. 90. Non-Gnostic examples of this practice are found (probably) in the *Didachē* ("The Teaching of the Lord through the Twelve Apostles to the Gentiles", which implies an expansion of the commission of Matt. 28:18–20) and (certainly) in the fourth-century Syriac manual of church order, *The Testament of our Lord*, which claims explicitly to reproduce Jesus' directions to the apostles before His ascension (cf. further pp. 120 f., 126).

[3] The Hierapolis of Col. 4:13, evangelized, with the other cities of the Lycus valley (Laodicea and Colossae), by Epaphras in the fifties of the first century.

[4] According to Irenaeus, Papias was not only a contemporary but a companion (ἑταῖρος) of Polycarp (*Heresies* v. 33.4, quoted by Eusebius, *Hist. Eccl.* iii. 39.1). If Polycarp's 86 years in the service of Christ, to which he bore witness at his martyrdom on February 23, A.D. 156 (*Mart. Polyc.* 9:3), are to be dated from his birth, he was born in A.D. 70.

[5] This work was still extant in the fourteenth century, if not later, but no copy of it is now known to survive. Extracts from it are preserved in quotations by Irenaeus and Eusebius.

[6] Quoted by Eusebius, *Hist. Eccl.* iii. 39.3 f. See the discussion by A. F. Walls, "Papias and Oral Tradition", *Vigiliae Christianae* 21 (1967), pp. 137 ff.

I will not hesitate to set down along with my interpretations all the things derived from the elders[1], for I learned them well and have remembered them well, and am confident of their truth. Unlike the majority, I did not find pleasure in those who have most to say but in those who teach the truth; not in those who recount other men's commandments but in those who recount the commandments given by the Lord to faith, commandments which proceed from the truth itself.[2] If ever there came my way someone who had associated with the elders, I used to inquire about the words of the elders: "What did Andrew or Peter say, or Philip or Thomas or James, or John or Matthew or any other of the Lord's disciples? What do Aristion[3] and the elder John, the Lord's disciples, say?" For I did not suppose that what I could get from books would be so helpful to me as what came from a living and abiding voice.

Many of the problems raised by this extract need not concern us here. It looks as if Papias makes a distinction between two groups of "disciples" – those who were dead when he prosecuted his inquiries and two who were still alive.[4] If so, one John seems to have belonged to the former group and another John to the latter.[5] What does concern us at present is the distinction which he draws between written records and oral tradition. His preference for the latter is not unnatural: while we may value, for example, a reliable biography of some outstanding figure of two or three generations ago – Alexander Whyte, for example, or Theodore Roosevelt – we welcome the opportunity of meeting someone who knew him and can give us a direct personal impression of him. Papias's interest was in the "oracles" of the Lord,[6] and he was eager to augment his stock. Two or three books were available to him – Matthew's collection of "oracles", for example, originally compiled in the "Hebrew speech" and translated by each man as best he could, and Mark's transcription of Peter's reminiscences, which followed the random order in which that apostle happened to mention things and did not pretend to be an orderly arrangement

---

[1] By "the elders" are meant the younger contemporaries of the apostles, who outlived them, on the analogy of "the elders who outlived Joshua" (Josh. 24:31; Judg. 2:7). See p. 21.

[2] Or perhaps "from the Truth Himself", since Papias stood in the Johannine tradition (cf. John 14:6; 3 John 12).

[3] This Aristion is otherwise unknown; B. H. Streeter's tentative identification of him with that Ariston who is listed as first bishop of Smyrna in the late fourth-century *Apostolic Constitutions* (vii. 46) lacks any substantial foundation (*The Primitive Church*, London, 1929, pp. 92 f., 130 ff.).

[4] He refers to the former in the aorist tense ("what did Andrew or Peter say?") and to the latter in the present tense ("what do they say?"). The tenses are relative rather than to the time when Papias was conducting his research than to the later time at which he was writing.

[5] A crucial question then is which John of the two is meant when "John the disciple of the Lord" is referred to without qualification by Irenaeus (*Heresies* ii. 22. 5, etc.) and others; possibly the reference is now to the one and now to the other.

[6] The word "oracles" (*logia*) in the title of Papias's work is presumably meant by him to bear the same sense as when he reports that "Matthew compiled the *logia* in the Hebrew speech, and everyone translated them as best he could" (quoted by Eusebius, *Hist. Eccl.* iii. 39.16). See p. 89.

of "the oracles of the Lord"[1] (Papias himself giving this account of both these documents).[2] But as for the information, not accessible in books, which he obtained from the "living and surviving voice" of those whom he interrogated, it does not appear to have amounted to much: Papias had plainly to scrape the bottom of the barrel of oral tradition. His most famous *agraphon* is the description of the supernatural fruitfulness which would mark the age to come:

> The days will come in which vines will grow with 10,000 shoots apiece, each shoot having 10,000 branches, each branch 10,000 twigs, each twig 10,000 clusters, and each cluster 10,000 grapes; and each grape when pressed will yield 200 gallons of wine. When any of the saints takes hold of one of their clusters, another cluster will exclaim, "I am a better cluster; take me, bless the Lord through me". Similarly a grain of wheat will produce 10,000 ears, and

[1] "Mark was Peter's interpreter and wrote down accurately all that he [Peter] recalled, whether sayings or doings of Christ – not, however, in order. For he was neither a hearer nor a companion of the Lord; but afterwards, as I said, he accompanied Peter, who adapted his teachings as necessity required, not as though he were arranging a compilation of the oracles of the Lord. So then, Mark was not mistaken when he wrote down in this way some things as he [Peter] recalled them; for his one concern was this – not to omit anything that he had heard, and not to include any false statement among them." This information (quoted by Eusebius, *Hist. Eccl.* iii. 39.15) Papias says he owned to "the elder" – conceivably "the elder John", but we cannot be sure. It may be that his information about Matthew was derived from the same source, but this is not stated in the fragment that survives. With the reference to what Peter "recalled" (Gk. μνημονεύω, ἀπομνημονεύω) may be compared Justin's description of the Gospels as "memoirs (ἀπομνημονεύματα) of the apostles" (*First Apology* 67:3; *Dialogue* 100:4, etc.).

[2] In addition to his information about Matthew and Mark, Papias may be the source behind the late second-century anti-Marcionite prologue to the Gospel of John, which has come down to us in an inaccurate Latin translation of a corrupt Greek text, but originally seems to have run as follows: "The gospel of John was published and given to the churches by John when he was still in the body, as a man of Hierapolis, Papias by name, John's dear disciple, has related in his five Exegetical books. He indeed wrote down the gospel correctly at John's dictation. But the heretic Marcion was thrust out by John, after being repudiated by him for his contrary sentiments. He had carried writings or letters to him from brethren who were in Pontus." (In the Greek copy from which the extant Latin of the prologue was translated the word ἐξηγητικοῖς, "exegetical", had been corrupted to ἐξωτερικοῖς, "external"; and the Latin rendering of the corruption, *externis*, was corrupted in its turn to *extremis*, "last".) The reference to Marcion is probably a confused reminiscence of an earlier statement that *Papias* had refused to countenance him. (It provides one of the starting-points for Robert Eisler's curious theory propounded in his *Enigma of the Fourth Gospel* [London, 1938], according to which Marcion was John's amanuensis, and was dismissed by him when he was discovered to have made heretical interpolations in the Gospel as he copied it!) But the most important feature of the prologue is its statement that "John" dictated the Gospel called by his name; if Papias indeed said this, we have here our earliest evidence for the Johannine authorship of the Gospel. But that Papias was the Evangelist's amanuensis is quite improbable. J. B. Lightfoot (*Essays on "Supernatural Religion"*, London, 1889, p. 214) made the very attractive suggestion that Papias wrote that the Gospel was "delivered by John to the Churches, which *they* wrote down from his lips", but that he was wrongly taken to mean "which *I* wrote down from his lips", since the Greek forms for "I wrote" and "they wrote" are identical in the imperfect tense (ἀπέγραφον) and similar in the aorist (1st singulat ἀπέγραψα, 3rd plural ἀπέγραψαν, perhaps written ἀπέγραψᾱ). The prologue agrees with Irenaeus (*Heresies* v. 33.4) in representing Papias as "a hearer of John", though Eusebius deduces from Papias's preface (quoted above) that "he had by no means been a hearer and eyewitness of the sacred apostles" (*Hist. Eccl.* iii. 39.2).

each ear will have 10,000 grains, and each grain will yield ten pounds of fine flour, bright and pure; and the other fruit, seeds and herbs will be proportionately productive according to their nature, while all the animals which feed on these products of the soil will live in peace and agreement one with another, yielding complete subjection to men.[1]

"This is credible", Papias added, "to those who believe", and he relates that when Judas expressed a measure of scepticism and asked when all this would come to pass, he was told: "Those who come to these times will see." (Judas himself, because of his treachery, was not destined to see them; Papias has an improbable tale to tell of Judas's last days.)[2] The passage we have quoted is consistent with Papias's reputation as a chiliast of a rather crude type;[3] more than that, it is closely paralleled in Jewish apocalyptic and rabbinical tradition.[4] It is in part an imaginative expansion of the poetic imagery of Psalm 72:16 ("May there be abundance of grain in the land; on the tops of the mountains may it wave"), but if this was the kind of thing with which oral tradition provided Papias in addition to the dominical oracles recorded in the "books" at his disposal, we can only conclude that the stream of genuine oral tradition had dried up almost entirely in his part of the world.

Irenaeus

But that oral tradition from the first century continued to be valued a generation after Papias, even when the formation of the New Testament canon was well advanced, is evident from the terms in which Irenaeus (c. A.D. 180) reminds his former acquaintance Florinus of their earlier days with Polycarp in Smyrna:

I remember the events of those days more clearly than those of recent date, for the things that have been learned from childhood grow up with the soul and become one with it. So I can describe even the place where the blessed Polycarp sat and held discourse, how he came in and went out, his manner of

---

[1] Papias, Book 4, quoted by Irenaeus, *Heresies* v. 33.3 f.

[2] Papias, Book 4, quoted by Apollinarius and reproduced in J. B. Lightfoot and J. R. Harmer, *The Apostolic Fathers* (1 vol. edition, London, 1891), pp. 523 f. (Greek), 534 f. (English), from J. A. Cramer, *Catena ad Acta SS Apostolorum* (Leipzig, 1838), pp. 12 ff., and from other sources given in O. Gebhardt, A. Harnack and T. Zahn, *Patrum Apostolicorum Opera* iii (Leipzig, 1877), p. 73. In the Lightfoot-Harmer volume there is a convenient collection of "The Fragments of Papias" (pp. 515–524, Greek and Latin; 527–535, English), and "The Reliques of the Elders preserved in Irenaeus" (pp. 539–550, Greek and Latin; 553–562, English).

[3] Cf. Eusebius, *Hist. Eccl.* iii. 39.12. Papias's eschatology is probably reproduced rather faithfully by Victorinus of Pettau (martyred A.D. 303) in his commentary on the Apocalypse.

[4] Cf. Apocalypse of Baruch 29:5–8; TB *Shabbat* 30b; *Ketubot* 111b; *Kallah Rabbati* 2; Midrash *Sifre on Deuteronomy* 315, 317. J. Klausner gives interesting discussions, with special reference to the rabbinic material, in *The Messianic Idea in Israel*, E. T. (London, 1956), pp. 505 ff., and *Jesus of Nazareth*, E. T. (London, 1929), pp. 400 ff.

life and personal appearance, the discourses which he delivered to the people, and how he reported his intercourse with John and with the others who had seen the Lord, how he recalled their words, and what he had heard from them about the Lord, His mighty works and His teaching, how he, Polycarp, had received[1] those things from the eyewitnesses of the word of life[2] and reported them all in conformity with the Scriptures. Even then I listened eagerly to these things by the mercy of God which was granted to me, making notes of them not on papyrus but in my heart; and by God's grace I always ruminate on them truly.[3]

Irenaeus does not put Polycarp's reminiscences on a level with apostolic tradition, but he appeals to them in an effort to persuade Florinus, who had by now embraced Valentinian Gnosticism, that he was out of step with apostolic tradition in departing so far from the teaching of "that blessed and apostolic elder" who was in such close touch with that tradition.

By calling Polycarp a "blessed and apostolic elder"[4] Irenaeus means that he was a disciple of the apostles[5] and implies that the John with whom Polycarp had held converse was John the apostle.[6] Polycarp may be the "elder, a disciple of the apostles" to whom Irenaeus refers elsewhere[7] as arguing (against Marcion) that the Creator-God of the Old Testament is identical with the Father of Jesus in the New Testament.[8]

But for Irenaeus apostolic tradition was more securely safeguarded than by chance personal links of this kind. It had been placed on permanent record in the sacred scriptures, and should the interpretation of the scriptures be disputed, a further safeguard was provided in those churches which could claim apostolic foundation and in which a regular succession

---

[1] Gk. παραλαμβάνω (see pp. 20, 30 ff.).

[2] Or "of the life of the Word"; the word-order (τῆς ζωῆς τοῦ λόγου) is different from that of I John 1:1 (περὶ τοῦ λόγου τῆς ζωῆς), but the difference may be nothing more than a stylistic variation.

[3] Quoted by Eusebius, *Hist. Eccl.* v. 20.4–7.

[4] Quoted by Eusebius, *Hist. Eccl.* v. 20.7.

[5] For the definition of elders as disciples of the apostles cf. Irenaeus, *Heresies* v. 5.1; *Demonstration* 3. See p. 109.

[6] As is further implied by his reference in *Heresies* iii. 3.4. to Polycarp as having been "not only instructed by apostles . . . but also appointed by apostles in Asia to be bishop in the church of Smyrna" – where "apostles" is probably a "generalizing plural".

[7] *Heresies* iv. 49.1.

[8] Other elders, presumably of Polycarp's generation, are brought by Irenaeus into close relation with "John the disciple of the Lord" (*Heresies* ii. 33.5; cf. v. 30.1; 33.3); "some of them, moreover, saw not only John but other apostles also, and heard these same things from them" (ii. 33.5). Since "these same things" were to the effect that Jesus lived to be between forty and fifty years old, "the reader may here perceive the unsatisfactory character of tradition where a mere fact is concerned" (W. W. Harvey, *ad loc.*). Irenaeus also mentions hearing something "from a certain elder, who had heard it from those who had seen the apostles, and from those who had learned it from them" (*Heresies* iv. 42.2); this man, who is later cited simply as "the elder" (iv. 46.1; 47.1), seems to have belonged to a later period than Polycarp and has been plausibly identified with the martyr Pothinus, Irenaeus's predecessor in the see of Lyons.

of elders[1] or bishops could be traced since that foundation. This is the principle of "apostolic succession", which was invoked not to enhance the pedigree of a particular church or to magnify the status of bishops but to defend the faith. The doctrine maintained in Irenaeus's day in a church of apostolic foundation might be safely assumed to be identical with what the founder-apostles had taught, further guaranteed as it was by the unbroken succession of bishops, unless it could be proved that at some point a change had been introduced – and the burden of proof rested on those who claimed that a change had in fact been introduced.

The church which Irenaeus held in highest honour in this regard was the church of Rome – in which he had no private interest, since he himself belonged to the province of Asia and spent the last two or three decades of his life (from A.D. 177 onwards) as bishop of Lyons. After invoking in general terms the principle of episcopal succession in the apostolic churches, he goes on:

> Since it would be tedious in such a volume as this to enumerate the successions in all the churches, we indicate the tradition derived from the apostles and the faith proclaimed to men, transmitted to our day through the successions of bishops, as it is held in the great, ancient and universally renowned church which was founded and established at Rome by the two most glorious apostles Peter and Paul. Thus we confound all those who in any way hold unauthorized meetings through evil self-will or vain glory or blindness and wrong judgement. With this church, on account of its superior authority, every church ought to agree – that is, the faithful everywhere, every church in which the apostolic tradition has been preserved by the faithful everywhere.[2]

There was nothing tendentious about this account of the matter. True, the church of Rome was in existence before any apostles visited the city,[3] but the association of both Peter and Paul with that church was well attested. Probably, too, the first few names in Irenaeus's succession-list represent colleagues on a board of presbyter-bishops rather than successive monarchical bishops.[4] But is was a fact of experience that the faith held in Rome was held by the other apostolic churches – Antioch, Ephesus, Thessalonica, Corinth and the rest. The same faith was held in Jerusalem –

---

[1] He uses the term "elders" (presbyters) in *Heresies* iii. 2.2, not in the above-mentioned sense of "disciples of the apostles" but with reference to office in the church, for which "bishops" (iii. 3.1 etc.) is a synonymous but commoner designation.

[2] *Heresies* iii. 3.1.

[3] Cf. Ambrosiaster, *Commentary on Romans* (preface): "They [the Roman Christians] had embraced the faith of Christ, albeit according to the Jewish rite, although they saw no sign of mighty works or any of the apostles."

[4] In view of Ignatius's insistence on the monarchical bishop in his letters to other churches, his silence on the subject in his letter to the Roman church suggests that the monarchical episcopate was not yet established at Rome (c. A.D. 110). The *Shepherd* of Hermas, produced at Rome early in the second century, makes mention of "the elders who preside over the church" and "the rulers and those who occupy the chief seats", but not of any one bishop (Vision 3.9.7).

which, in view of its new and Gentile foundation after A.D. 135, could not now strictly be called an apostolic church, though it no doubt served itself heir to the primitive church of that city[1] – and in Alexandria, where the Christian establishment was orthodox by Irenaeus's time, whatever its doctrine may have been in earlier days.[2] Differences about the dating of Easter, such as existed between Rome and some of the Asian churches,[3] did not affect the essence of the faith. No matter in how many languages the faith might be taught, "yet the force of the tradition is one and the same. For the churches planted in Germany have not believed or handed down anything different, nor yet the churches among the Iberians or the Celts, nor those in the east, nor yet in Egypt and Libya, nor those established in the centre of the world".[4]

What then was the faith which the worldwide church "received from the apostles and their disciples"? Irenaeus summarizes its content thus: it is the faith

> in one God, the Father Almighty, who made heaven and earth and the seas, and all that is in them; and in one Christ Jesus, the Son of God, who was made flesh for our salvation; and in the Holy Spirit, who through the prophets announced the dispensations and the advents, and the birth from a virgin, the passion and the rising from the dead, and the bodily assumption into the heavens of our beloved Lord Jesus Christ, and his coming from the heavens in the glory of the Father "to bring all things into one"[5] and to raise up all flesh of all mankind, in order that to Christ Jesus our Lord and God and Saviour and King, according to the decree of the invisible Father, "every knee should bow, of beings in heaven and on earth and under the earth, and that every tongue should acknowledge him",[6] and that he should execute righteous judgement among all, sending into the eternal fire the "spiritual hosts of wickedness"[7] and the angels that transgressed and were involved in rebellion, with the ungodly and unrighteous and lawless and slanderers among men, but bestowing life and immortality as a gift of grace on the righteous and holy, and on those who have kept his commandments whether from the beginning or after repentance, and investing them with eternal glory.[8]

Irenaeus elsewhere gives us two shorter summaries,[9] Tertullian (c.

---

[1] Cf. F. C. Burkitt, *Christian Beginnings* (London, 1924), pp. 65 ff.

[2] Until the establishment of the catechetical school of Alexandria by Pantaenus (c. A.D. 170) the principal figures in Alexandrian Christianity were more gnostic than catholic in their doctrine. The story of the foundation of the Alexandrian church by Mark (Eusebius, *Hist. Eccl.* ii. 16) is probably a late invention designed to substitute an orthodox account of its beginning for one which, though more in accordance with historical fact, was less theologically reputable by later standards. Cf. W. Bauer, *Rechtgläubigkeit und Ketzerei im ältesten Christentum*[2] (Tübingen, 1964), pp. 49 ff.; A. Ehrhardt, *The Framework of the New Testament Stories* (Manchester, 1964), pp. 174 ff.

[3] Cf. Eusebius, *Hist. Eccl.* v. 23 f.

[4] Irenaeus, *Heresies* i. 3. The "centre of the world" is probably Rome and the rest of Italy, though it has also been taken to mean Jerusalem and the rest of Palestine.

[5] Eph. 1:10.   [6] Phil. 2:10 f.   [7] Eph. 6:12.

[8] *Heresies* i. 2.   [9] *Heresies* iii. 4.1; iv. 53.1.

160–220) gives us three,[1] and Origen (185–254), in the preface to his treatise *On First Principles*, gives a full and detailed outline of "the features clearly delivered in the teaching of the apostles".[2] This outline, which might equally well be called an outline of the church's faith, Origen regards as summarizing one self-consistent body of doctrine based on what one "has discovered in Holy Writ or has deduced by drawing logical inferences from it in accordance with a correct method".[3] It does not occur to him that any other body of doctrine could fairly be derived from scripture.

In Irenaeus, Tertullian and Origen alike this summary of the content of the apostles' teaching is in three sections, relating respectively to God the Father, to the Son, and to the Holy Spirit. This is comparable to the primitive baptismal confession of the Gentile churches, which consisted of an affirmative answer to the threefold question, framed more or less like this:

> Do you believe in God the Father?
> And in his Son Jesus Christ?
> And in the Holy Spirit?[4]

The response to this threefold question forms the skeleton on which were built up the early creeds, best known of which is the Roman creed, the ancestor of what we call the Apostles' Creed.[5] But even the old Roman

---

[1] *Against Praxeas* 2; *Prescription against Heretics* 13:1–6; *Veiling of Virgins* 1:3. Translations of these three passages, preceded by translations of the three passages from Irenaeus, are given in R. P. C. Hanson, *Tradition in the Early Church* (London, 1962), pp. 86 f. This work by Bishop Hanson is of the highest importance for the subject of this chapter. See also E. Flesseman-van Leer, *Tradition and Scripture* (Assen, 1954); H. E. W. Turner, *The Pattern of Christian Truth* (London, 1954).

[2] Origen, *Princ.*, preface 4–10. At the end of his summary of the apostles' teaching Origen adds what he claims they taught about the after-life of the soul (discussing at the same time the provenance of the soul and the freedom of the will) and the resurrection of the body (he avoids the word "flesh" in this connexion); about the devil and his angels; about the creation and coming dissolution of the world; about the Holy Scriptures (indited by the Spirit of God in such a way that they have a spiritual sense, accessible only by the Spirit's grace, in addition to their surface and literal sense) and about the angels of God, "his servants in accomplishing the salvation of men", whose origin, nature and mode of existence are unknown. But here we discern Origen's own doctrine rather than the tradition of the apostles or of the church at large. Cf. for a full examination of his position R. P. C. Hanson, *Origen's Doctrine of Tradition* (London, 1952) and *Allegory and Event: A Study of the Sources and Significance of Origen's Interpretation of Scripture* (London, 1959).

[3] *Princ.*, preface 10.

[4] Compare the trinitarian formula for Gentile baptism in Matt. 28:19 (*Didachē* 7:1, 3). At an earlier stage, and especially in the Jewish mission, baptism was "into the name of the Lord Jesus" (Acts 8:16; 19:5; cf. 2:38; 10:48) and confession of Jesus as Messiah or as Lord sufficed (cf. the Ethiopian's confession in Acts 8:37 which, while a Western addition to the original text, dates probably from the early second century). Cf. G. F. Moore, *Judaism in the First Centuries of the Christian Era* i (Cambridge, Mass., 1927), pp. 188 f.

[5] Cf. J. N. D. Kelly, *Early Christian Creeds* (London, 1950), pp. 30 ff., 100 ff., *et passim*, for a critical study of these and related questions; his scrutiny of widely held assumptions is specially valuable.

creed, and to a much more marked degree the creeds of the eastern
churches (culminating in the Creed of Nicaea and what we traditionally
call the Nicene Creed)[1] amplify the original threefold response by means
of such a summary of the faith as we find in Irenaeus, Tertullian
and Origen. Thus, even if the baptismal confession and the "rule of faith"
were independent in origin, they came in time to interpenetrate each
other, until from the fourth century onward the ecumenical creed super-
sedes the appeal to the rule of faith.

If, in the language of Article VIII, the historical creeds "may be proved
by most certain warrants of holy Scripture", the same might be said of
the rule of faith. This, at least, was believed, or indeed taken for granted,
by the fathers who have been referred to. Origen's observation to this
effect has been mentioned already.[2] As for Irenaeus, this rule was the
tradition which was safeguarded by the episcopal succession in the apostolic churches:

> even if the apostles had not left us the scriptures, would it not be our duty to
> follow the order of tradition which they delivered to those to whom they
> entrusted the churches? Many barbarian nations which believe in Christ assent
> to this tradition, having [the way of] salvation written in their hearts through
> the Spirit, without paper or ink, and diligently keeping the ancient tradition.[3]

The way of salvation and the tradition are in practice synonymous.
But Irenaeus attached supreme importance to what was written with paper
and ink. The apostolic tradition is for him the proper and natural interpretation of Scripture: the faith which he summarizes and expounds is
what Scripture teaches. He is convinced of the perspicuity of Scripture;
any honest student of Scripture must agree that this is its meaning. Heretics may appeal to Scripture, but if they construct from Scripture something different from the apostolic tradition as preserved in the church
their appeal is invalid.

> Not only do they try to derive their proofs from the evangelic and apostolic
> writings, perverting their meaning and interpreting them corruptly, but from
> the law and the prophets as well, for in the latter there are many parables and
> allegories which can be pulled in many directions because of the ambiguity
> of their interpretation. Thus the more readily do they craftily adapt the scrip-
> tures to their own fictions and lead captive away from the truth those who do
> not firmly guard the faith in one God the Father Almighty and in one Lord
> Jesus Christ the Son of God.[4]

---

[1] What we popularly call the Nicene Creed is not the formula adopted by the Council of
Nicaea (A.D. 325) but one sanctioned by the Council of Chalcedon (A.D. 451). See J. N. D.
Kelly, *Early Christian Creeds*, pp. 205 ff.

[2] See p. 115; cf. also *Against Celsus* ii. 71, where Origen treats passages like Luke 10:22;
John 1:18; 4:24 and I John 1:5 as starting-points (ἀφορμαί) for theological construction.

[3] *Heresies* iii. 4.1.

[4] *Heresies* i. 1.6.

Their treatment of the Scriptures resembles the behaviour of people who dismember a mosaic likeness of the emperor, and reconstruct the pieces to make a picture of a dog or a fox.[1]

The Church's Norm

Heretics and those who are outside the church are incompetent to interpret the Scriptures for they repudiate the one key that unlocks its meaning. This is elaborated by Tertullian's *Prescription against Heretics*,[2] in which he uses a legal argument to debar heretics from the right of appealing to Scriptures, and it is carried to its logical conclusion by Cyprian (died A.D. 258), who insists that outside the church there is no salvation, either for heretics or for schismatics.[3] Separated brethren like Novatians might be more strictly orthodox in their theology than many members of the Church Catholic,[4] but in Cyprian's eyes that did them no good if they were out of communion with the Church Catholic: even their baptism was invalid, for whatever they meant when in their baptismal creed they confessed their faith in "the holy church", their "holy church" was not the true church, and since salvation could be found only within the true church, they were cut off from all share in it.

When the summary of the apostolic tradition is called the rule of faith or the rule of truth,[5] the implication is that this is the church's norm, the

---

[1] *Heresies* i. 1.15.

[2] In this document "prescription" (Latin *praescriptio*) is a technical term of Roman law (familiar to a jurist like Tertullian) meaning a demurrer or formal objection. In the *Prescription* Tertullian carries his argument so far as to refuse to appeal to Scripture in debating with heretics, since they do not share the premises on which alone Scripture can be properly used. But in other treatises against heretics he freely appeals to Scripture: indeed, in one place (*Against Marcion* i. 22) he treats "mere prescription" as inadequate for their confutation.

[3] Cyprian, *Epistles* 4.4.3; 73.21.2. More than once he uses as an analogy Noah's ark, outside which there was no salvation from the flood (*Epistle* 74.11; *Unity of the Church* 6, where he also affirms that "no one can have God for his Father who has not the church for his mother").

[4] Novatian's treatise *On the Trinity* (c. A.D. 250), the earliest extant work dealing with the subject of its title, marks an important advance in the definition of the catholic doctrine of God: he expounded the three articles of the rule of faith, dealing with the relation between the Father and the Son and adding a brief independent exposition of the doctrine of the Spirit. Yet hereby (in Cyprian's eyes) he was not justified, because he was a schismatic, and "he who is not in the church of Christ is not a Christian" (*Epistle* 55).

[5] It is denoted by a variety of expressions. Irenaeus occasionally calls it "the rule ($\kappa\alpha\nu\omega\nu$) of truth" (e.g. in *Heresies* i. 1.20), as also does Novatian (*On the Trinity* 1). In *Demonstration* 3 it is called "the rule of the faith" but since this treatise is extant only in an Armenian version we cannot be certain what Irenaeus's Greek wording was here. In the full title of this treatise (*Demonstration of the Apostolic Preaching*) it is called "the apostolic preaching ($\kappa\eta\rho\upsilon\gamma\mu\alpha$)"; indeed, this whole treatise may be called "a commentary on the rule of faith" (R. P. C. Hanson, *Tradition in the Early Church*, p. 108). Tertullian frequently speaks of "the rule of faith" (*regula fidei*). Hippolytus speaks of "the definition ($\delta\rho\sigma\varsigma$) of truth" (*Refutation* x. 5.1 f.). Clement and Origen of Alexandria use the word "rule" ($\kappa\alpha\nu\omega\nu$) of the rule of faith with or without further qualification. Cyprian speaks of "the maintenance of the faith" (*tenor fidei*) with similar, though not identical, sense to Tertullian's *regula fidei* (cf. Cyprian, *Epistle* 74.9.1: "if there be among us the fear of God, if the maintenance of the faith prevail, if we keep the precepts of Christ").

standard by which everything must be judged that presents itself for Christian faith or claims to be Christian doctrine, the criterion for the recognition of truth and exposure of error. If at times it is formally distinguished from Scripture in the sense that it is recognized as the interpretation of Scripture, at other times it is materially identical with Scripture in the sense that it sums up what Scripture says. Plainly what was written down by the apostles in their letters and what was delivered by them orally to their disciples and handed down in the church's tradition must be one and the same body of teaching. As R. P. C. Hanson puts it, the rule of faith invoked by the church fathers is "a graph of the interpretation of the Bible by the Church in the second and third centuries",[1] a statement of what was generally believed to be the essence of Scripture.[2] It was not that the apostolic writings were unintelligible in themselves;[3] only the Christian Platonists of Alexandria, with their predilection for allegorical interpretation, found themselves led on occasion by the course of their arguments to say something like this.[4] But when they are being Christians rather than Platonists they speak to the same effect as the other fathers: "we have as the source of teaching", says Clement (c. A.D. 180), "the Lord, leading us by the prophets, the gospel and the blessed apostles, 'in many ways and many parts', from the beginning of knowledge to the end . . . He, then, who spontaneously believes the Scripture and the voice of the Lord . . . is rightly held to be faithful." Heresy is revealed by its being in opposition to the Scriptures; heretics fail to "follow God wherever he leads – and he leads us in the inspired Scriptures." They may fall into heresy through wilful opposition to what the Scriptures teach, or through a propensity to sloth; "for they are guilty of sloth when they have it in their power to provide themselves with proper proofs for the divine Scriptures from the Scriptures themselves but select only what serves their own pleasure." Clement's "true Gnostic", his ideal Christian

---

[1] *Tradition in the Early Church*, p. 127. Elsewhere he suggests as a generally adequate, though not entirely comprehensive, definition: "that which regards it as an account of the teaching of the Church as it is known to the writer who uses the concept of the rule, believed to be continuous or virtually identical with the teaching which the Church has been giving from the very beginning, from the time of the apostles" (*op. cit.*, pp. 124 f.)

[2] Much depends, of course, on one's conception of what the essence of Scripture is. E. Flesseman-van Leer compares the fathers' use of the rule to the Reformers' principle of biblical interpretation according to "the analogy of faith" – the main thrust of Scripture, as they understood it (*Tradition and Scripture*, p. 194). Compare Luther's appeal to *was Christum treibet*, and cf. the references on pp. 145 f. to N. H. Snaith and E. J. Carnell.

[3] For Cyprian the church's teaching was the same as the teaching of Scripture: to "have recourse to the fountain of truth" is to "seek the head" and to "keep the teaching of the heavenly Master" (*Unity of the Church*, 3).

[4] Clement on occasion claims to be in possession of a secret tradition independent of Scripture, a *gnōsis* "which has come down by transmission to a few, having been imparted unwritten by the apostles" (*Stromata* vi. 7). But in this gnosticizing claim he is unique among the fathers. In so far as the character of his secret *gnōsis* can be ascertained, it may have consisted of a tradition of midrashic interpretation (cf. J. Daniélou, *Théologie du judéo-christianisme*, Paris, 1958, pp. 62 f.).

(by contrast with devotees of "the *gnosis* which is falsely so called"), "having grown old in the Scriptures, and maintaining apostolic and ecclesiastical orthodoxy in his doctrines, lives most correctly in accordance with the gospel, and derives from the law and the prophets the proofs for which he has made search . . . For the life of the Gnostic, in my view, consists simply in deeds and words which correspond to the tradition of our Lord."[1]

Ethical Tradition

The tradition of Christian ethics founded on the teaching of Jesus, which was recorded by the evangelists and expounded and applied by the apostles, was further developed in the post-apostolic age. The narratives and laws of the Old Testament, which provided the New Testament writers with illustrations for their ethical injunctions, were further pressed into service by the Apostolic Fathers, frequently with liberal use of allegorization. Paul had used the experience of Israel in the wilderness as a warning to his self-confident Corinthian converts to take heed lest they should fall[2] and had appealed to the law against muzzling an ox when it was treading out the grain to confirm that preachers of the gospel should live by the gospel.[3] The writer to the Hebrews invoked the faith of the saints from Abel to the Maccabaean martyrs in order to encourage his readers to cultivate similar faith,[4] while in Jude and II Peter classic instances of judgement in Old Testament times – the fall of the angels, the flood of Noah's day, the destruction of Sodom, and so forth – prefigure the eschatological judgement of the ungodly.[5] So Clement of Rome adduces from the Old Testament instances of the terrible consequences of jealousy and envy to warn the church of Corinth against these vices,[6] and recommends them to imitate Abraham, David, Elijah, Elisha and other Old Testament characters, and above all to imitate Christ.[7] The Epistle of Barnabas allegorizes the ceremonial laws, especially those relating to various animals, so as to draw moral lessons from them:[8] for example, the commandment to eat the flesh only of those animals that chew the cud and are cloven-hoofed means that one should consort with people who meditate on the word of the Lord and look forward to the coming age while walking in this world.[9]

The Epistle of Barnabas, together with the more or less contemporary

---

[1] *Stromata* vii. 16.
[2] I Cor. 10:1-12 (see p. 84).
[3] I Cor. 9:8-10 (see p. 33).
[4] Heb. 11:4 ff.
[5] Jude 5 ff. (see pp. 84, 130); II Peter 2:4 ff.
[6] I Clement 4:1 ff.
[7] I Clement 10:1 ff.
[8] Barn. 7:1 ff.
[9] Barn. 10:11.

Didache, incorporates a code of ethical practice, less imaginative and more pedestrian in style, in the catechesis of the Two Ways – the way of light and life and the way of darkness and death.[1] As the catechesis of the Two Ways appears in two different recensions in the Epistle of Barnabas and the *Didache,* it is manifestly earlier than either of them, and in fact it seems to be a christianized edition of an originally Jewish manual, going back to the pre-Christian era. Traces of it appear in the Qumran texts and in the *Testaments of the Twelve Patriarchs.*[2] The dichotomy expressed in the construction and title goes back to the Wisdom literature[3] and beyond that to Deuteronomy;[4] the contents include expositions both of the Decalogue and of the Sermon on the Mount. The way of life is summed up in the twofold commandment of love to God and love to one's neighbour, combined with the negative form of the Golden Rule ("whatsoever you would not have done to yourself, do not to another").[5]

Whether it was conveyed by allegorical interpretation or by prosaic injunctions, there was a well established and widely accepted tradition of Christian ethics, distinguished in some degree from the extreme asceticism of the Montanists and some Gnostic groups[6] and much more radically from the libertinism of other Gnostic groups. But from the Jerusalem decree of apostolic times onwards we can trace an increasing tendency to replace the freedom of the Spirit by the bondage of the letter.[7]

---

[1] Barn. 18:1–20:2; *Didachē* 1:1–6:3. In the former the two ways are the way of light and the way of darkness; in the latter they are the way of life and the way of death. Cf. R. A. Kraft, *The Apostolic Fathers* III: *The Didache and Barnabas* (New York, 1965), pp. 4 ff.

[2] Cf. 1 QS iii. 18–iv. 26; *Test XII Judah* 20:1–5; *Test. XII Asher* 1:3–6:6. On the use of the "two ways" catechesis in early Judaeo-Christian baptismal instruction see J. V. Bartlet, *The Apostolic Age* (Edinburgh, 1929), pp. 250 ff., 313.

[3] Cf. Proverbs 2:12, 20, etc.

[4] Cf. Deut. 30:15, 19.

[5] *Didachē* 1:2. For the negative golden rule cf. Tobit 4:15, Hillel in TB Shabbat 31*a*, and the Western text of Acts 15:20, 29.

[6] The tendency to asceticism increased from the apostolic age onwards, but it was thought by those who practised it to be part of the apostolic tradition. Compare the fasting injunction in *Didachē* 8:1 ("Let not your fasts be with the hypocrites, for they fast on Mondays and Thursdays, but do you fast on Wednesdays and Fridays"). Tertullian, in his Montanist days (*On Fasting,* 13:1) argues against the criticism that the Montanists impose asceticism beyond what the apostolic tradition commands, that his critics themselves observe appointed fasts beyond those contemplated for "the days when the bridegroom is taken away" (Mark 2:20; see p. 61). Elsewhere he indicates that the Montanist prohibition of remarriage is in line with "catholic tradition" (*On Monogamy* 2:2), although in the same context he makes provision for a development of what was only implicit in the tradition (equivalent to the apostolic writings) by appealing to Jesus' promise that the Paraclete would lead His followers into truth which at the time would have been too burdensome for them (John 16:12 f.). Tertullian might have found partial biblical authority for his case in the stipulation in the Pastoral Letters that bishops or elders, and deacons, must be "husbands of one wife" (I Tim. 3:2, 12; Tit. 1:6), interpreted in RSV as "married only once" (cf. the parallel qualification for enrolment as a "widow" in I Tim. 5:9).

[7] We may contrast the decree's uncompromising ban on the eating of *eidolothyta* with Paul's treatment of the problem in terms of personal relationships (I Cor. 8:1 ff.; 10:14 ff., especially verse 23).

Church Order: the "Didache"

Mention of the *Didache* brings us to another important phase of apostolic tradition in the early church, the phase that relates to church order and worship.

The *Didache* purports to be "the Lord's teaching through the twelve apostles to the Gentiles",[1] which suggests that it aims at expanding His commission to them to "make disciples of all the nations . . . teaching them to observe all that I have commanded you" (Matt. 28:19 f.). It is a composite work, illustrating the development of tradition within a Christian community or group of communities – perhaps in some country district of Syria, though Egypt cannot be ruled out. Some of its material is manifestly primitive, belonging probably to the first century, but the work as we have it includes some later elements and may be dated about the middle of the second century.[2] Even if we can see the tradition growing as we read the *Didache,* the tradition is presented throughout as dominical.

What, then, are the topics on which our Lord is thought to have given the apostles instruction for the Gentiles? After the catechesis of the Two Ways comes instruction about food, where changing conditions made it difficult to keep all the traditions ("concerning food, bear what you can, but at any rate avoid what is sacrificed to idols, for that is the worship of dead gods"),[3] and baptism, where Matthew's trinitarian formula is reproduced and concessions are made regarding the character and quantity of the water to be used (running water is best, but static water will do; warm water is permitted if cold is out of the question; affusion is acceptable is there is not enough water for dipping.)[4] Two of the religious practices of Matt. 6:1–18 are then dealt with: fasting[5] (in a way which ludicrously misinterprets the injunction of Matt. 6:16–18 not to fast like "hypocrites")[6] and prayer (the Lord's Prayer, in a form closely approximating to that of Matt. 6:9–13, with a shorter doxology than that added in the Caesarean and later texts, is to be said three times a day).[7]

---

[1] The silence about Paul's apostleship to the Gentiles may be intentional. Further attention should be paid to the two traditions of the apostolate of the Twelve – presumably the eleven of Matt. 28:16 augmented by Matthias (Acts 1:26) – to the Gentiles and the restriction of their apostolate to "the circumcision" (Gal. 2:7–9, with which the representation of Acts largely agrees).

[2] Cf. R. A. Kraft, *The Didache and Barnabas,* pp. 57 ff.

[3] *Didachē* 6:3.

[4] *Didachē* 7:1–3.

[5] The subject of fasting is introduced by the direction that before baptism the candidate should fast (for one or two days) along with the baptizer and "any others who can" (7:4).

[6] See p. 120, n. 6.

[7] *Didachē* 8:2 f.

The instruction concerning the Eucharist is specially valuable:[1] the thanksgiving for the cup precedes that for the bread,[2] each thanksgiving being given in full, as is also the prayer of thanksgiving "after you have been filled". This prayer ends with the same doxology as concludes the Lord's Prayer, "For thine is the power and the glory for ever", followed by three versicles and responses:

> Let grace come and let this world pass away.
> Hosanna to the God of David!
> If any one is holy, let him come.
> If any one is not, let him repent.
> Marana-tha.[3]
> Amen.

These concluding words suggest that this prayer, both "fencing the table" and invoking the Lord's real presence, preceded the Eucharist proper; if so, then the clause "after you have been filled" refers not to participation in the sacramental bread and wine, but to a preceding meal.[4]

The composite nature of the *Didache* is illustrated by the fact that, after directions about hospitality to itinerant apostles and prophets,[5] further injunction is given about breaking bread and giving thanks (holding eucharist) "on the Lord's Day of the Lord", after confession of sins and mending of quarrels.[6] The treatise then ends with directions for the appointment of bishops and deacons[7] and an eschatological admonition: lawlessness will increase, Antichrist will hold sway, all mankind will come to the fiery trial, which only the faithful will survive;[8] then comes the Parousia, heralded by three signs: (i) the sign spread out in heaven,[9] (ii) the sound of the trumpet and (iii) the resurrection of the dead.[10]

On many of these subjects the Lord does give instruction in the gospel tradition, but not on church order. Yet those who received and delivered these directions on this subject were probably convinced that it was genuine dominical tradition that they were receiving and delivering. They did not rationalize their conviction as they might have done had it

---

[1] *Didachē* 9:1–10:7.

[2] Cf. I Cor. 10:16; also the order of the shorter text of Luke 22:17–19.

[3] For the Aramaic *Marana-tha* ("Our Lord, come!") cf. I Cor. 16:22 (its Greek equivalent occurs in Rev. 22:20). The use by Greek-speaking Christians of this Aramaic invocation points to the Palestinian origin of the ascription to Jesus of the title "Lord"; it confirms the place given to the exalted and expected Christ in the worship of the most primitive church.

[4] Cf. I Cor. 11:20 ff., where Paul urges the discontinuance of this communal pre-eucharistic meal at Corinth because of abuses which attended it there.

[5] *Didachē* 11:1–13:7.

[6] *Didachē* 14:1–3.

[7] *Didachē* 15:1–4.

[8] *Didachē* 16:1–8.

[9] Cf. Matt. 24:30, "then will appear the sign of the Son of Man in heaven".

[10] For the trumpet as resurrection-signal see I Cor. 15:52; I Thess. 4:16; Rev. 11:15 ff. (cf. also Matt. 24:31 and its OT antecedent, Isa. 27:13).

been brought home to them that it had no firm foundation in the teaching of Jesus. They had no thought of appealing to the continuing ministry of Jesus from His place of exaltation, or to His Spirit's guidance into further truth, or to the development of doctrine after the analogy of the acorn and the oak. They simply assumed that the practice which was familiar to them was apostolic practice, as many Christians do today, whether the practice they have in mind be that (say) of the Roman Catholic Church or (say) of the Exclusive Brethren of Mr. James Taylor's connexion.

"Didascalia"

The pattern of the *Didache* is reproduced in a series of later manuals. One of these, the *Didascalia Apostolorum,* was composed in Greek early in the fourth century, but it is extant in its entirety only in a Syriac version.[1] It presents a vivid and detailed picture of church life in the third century. The authority which it claims is more comprehensive than that of the *Didache,* for Paul and James the Just are co-opted along with the Twelve:

> We, the twelve apostles of the only Son, the everlasting Word of God, our Lord and God and Saviour Jesus the Christ, being assembled with one accord in Jerusalem, the city of the great King, and with us our brother Paul, the apostle of the Gentiles, and James the bishop of the above-mentioned city, have established this *Didascalia . . .*[2]

The work then lays down the basic rules of Christian conduct, the qualifications and duties of a bishop, the election of elders and deacons, the ministry of widows, the care of orphans and giving of alms, the regard to be paid to confessors and martyrs, the paschal fast (the directions on this presuppose the calendar according to which our Lord kept the Last Supper with the disciples on Tuesday evening, appeared before Caiaphas on Wednesday and before Pilate on Thursday, and was crucified on Friday),[3] the upbringing of children, heresy and schism. The *Didascalia* takes heresy and schism seriously and warns those who are guilty of these

---

[1] Its Greek text can be reconstructed in part from the *Apostolic Constitutions* (see p. 125). Its Greek title was evidently Διδαχὴ ᾿Αποστόλων (as given at the end of the Syriac version); the alternative title *Didascalia* also appears at the end of the Syriac version ("we leave this *Didascalia,* holy and catholic, justly and righteously to the catholic church and for the assurance of believers") and elsewhere (e.g. in the preface: "We begin to write the book *Didascalia* . . ."). The Syriac version was edited by M. D. Gibson in *Horae Semiticae* i (London, 1903) and translated by her in *Horae Semiticae* ii (London, 1903). The references here are given according to her chapter-headings. Cf. also R. H. Connolly, "The Use of the *Didache* in the *Didascalia*", *JTS* 24 (1922–3), pp. 147 ff.

[2] Preface.

[3] Cf. on this calendar A. Jaubert, *La date de la Cène* (Paris, 1957), pp. 79 ff.; she relates it to the calendar of the book of Jubilees and of the Qumran community.

offences that they will suffer the fate of Korah, Dathan and Abiram, who were swallowed up by the earth and went down alive into Sheol.

The *Didascalia* is not couched in the pedestrian style of a manual of church order, but breathes a hortatory, and almost prophetic, spirit throughout. It is a matter of literary interest that the apocryphal composition which we know as the *Prayer of Manasseh* makes its first extant appearance as a quotation in the course of a direction to the bishops about granting absolution to penitent sinners.[1]

Manasseh worshipped evil idols zealously, and killed the righteous, but when he repented, the Lord forgave him; although there is no sin worse than the worship of idols, yet a place for repentance was given. But to him who says, "Good things shall happen to me though I walk in the perverse will of my heart",[2] thus says the Lord: "I will stretch out my hand against him, and he shall become a by-word and a proverb"[3] – because Amon son of Manasseh, having taken counsel with the counsel of law-breaking, said: "My father from his childhood was very wicked, and good in his old age; I also will act now according to the lusts of my soul, and at the end I will repent towards the Lord." So he did what was evil before the Lord,[4] but he reigned only two years: the Lord God destroyed him from the good land. Therefore take heed, you who are without faith . . .

This note of exhortation is sustained throughout the *Didascalia,* an d in this sense at least it stands within the authentic apostolic tradition. J. V. Bartlet draws attention to its affinity in this respect with the Epistle of James.[5]

"Apostolic Tradition" and Kindred Works

There is a tendency for later church orders, while standing formally in the succession of the *Didache,* to be less closely related to the practical realities of church life. Such is the work of Egyptian provenance called the *Apostolic Church Order* (or *Ecclesiastical Canons*), written in Greek in the early fourth century.[6] As in the *Didache,* the catechesis of the Two Ways comes first, followed by church rules probably intended to replace those of the *Didache,* which were no longer applicable to the contemporary situation. The authority of various individual apostles is invoked for the rules.

[1] Ch. 7.
[2] Deut. 29:19.
[3] Cf. Deut. 28:37; I Kings 9:7.
[4] Cf. II Kings 20:19 ff.; II Chron. 33:21 ff.
[5] J. V. Bartlet, *Church-Life and Church-Order during the First Four Centuries* (Oxford, 1943), p. 78. (This posthumously published work has much of importance to say about the eastern church orders of this period.)
[6] Cf. J. P. Arendzen, "An Entire Syriac Text of the 'Apostolic Church Order'," *JTS* 3 3 (1901–2), pp. 59 ff.; R. H. Connolly, *art. cit., JTS* 24 (1922–3), pp. 155 f.; J. V. Bartlet, *Church-Life and Church-Order,* pp. 100 ff.

A later and larger compilation is that called the *Apostolic Constitutions,* a late fourth-century work in eight books, purporting to come from "the apostles and elders to all those who from among the Gentiles have believed in the Lord Jesus Christ".[1] Books I–VI are an expansion of the *Didascalia* and Book VII is an enlargement of the *Didache,* among the additions being an account of the bishops who were ordained in the churches by the respective apostles – a testimony to contemporary tradition, not to first-century fact. Where more apostles than one were associated with a church, due regard was paid to this: thus "of Antioch Euodius [was bishop], ordained by me Peter, and Ignatius by Paul; . . . of the church of Rome, Linus the son of Claudia was the first,[2] ordained by Paul, and Clement was second, after the death of Linus, ordained by me Peter; of Ephesus, Timothy, ordained by Paul, and John, by me John."[3]

Book VIII of the *Apostolic Constitutions* stands in another tradition than that of the *Didache* and *Didascalia,* but one which equally claims to stem from the apostles. Large sections of this book are based on the *Apostolic Tradition* of Hippolytus of Rome, a manual of church order which has come down to us from the beginning of the third century.[4] Hippolytus, the greatest Christian scholar of the generation after Irenaeus, was bishop of a body of Roman Christians who for some years were in schism from the church of Rome, but his theology was completely in line with what the church of Rome acknowledged as apostolic doctrine,[5] and in due course the Roman church, turning a blind eye to his schismatic deviation, canonized him as a catholic doctor and martyr. It may reasonably be concluded that his *Apostolic Tradition* represents contemporary practice in the church of Rome. To say that the *Apostolic Tradition* of Hippolytus "has come down to us" may be an over-statement; we wish it had come down to us in its original Greek text. What has actually come down to us is a series of later documents which (like Book VIII of the *Apostolic Constitutions*) incorporate it or draw upon it – particularly "the

---

[1] *Apostolic Constitutions* i. i.

[2] Probably an inference from II Tim. 4:21.

[3] *Ap. Const.* vii. 46. The closing words evidently distinguish John the elder (bishop of Ephesus) from John the apostle (who is said to have ordained him). The Peshitta MS. Mingana Syriac 540 has a prefatory note to the Fourth Gospel: "The holy Gospel of our Lord Jesus Christ – the teaching of John the *younger*" (while he had the status of "elder" as a disciple of apostles, he was "John the younger" in relation to his apostolic namesake). See A. Mingana, "The Authorship of the Fourth Gospel", *BJRL* 14 (1930), pp. 333 ff.

[4] The list of Hippolytus's works engraved on the back of his seated statue (rediscovered in 1551) includes περὶ χαρισμάτων ἀποστολικὴ παράδοσις. It is disputed whether this is one title ("Apostolic tradition concerning grace-gifts") or two ("Concerning grace-gifts" and "Apostolic tradition").

[5] Hippolytus actually charged Callistus, bishop of Rome, with disciplinary laxity and erroneous doctrine and withdrew from his communion, regarding his own following as the catholic church and the "Callistians" as schismatics. Together with Pontianus, a later bishop of Rome, Hippolytus was sent in 235 into penal servitude in Sardinia, where they died reconciled to each other.

E

so-called Egyptian Church Order and derived documents",[1] as Dom R.
H. Connolly called them – from which it is possible with considerable
confidence to reconstruct it.[2] The Egyptian (Coptic) Church Order is a
work of the fifth century, from which are derived later Coptic editions
(Sahidic and Bohairic) and Arabic and Ethiopic versions. Other witnesses
to the text of the *Apostolic Tradition* are a corpus of church rules called
the *Canons of Hippolytus*, extant only in Arabic, the *Testament of our Lord*
(a work of c. A.D. 400 composed in Greek but extant in Syriac)[3] and a
Latin version of the late fourth or early fifth century which, in the opinion
of some, was made for the use of Arian congregations (although it contains no distinctive Arianism).[4]

The document as reconstructed comprises (i) the order for the consecration of bishops, the eucharistic liturgy (from which we have already
quoted),[5] the blessing of food, and ordination to various ministries in the
church; (ii) regulations for the laity, for baptism and confirmation (which
belong together in a single service) and for communion; (iii) ecclesiastical practices and customs. If all this is subsumed under apostolic tradition,
then apostolic tradition must have constituted the rule of practice as well
as the rule of faith.[6]

There is some evidence in the *Apostolic Tradition* of features more characteristic of Judaism than of historic Christianity, and of "nonconformist
Judaism" rather than "normative Judaism". For example, those who are
to receive baptism on a particular Sunday (possibly Easter Day) are required to undergo a purificatory bath the preceding Thursday.[7] This
pre-baptismal bath has no warrant in the apostolic writings but is in line
with the practice of some Jewish sects; Cardinal Daniélou has expressed
the view that it is a heritage from Essenism.[8] Again, women are required
at baptism to lay aside their jewellery and wear their hair unbound; a
similar rule is attested in the Mishnah for Jewish ritual washings.[9] The

[1] In the title of his contribution to *Texts and Studies* viii. 4 (Cambridge, 1916).
[2] Cf. editions by G. Dix, *The Apostolic Tradition of St. Hippolytus of Rome* (London, 1937),
reissued with corrections, preface and bibliography by H. Chadwick (London, 1968); B.
Botte, *La Tradition Apostolique de Saint Hippolyte: essai de reconstruction* (Münster, 1963).
[3] Edited by J. Cooper and A. J. Maclean, *The Testament of our Lord* (Edinburgh, 1902). See
p. 108.
[4] Cf. A. F. Walls, "The Latin Version of Hippolytus' Apostolic Tradition", *Studia Patristica*
iii = *TU* 78 (Berlin, 1961), pp. 155 ff.
[5] See p. 34.
[6] Sometimes, however, as in Polycrates and Cornelius, "the rule of faith" meant the church's
practice, not its doctrine (cf. R. P. C. Hanson, *Tradition in the Early Church*, p. 125).
[7] *Ap. Trad.* 20:5.
[8] J. Daniélou, "La communauté de Qumrân et l'organisation de l'Eglise ancienne", *RHPR*
35 (1955), pp. 104 ff.; cf. R. J. Zwi Werblowsky, "On the Baptismal Rite according to St.
Hippolytus", *Studia Patristica* ii = *TU* 64 (Berlin, 1957), pp. 93 ff.; M. Black, *The Scrolls and
Christian Origins* (London, 1961), pp. 99 ff., 114 f.
[9] *Ap. Trad.* 21:5; cf. Mishnah *Shabbat* 6:1. See W. C. van Unnik, "Les cheveux défaits
des femmes baptisées: un rite de baptême dans l'Ordre ecclésiastique d'Hippolyte", *Vigiliae
Christianae* 1 (1947), pp. 77 ff.

odd regulation that when fruits are brought to the bishop to be blessed, pumpkins, melons, cucumbers, onions, garlic *et hoc genus omne* must not be included among them, may reflect a contemporary synagogue regulation based on the Israelites' ungrateful preference of these vegetables to manna in Num. 11:5.[1] Hippolytus thus bears witness to the Jewish base of the Roman church in its earliest days and to a continuous tradition of practice originating in those earliest days. To that extent his "tradition" is "apostolic" – if not in the sense of being delivered by the apostles, at least in the sense of going back to apostolic times. But alongside these archaic features are others which show no such Jewish affinities; some indeed may be the work of Hippolytus himself, shaped of course from pre-existent material, like the *anaphora* or prayer of thanksgiving in the eucharistic liturgy.[2]

The *Apostolic Tradition* bears witness also to a strict church discipline: a variety of pagan crafts and professions are taboo to Christians – actors, charioteers, gladiators, manufacturers of idols, magicians and so forth. Military officers must not execute men, even if ordered to do so; Christians who volunteer to become soldiers are to be excommunicated.[3] A more kindly consideration is shown towards another honourable profession: "if a man teaches children secular knowledge, it is well if he desists. But if he has no other craft to live by, let him be forgiven."[4]

In matters of doctrine, ethics or church order, it was axiomatic that whatever the apostles taught was right and regular, and it was not difficult to argue backwards and say that whatever was right and regular (or was believed to be so) in a Christian context must have been practised or taught by the apostles. This tendency reaches a point where we find, as in Basil of Cappadocian Caesarea (329–379), what looks at first sight "like an attempt to turn Christianity into a mystery-religion or an ecclesiastical freemasonry and to canonize a tradition of custom which earlier Christian ages had regarded as wholly secondary".[5]

Even so, the kind of "apostolic tradition" at which we have been looking was treated differently from the canon of apostolic writings. As Bishop Hanson says: "In the early Church the Christian showed his veneration for his Bible by copying it out; he showed his respect for his

[1] *Ap. Trad.* 28:6.
[2] *Ap. Trad.* 4:4 ff.
[3] *Ap. Trad.* 16:9 ff.
[4] *Ap. Trad.* 16:13.
[5] R. P. C. Hanson, *Tradition in the Early Church*, p. 184. But cf. the reply by E. Amand de Mendieta in *The "Unwritten" and "Secret" Apostolic Traditions in the Theological Thought of St. Basil of Caesarea* (Edinburgh, 1965). He translates and analyses the relevant passages in Basil, and concludes that the criticisms are too sweeping. As a man of the fourth century, Basil could not be expected to manifest that historical sense for lack of which he ascribes to the apostles many of the sacramental, ritual and doctrinal traditions of his own day. There are other traditions which he does not ascribe to them, and he does not "give a status as *de fide* to *all* existing custom or rite in use in the Eastern Orthodox Churches of his time, especially in his own diocese" (p. 56).

manual of traditional practice by putting interpolations into it. This is the difference between Scripture and tradition."[1]

Yet the living tradition, the continuity of Christian life, is indispensable. Without it, Scripture would have had no context. If we could suppose that the church had been wiped out in the Diocletianic persecution and the church's scriptures lost, to be rediscovered in our own day like the Dead Sea Scrolls, would the rediscovered scriptures once more have the effect which we know them to have in experience, or would they, like the Scrolls, be an archaeological curiosity and a subject for historical debate?[2]

On the other hand, the living tradition without the constant corrective of Scripture (or, in more modern language, without the possibility of "reformation according to the word of God"), might have developed out of all recognition if it had not indeed slowly faded and died.

---

[1] *Tradition in the Early Church*, p. 173.

[2] The supposition is formulated by N. Pittenger, *The Word Incarnate* (London, 1959), pp. 57 f. Compare H. J. Schonfield's claim, in his *Authentic New Testament* (London, 1955) to approach the documents "as if they had recently been recovered from a cave in Palestine or beneath the sands of Egypt, and had never previously been given to the public".

CHAPTER VIII

TRADITION AND THE CANON
OF SCRIPTURE

W E RETURN NOW TO LOOK FURTHER AT THOSE SCRIPTURES
which provide a corrective to unwritten tradition, a standard or
"canon" by which it may be tested: in other words, we must
consider the relation between our general subject and the "canon" of
Scripture. When we speak of the "canon" of Scripture we use the word
in a different sense from that of "rule" or "standard"; the "canon" of
Scripture is originally the "list" of books recognized by the church as
her sacred writings – a use of the word first attested, it appears, in Athanasius.[1] But inevitably, because of the close relation between Scripture
and the rule of faith, something of the sense of authority has come to be
attached in common usage to the terms "canon" and "canonical" when
they refer to the books of the Bible.

This is an area in which the most biblicist and anti-traditionalist Christian communities rely perforce upon tradition – a tradition which in
fact is more essential the more biblicist a community is, for the more
dependent it is for its authority on *sola scriptura,* the more necessary it is
to define *sola scriptura.* In other words, the more Christians aim at being
"men of one book", the more important it is for them to know the limits
of that one book.

Delimiting the Canon

There are some churches in which the limits of the canon are laid down
by authority: their members (formally, at any rate) accept these limits
because their church has defined them. This is true, for instance, of the
Roman Catholic Church, the Church of England, and those churches
which adhere to the Westminster Confession of Faith. But what of
churches which do not have the canon of Scripture delimited for them in
this way? (I write now of my own heritage.) On what authority (say) do
we accept the thirty-nine books of the Old Testament, as commonly
reckoned, either rejecting the Apocrypha altogether or else relegating
them to an inferior or "deuterocanonical" status? "We accept these thirty-
nine books," it may be said, "because they make up the Hebrew Bible
which our Lord and the apostles acknowledged." True: there seems to

---

[1] Athanasius, *Thirty-Ninth Festal Letter* (see p. 134). Cf. T. Zahn, *Grundriss der Geschichte des
neutestamentlichen Kanons*[2] (Leipzig, 1904), p. 87, cited by H. Oppel, *KANΩN (Philologus,*
Suppl. 30, Heft 4, Leipzig, 1937), pp. 70 f., cited by R. P. C. Hanson, "Origen's Doctrine of
Tradition", *JTS* 49 (1948), p. 23.

have been common ground between our Lord and the Jewish scribes of His day on the content of Scripture, however much they differed on its interpretation and application. We may be sure that He and they accepted the threefold corpus of Law, Prophets and Writings as it was known from the second century B.C. if not earlier.[1] But, in view of the fact that the precise limits of the third group, the "Writings", do not appear to have been fixed by Jewish authority until the last quarter of the first century A.D., can we be quite sure that our Lord accepted (say) Ecclesiastes or Esther? If (as the argument from silence might suggest) Esther was unknown as a canonical book to the Qumran community,[2] would it be surprising to discover that it was similarly unknown in our Lord's circle? Yet we accept Ecclesiastes and Esther as part of Holy Scripture. Why? Not, in our case, because ecclesiastical authority so directs us – stubborn individualists as many of us are, if ecclesiastical authority did so direct us, that in itself might stimulate us to refuse the direction. No: we accept them, I suppose, because we have "received" them as included in Holy Writ: in other words, because of our tradition. Our tradition is not inviolably sacrosanct, but unless strong reason is shown for rejecting something that we so receive, like the canonicity of these books, we go along with it.

Take an example of another kind: the book of Enoch.[3] We do not accept this book as canonical: it is not so accepted either by western Catholicism (the rock from which *we* were hewn) or by eastern Orthodoxy, although it is part of the Bible of the monophysite Ethiopic church. Yet it is quoted, and quoted as authoritative, by a New Testament writer.[4] We cannot dismiss Jude's Enoch quotation as on a level with Paul's quotations from Menander[5] or Epimenides;[6] Jude quotes from the book of Enoch as other New Testament writers quote the Hebrew prophets, treating the words as a divine oracle.[7] No doubt it would put too great

---

[1] The Law comprises the Pentateuch (Genesis-Deuteronomy); the Prophets comprise the Former Prophets (Joshua, Judges, Samuel, Kings) and the latter Prophets (Isaiah, Jeremiah, Ezekiel, the book of the Twelve Prophets); the Writings comprise Psalms, Proverbs, Job, with the five *Megillôt* or "Rolls" (Canticles, Ruth, Lamentations, Ecclesiastes, Esther) and Daniel, Ezra-Nehemiah and Chronicles: twenty-four books in all.

[2] Esther is the only book of the Hebrew Bible unrepresented among the Qumran manuscripts.

[3] That is, the "Ethiopic Enoch" (a compilation so called because it is extant in its entirety only in the Ethiopic version), distinguished as I Enoch from the much later II Enoch (the "Secrets of Enoch", originally composed in Greek but extant only in Slavonic) and II Enoch (a Hebrew mystical treatise). Aramaic fragments of I Enoch have been found among the Qumran manuscripts; rather more than one-third of the work is extant in a Greek version.

[4] I Enoch 1:9 is quoted in Jude 14 f.

[5] I Cor. 15:33.   [6] Titus 1:12; cf. Acts 17:28a.

[7] As John Bunyan reckoned it his duty to take comfort from Ecclesiasticus 2:10, even if it was an apocryphal work, because it was "the sum and substance of many of the promises" (*Grace Abounding*, 65), so it could be said that I Enoch 1:9 may well rank as a divine oracle, because it is the sum and substance of many of the prophetic warnings of judgement. Tertullian, accepting an antediluvian date for I Enoch, and regarding Jude's quotation as lending authority to the book (since Jude is in his eyes an apostle), adds the further consideration that "nothing which pertains *to* us must be rejected *by* us" (*On the Apparel of Women*, 3).

a strain on our intellectual agility to defend the divine inspiration of the whole book of Enoch, even if other parts of it have influenced thought and language elsewhere in the New Testament.[1] But it is not because of the difficulty of defending the inspiration of the book of Enoch that we do not accept it; it is primarily because our tradition does not recognize it: we have not "received" it. Certainly, if valid arguments were forthcoming for the acceptance of this book, we might revise our tradition and accept it; otherwise we go along with our tradition.

However, Jude's quotation of a passage from the book of Enoch as a divine oracle might prompt the query whether the Letter of Jude itself should be accepted as canonical. It was one of the "disputed" books in the early church,[2] and Luther put it among the four New Testament books to which he accorded a lower canonical status than the other twenty-three.[3] But this raises the problem of the New Testament canon – a knottier problem than that of the Old Testament canon. Apart from such questions as might be raised about "marginal" books like Ecclesiastes and Esther, the Christian biblicist can properly say that he accepts the Old Testament not on the authority of ecclesiastical tradition but on that of our Lord and the apostles. He has no such short answer to the question of the New Testament canon.

These, then, are some of the questions which arise when this subject is under consideration.

The Old Testament Canon

The earliest Christians, as we have seen, found their sacred writings ready to hand in the books of the Hebrew Bible, either in their original text or in the Greek version. The acceptance of the Old Testament was indubitably something which they "received from the Lord" – by example as well as by instruction. For, to reproduce a purple passage from a distinguished Old Testament scholar of a past generation:

> For us its supreme sanction is that which it received from Christ Himself. It was the Bible of His education and the Bible of His ministry. He took for granted its fundamental doctrines about creation, about man and about righteousness; about God's Providence of the world and His purposes of grace through Israel. He accepted its history as the preparation for Himself, and taught His disciples to find Him in it. He used it to justify His mission and to illuminate the mystery of His Cross. He drew from it many of the examples and most

---

[1] Not only the references to fallen angels in Jude 6 and II Peter 2:4 (cf. the "spirits in prison" of I Peter 3:19) – i.e. to the trespassing "sons of God" of Gen. 6:2, 4, on whose sin and penalty I Enoch enlarges – but also the portrayal of the "Son of Man" in the independent section called the "Similitudes of Enoch" (I Enoch 37–71); cf. M. D. Hooker, *The Son of Man in Mark* (London, 1967), pp. 33 ff.

[2] See p. 142.   [3] See p. 145.

of the categories of His gospel. He re-enforced the essence of its law and res-
tored many of its ideals. But, above all, He fed His own soul with its contents,
and in the great crises of His life sustained Himself upon it as upon the living
and sovereign Word of God. These are the highest external proofs – if indeed
we can call them external – for the abiding validity of the Old Testament in
the life and doctrine of Christ's Church. What was indispensable to the Redeemer must always be indispensable to the redeemed.[1]

In the apostolic age there is no sign that Christians felt the need of a
New Testament in the sense of a collection of writings. They had the
sacred writings which their Lord used and fulfilled, writings which not
only conveyed the way of "salvation through faith in Christ Jesus" but
which also, being divinely inspired, were "profitable for teaching, for
reproof, for correction, and for training in righteousness, that the man of
God may be complete, equipped for every good work."[2] These writings,
until well into the second century, constituted the church's Bible, read,
of course, through Christian spectacles. From them the apostles of the
first century and the apologists of the second century drew their basic
texts as they proclaimed and defended the gospel; the reading of them was
sufficient to convince a number of educated pagans of the truth of Christianity.[3]

One thing which does not seem to have greatly concerned those early
Christians was the precise delimitation of their Bible. Actually, there
was no particular reason why they should be greatly concerned; they were
all agreed about its main contents. It is commonly supposed that the threefold division of the Hebrew Bible corresponds to three stages in the
growth of the Hebrew canon.[4] The Law and the Prophets were firmly
established as well-defined bodies of canonical literature long before the
Christian era, and so were most of the "Writings". The grandson of Jesus
ben Sira tells how his grandfather, at the beginning of the second century
B.C., was a student of "the law and the prophets and the other books of
our fathers".[5] Our Lord apparently knew His Bible as beginning with
Genesis and ending with Chronicles,[6] as the Hebrew Bible traditionally

---

[1] G. A. Smith, *Modern Criticism and the Preaching of the Old Testament* (London, 1901), p. 11.

[2] II Timothy 3:15–17.

[3] "One of the extraordinary features of the early Church is the number of men who were converted by reading the Old Testament" (W. Barclay, *The Making of the Bible*, London, 1961, p. 41).

[4] See, e.g. O. Eissfeldt, *The Old Testament: An Introduction*, E. T. (Oxford, 1965), pp. 560 ff.

[5] Ecclesiasticus, prologue. It is evident from Ecclesiasticus 48:22–49:10 that Ben Sira knew all the "Latter Prophets" – Isaiah, Jeremiah, Ezekiel and the Twelve – as canonical. In the first half of the first century A.D. Philo of Alexandria speaks of the Therapeutae as studying "laws, and oracles uttered through prophets, and hymns and the other things by which knowledge and piety are increased and brought to perfection" (*On the Contemplative Life*, 25).

[6] This is the most natural inference from His language about "the blood of all the prophets shed from the foundation of the world ... from the blood of Abel to the blood of Zechariah" (Luke 11:50 f.) – Zechariah being best identified with the martyred prophet of II Chron. 24:20–22.

does; and He is recorded as speaking of "everything that is written . . . in the law of Moses and the prophets and the psalms" (Luke 24:44). Since the Psalter is the first book of the "Writings", it has sometimes been thought that "the psalms" here might indicate the whole group of documents which it introduces, but this is uncertain. This third group was not authoritatively "closed" until after the catastrophe of A.D. 70, when the rabbis of Jamnia, Yochanan ben Zakkai and his colleagues, undertook the reconstitution of the Jewish polity on a religious basis. But although the "Writings" had remained open until then, so that they could freely discuss the admission of fresh documents or the eviction of others, their final decision seems to have been the confirmation of traditional practice.[1] Josephus, writing towards the end of the first century, treats the whole canon of Hebrew scripture as closed and reckons its contents to be twenty-two books in all (a total designed to coincide with the number of letters in the Hebrew alphabet).[2]

Christians, however, and particularly Gentile Christians, would not feel bound by the decrees of Jamnia. The rank and file who used the Greek version might include among their sacred books works which were closely associated with those of whose canonicity there was no doubt, although the better informed made a distinction – in theory, at least – between those which were part of the Hebrew Bible and those which were not. Here and there in the New Testament we find introduced by a formula which normally indicates a Scripture quotation something which cannot be identified in any Old Testament text known to us (or, for the matter of that, in any other text known to us).[3] Jude not only quotes from the book of Enoch,[4] but also alludes to an incident which was probably recorded in the *Assumption of Moses*.[5] It is striking, however,

[1] The upshot of their debates was that, in spite of objections, Proverbs, Ecclesiastes, Canticles and Esther were acknowledged as canonical; Ecclesiasticus was not acknowledged (TB *Shabbat* 30b; Mishnah *Yadaim* 3:5; TB *Megillah* 7a; TJ Megillah 70d). The Jamnia debates "have not so much dealt with the acceptance of certain writings into the Canon, but rather with their right to remain there" (A. Bentzen, *Introduction to the Old Testament*, i [Copenhagen, 1948], p. 31). There was some argument earlier in the school of Shammai about Ezekiel, long since included among the Prophets, but when an ingenious rabbi showed that he did not really contradict Moses, as had been alleged, misgivings were allayed (TB *Shabbat* 13b).

[2] *Against Apion* 1. 37–43. Since Josephus does not name the individual books, but classifies them in three groups of five, thirteen and four respectively, we cannot say positively that his canon coincided precisely with that laid down at Jamnia, but if he reckoned Ruth as an appendix of Judges and Lamentations of Jeremiah, his total of twenty-two would correspond with the traditional twenty-four. Canonicity for him depends on prophetic inspiration, which dried up in the reign of Artaxerxes I: "Our history has also been written in detail from Artaxerxes to our own times, but is not esteemed as of equal authority with the books already mentioned, because the exact succession of prophets failed."

[3] E.g. the utterance of "the Wisdom of God" in Luke 11:49; the passage beginning "What no eye has seen . . ." in I Cor. 2:9 (cf. p. 106) and the "scripture" quoted in James 4:5.

[4] See p. 130.

[5] Jude 9; cf. Clement of Alexandria, *Adumbrations on Jude*.(The relevant part of the *Assumption of Moses* is no longer extant.)

that from "the Books commonly called Apocrypha" no quotation appears to be made by any New Testament writer.[1]

The earliest Christian list of Old Testament books, compiled about A.D. 170 by Melito, bishop of Sardis, was based on information which he received while travelling in Syria;[2] it comprises all the books of the Hebrew Bible except Esther.[3] Just a little later is a list preserved in a manuscript in the Library of the Greek Patriarchate in Jerusalem, in which the title of each book is given both in Hebrew (or Aramaic) and in Greek.[4] Origen (c. A.D. 230) also gives us a list of Old Testament books with their Hebrew and Greek titles; the book of the Twelve Prophets is accidentally omitted from the textual tradition of his list but is required to make up his total. "Outside these," he adds, "are the books of Maccabees".[5] Athanasius (A.D. 367) communicated to his fellow-bishops a list of canonical books, including all the books of the Hebrew Bible except Esther; Esther he includes, along with Wisdom, Ben Sira, Judith and Tobit, among those "other books outside our list which are not canonical, but have been handed down from our fathers as suitable to be read to new converts".[6]

As late as the second half of the fourth century, then, there survived in the church a strong tradition putting the books contained in the Hebrew Bible on a higher level than those not contained in it, although doubts persisted regarding the status of Esther.

The question of the Old Testament canon is discussed by Jerome in the prologues to his Latin translation of the books of Samuel (or, as he called them, I and II Kings), of the Solomonic books and of Daniel. Jerome's acquaintance with Hebrew was far in advance of that of any

[1] The "Books commonly called Apocrypha" (Westminster Confession i. 3) are I and II Esdras (III and IV Esdras in the Vulgate), Tobit, Judith, additions to Esther, Wisdom of Solomon, Ecclesiasticus (Wisdom of Jesus ben Sira), Baruch, Letter of Jeremiah, Additions to Daniel (The Prayer of Azariah and the Song of the Three Young Men, Susanna, Bel and the Dragon), Prayer of Manasseh (see p. 124), I and II Maccabees. There may be allusions to Wisdom in Rom. 1:18–2:16, but if so they express dissent as well as assent. The martyrs of the Maccabaean struggle (cf. II Macc. 6–7) are probably in view in Heb. 11:35b–38, the author of which indeed was probably acquainted with IV Maccabees, but IV Maccabees was never accounted a canonical book. If the argument from silence is pressed, it should be realized that one could apply it to Canticles and Esther, which are not quoted in the New Testament (there may be allusions to Ecclesiastes in Rom. 8:20 and I Cor. 15:32).

[2] Quoted by Eusebius, Hist. Eccl. iv. 26.14.

[3] See p. 130. One objection to the canonical acceptance of Esther was the fact that the name of God makes no appearance in it; another (voiced naturally among Jews rather than among Christians) was its record of the institution of a new festival (Purim), which conflicted with the view that all the festivals were instituted by Moses. Lamentations and Nehemiah are not specifically mentioned by Melito, but they may have been included with Jeremiah and Ezra respectively.

[4] Cf. J. P. Audet, "A Hebrew-Aramaic List of Books of the Old Testament in Greek", JTS n.s. 1 (1950), pp. 135 ff. Lamentations is not mentioned by name but may have been counted as an appendix to Jeremiah. This list makes the total twenty-seven.

[5] Quoted by Eusebius, Hist. Eccl. vi. 25:2. Origen's total, like Josephus's, is twenty-two.

[6] Athanasius, Thirty-Ninth Festal Letter. His total also is twenty-two. To the five recommended books "outside our list" he adds the Shepherd of Hermas (see p. 140).

other father of the western church – far in advance, one might say, of that of any other church father in west or east after the time of Origen – and he attached high importance to the "Hebraic verity", as he put it. It was he who first used the adjective "apocryphal" of the books outside the Hebrew canon,[1] indicating not that they were in any sense spurious but that although the church "does not receive them within the canonical scriptures", yet she "reads them for the edification of the people, not to confirm the authority of ecclesiastical dogmas".[2]

But Jerome's careful distinction tended to be forgotten by others who had no direct access, as he had, to the Hebrew Bible and who had received the books which he called the Apocrypha together with those which belonged to the Hebrew canon. Augustine, for example, reckons the Old Testament books as forty-four in number (including Tobit, Judith, Wisdom, Ecclesiasticus, I and II Maccabees),[3] and the same view was accepted in his time by the Synod of Hippo (393) and the Third Synod of Carthage (397).

But the law was not laid down dogmatically about the limits of the Old Testament canon: they remained a matter of tradition until the sixteenth century.[4] It was in the Reformation period that a serious issue was made of them. While the Anglicans and Lutherans generally followed the precedent of Jerome,[5] treating the apocryphal books as unsuitable for the establishment of doctrine, the Council of Trent (1546) ignored his precedent and declared that all the books in the Vulgate were canonical without distinction,[6] and at the opposite extreme the Reformers who

[1] Prologue to Samuel (*Prologus Galeatus*). The adjective "apocryphal" (Gk. ἀπόκρυφος, "hidden") had previously been used to denote books which were esoteric in content or withdrawn from general reading (cf. II Esdras 14:46 f.); Jerome uses it of those books which other church fathers called "ecclesiastical" (i.e. suitable for reading publicly in church).

[2] Prologue to books of Solomon. This is the passage referred to in Article VI: "And the other books (as Hierome saith) the Church doth read for example of life, and instruction of manners; but yet doth it not apply them to establish any doctrine."

[3] Augustine points out that the books of the Maccabees (and others) "are held as canonical not by the Jews but by the church" (*City of God* xviii. 36). He further explains that books like I Enoch have no place in the canon "because their antiquity brought them under suspicion, and it was impossible to ascertain whether these were his [Enoch's] genuine writings" (*City of God* xv. 23; cf. xviii. 38).

[4] The distinction between the Apocrypha and the books contained in the Hebrew Bible was preserved by some medieval scholars, especially those who knew Hebrew or at least paid attention to Jerome. Thus Hugh of St. Victor (died *c*. 1141) in a chapter *De numero librorum sacri eloquii* enumerates the books of the Hebrew Bible and adds: "There are also in the Old Testament certain other books which are indeed read [i.e. in church] but are not inscribed in the body of the text or in the canon of authority: such are the books of Tobit, Judith and the Maccabees, the so-called Wisdom of Solomon and Ecclesiasticus" (*De Sacramentis* i, Prologue, ch. 7: *Patrologia Latina* 176, cols. 185–186 D).

[5] Richard Hooker defends the Anglican attitude in his *Laws of Ecclesiastical Polity* v (London, 1597), 20.

[6] Sessio iv, *Decretum de canonicis scripturis*. III and IV Esdras and the Prayer of Manasseh are not included in these books: III and IV Esdras (= I and II Esdras of the "Protestant" Apocrypha) are placed in an appendix to the Vulgate and versions translated from it. (The Eastern Church confirmed the canonicity of the apocryphal books included in the Septuagint in 1642 and 1672.)

followed the pattern of Geneva ultimately took the line that "the Books commonly called Apocrypha, not being of divine inspiration, are not part of the canon of the Scripture; and therefore are of no authority in the church of God, nor to be any otherwise approved, or made use of, than other human writings".[1]

The position taken up at Trent was reaffirmed at Vatican Council I (1869–70),[2] but in practice the distinction made by Jerome is observed today by many Roman Catholic scholars, who find it convenient to use the old classification of biblical books into "protocanonical" and "deuterocanonical".[3] But positions taken up in an atmosphere of controversy tend to be maintained as party traditions: there are, for example, some people even today who, not being well versed in the history or status of the apocryphal books, think of them as in some sense the perquisite of Rome. Thus a reviewer of the New English Bible, criticizing it for including these books, remarked: "Rome can rightly rejoice that at last her view of the canon of Scripture has displaced that of the Apostolic Church"[4] – as though all the major Protestant versions of the complete Bible, from Coverdale to the Revised Standard Version, had not included the Apocrypha as a matter of course.

The New Testament Canon

While the Old Testament constituted the church's earliest Bible, it was the Old Testament read and applied in the light of the gospel.[5] The gospel – God's final and perfect word to men – was supremely authoritative, since it was embodied in Christ Himself, the church's Lord. But for a generation and more there was no need to appeal to a written record

[1] Westminster Confession of Faith i. 3. The word "ultimately" is used deliberately: earlier representatives of the Geneva tradition are not so uncompromising. Coverdale (1535), who first gathered the apocryphal books together as an appendix to the Old Testament, says he did so because "there be many places in them, that seme to be repugnaunt vnto the open and manyfest trueth in the other bokes of the byble", yet will not "haue them despysed, or little sett by" because if they are read in the light of the canonical books "they shulde nether seme contrary, ner be vntruly & peruersly alledged". The Geneva Bible (1560), following Jerome, says that "as bokes proceding from godlie men" they "were receiued to be red for the aduancement and furtherance of the knowledge of the historie, & for the instruction of godlie maners: which bokes declare that at all times God had an especial care of his Church and left them not vtterly destitute of teachers and meanes to confirme them in the hope of the promised Messiah, and also witnesse that those calamities that God sent to his Church, were according to his prouidence, who had bothe so threatened by his Prophetes, and so broght it to passe for the destruction of their enemies, and for the tryal of his children."

[2] *Dogmatic Constitution on the Catholic Faith:* ch. 2, "Of Revelation". Vatican II does not go into detail about the Old Testament canon.

[3] Cf. C. Lattey, *The Book of Daniel*, Westminster Version (Dublin, 1948), where the historicity of the protocanonical narratives is defended, whereas the deuterocanonical ones "are strange, and while it would be wrong to join in deriding them, it may be felt wiser not to close the door absolutely to an explanation which would allow an element of fiction in them" (p. iii).

[4] I. R. K. Paisley, *The New English Bible – Version or Perversion?* (Belfast, 1961), p. 3.

[5] See pp. 78 ff.

of the gospel: even if from an early date there were notes or digests of the ministry or teaching of Jesus, compiled for the use of preachers or teachers,[1] no particular authority attached to such notes or digests. The authority belonged to the message which they documented, and ultimately to the Lord whom the message proclaimed. His authority could not be rated below that of the prophets who foretold His coming: Clement of Rome, for instance, quotes "the words of the Lord Jesus" on the same level as the Spirit's utterances through Jeremiah and Hannah.[2]

The authority of the Lord was exercised by His specially commissioned apostles, as may be seen both in those whose base was Jerusalem and in Paul as he pursued his Gentile mission and directed his Gentile churches. The Jerusalem decree of Acts 15:29 is an early example of the authority wielded by the Jerusalem apostles,[3] and a careful reading of Paul's letters indicates that they – or, if not themselves in person, then others in their name – tried to extend their authority over his mission field.[4] Paul, for his part, teaches his converts to recognize in his writings "a command of the Lord" (I Cor. 14:37) and indicates that he lays down one "rule in all the churches" (I Cor. 7:17; cf. 11:16; 14:33b). But in writing to a church outside the area of his own apostolic responsibility he shows the restraint and delicacy that he would have liked his fellow-apostles to exhibit in their approach to his churches.[5]

After the apostolic age, however, the recognition of separate spheres of apostolic service disappeared. While in the second century we find Marcion, on the one hand, venerating Paul as the only faithful apostle of Jesus,[6] and the Ebionites, on the other hand, execrating the memory of Paul and exalting the names of Peter and especially James the Just,[7] the church as a whole carried out in practice Paul's own exhortation to recognize that all the apostles and teachers – "whether Paul or Apollos or Cephas" – belonged to them all (I Cor. 3:22). However unhistorical we may judge the claim of the churches of Rome and Corinth to be joint-foundations of Peter and Paul,[8] the *attitude* expressed in such a claim was a sound one. And this attitude finds expression in the New Testament

---

[1] Cf. what is said about the sayings collection on pp. 65, 66.

[2] I Clement 13:1 f.

[3] Cf. F. J. A. Hort, *The Christian Ecclesia* (London, 1897), pp. 82 f.; G. K. Barrett, "Christianity at Corinth", *BJRL* 46 (1963–64), pp. 269 ff.; "Things Sacrificed to Idols", *New Testament Studies* 11 (1964–65), pp. 138 ff.

[4] Cf. II Cor. 10:7 ff. (F. F. Bruce, "Paul and Jerusalem", *Tyndale Bulletin* 19, 1968, pp. 3 ff.; *Corinthians*, Century Bible, London, 1971, *ad loc.*).

[5] Cf. Rom. 1:8 ff.; 15:14 ff.

[6] Cf. A. Harnack, *Marcion* (Leipzig², 1924); *Neue Studien zu Marcion* (Leipzig, 1923).

[7] Cf. H. J. Schoeps, *Theologie und Geschichte des Judenchristentums* (Tübingen, 1949), p. 120, where Paul is seen as "beyond question" the "enemy" (ἐχθρὸς ἄνθρωπος) of the Ebionite *Epistle of Peter to James*, 2.

[8] Cf. Irenaeus, *Heresies* iii. 3.1; Dionysius of Corinth, quoted by Eusebius, *Hist. Eccl.* ii. 25.8.

canon, where every document that could colourably be called apostolic found its place in due course.

The gospels, anonymous though they were, were recognized as transcripts of the apostolic witness to Christ and, from an early point in the second century, were brought together, so that they no longer circulated separately in their respective constituencies but as a fourfold collection. It is difficult to say how far advanced this process was in the time of Ignatius, but he clearly had a written gospel to appeal to, and equally clearly he had to contend with more conservative brethren who disapproved of the idea of appealing to any written authority alongside the Old Testament scriptures as interpreted in the church's oral tradition. This is the point of the reference in his Letter to the Philadelphians to those people who asserted: "If I do not find it in the archives [the Old Testament], I do not believe it [if it is contained] in the gospel." To which he replied "It is written" – "Scripture says" (meaning that the gospel is "scripture"). But they say, "That is the very point at question" – i.e. is the gospel "scripture"? And then Ignatius, like many another debater driven into a corner, takes refuge in rhetoric:

> But my archives are Jesus Christ; the inviolable archives are His cross, His death, His resurrection, and the faith which is exercised through Him . . .[1]

Plainly Ignatius regarded Jesus Christ as his "tradition". Within that tradition everything had a place which bore true witness to Him – the Old Testament scriptures because they pointed forward to Him, the written gospel because it was the record of His incarnation and passion, the letters of the apostles because they were His delegates, and the church's faith and worship because they had their source in Him. Plainly, too, Ignatius had not thought his tradition through to first principles, so that he could give a logical defence of it in every part, including his recognition of the gospel as "scripture". The earliest recognition of the New Testament writings was spontaneous and instinctive: the rationale of the canon came later. Hence the history of the canon at its outset has untidy edges: we cannot give a cut-and-dried account of its first formation any more than Ignatius or his contemporaries could have done.

The necessity of a canon of written documents as a check on the corruption of oral tradition was as apparent to many Gnostics as it was to those who maintained the tradition of the apostolic churches. Valentinus, according to Tertullian, used the whole New Testament canon,[2] and the substantial truth of this statement has been confirmed in recent years by the evidence of Valentinian documents found among the Nag Hammadi papyri. The *Gospel of Truth*, for example, acknowledges the authority of

[1] Ignatius, *Philadelphians* 8:2.
[2] Tertullian, *Prescription against Heretics*, 38.

every major section of the New Testament except the Pastoral Epistles.[1] It was in their interpretation of the documents, not in their recognition of them, that the Valentinians were distinguished from the catholic church.[2]

Marcion, for his part, also knew the value of an authoritative written canon and, strong in his cast-iron presuppositions, he promulgated his edition of the *Euangelion* and *Apostolikon* as (in his view) they must originally have been, thus creating a new tradition for his followers. The catholic leaders had an older tradition, but no doubt it was the promulgation of Marcion's canon that stimulated them, and especially the leaders of the Roman church, to define that tradition more precisely than they had thus far felt necessary. Whereas Marcion's canon expressed his exclusive devotion to Paul (Luke the evangelist enjoying special credit because of his association with Paul),[3] the catholic canon was catholic in a further sense, comprising the writings of other apostles or "apostolic men" alongside Paul, and of three other evangelists alongside Luke, and binding the *Euangelion* and *Apostolikon* together with Luke's second volume, henceforth called the Acts of the Apostles, which provided the sequel to the gospel story and the historical context of the apostolic letters, presenting independent evidence for the genuineness of Paul's apostolic claims[4] and for the loyal witness of other apostles whom Marcion had denigrated. Acts was thus, as Harnack aptly put it, the "pivot" of the New Testament.[5]

Justin Martyr attests the use of an informal New Testament canon: he tells how "the memoirs of the apostles", otherwise called "gospels", were read in church in the same way as "the compositions of the prophets"[6] and quotes Old Testament texts together with passages from the writings of the new covenant (especially sayings of Jesus) as though they shared the same authority.[7] If here and there his works contain traces of materials from the pseudonymous Gospels of Peter or Thomas, these are very few in comparison with his use of the fourfold Gospel.

Justin's disciple Tatian is best known for his *Diatessaron* or Harmony of

---

[1] Cf. W. C. van Unnik, "The 'Gospel of Truth' and the New Testament", in *The Jung Codex*, ed. F. L. Cross (London, 1955), pp. 81 ff., 124.

[2] As in the commentary on John by the Valentinian Heracleon (*c.* 175), the earliest commentary on that Gospel, quoted repeatedly by Origen in his commentary on John.

[3] Marcion's *Euangelion* was a revision of the Third Gospel, beginning at Luke 3:1 and going straight on from there to 4:31 so as to exlcude all suggestion that the story of Jesus is linked with preceding history or that He came into the world by birth: "In the fifteenth year of Tiberius Caesar Jesus came down to Capernaum, a city of Galilee" (Tertullian, *Against Marcion* iv. 7.1).

[4] Cf. Tertullian, *Prescription against Heretics*, 22 f.

[5] A. Harnack, *The Origin of the New Testament*, E. T. (London, 1925), pp. 53, 63 ff.

[6] Justin, *First Apology* 66:3; 67:3. He refers elsewhere (*Dialogue* 106:3) to the "memoirs" of Peter, meaning either the Gospel of Mark or the pseudonymous Gospel of Peter (see pp. 109 f., 142), the latter of which he seems to quote (from 3:6 f.) in *First Apology* 35:6.

[7] E.g. *First Apology* 63:1-8, where Isa. 1:3; Matt. 11:27; Luke 10:16 (or rather something like it) and Ex. 3:6 ff. (abridged) are quoted together.

the four Gospels, which provides sufficient evidence of the separate level on which these four records were placed in his time. In places Tatian appears to have amplified the fourfold record by means of the *Gospel according to the Hebrews,* which may have been a sectarian revision of Matthew, but not to an extent which impairs the fourfold pattern of his Harmony.[1]

For Irenaeus the fourfold Gospel is one of the facts of life, as axiomatic as the four pillars of the earth or the four winds of heaven.[2] This shows how thoroughly he and his contemporaries took it for granted that there were, and could be, only four gospel-writings. Even more thoroughly did they take it for granted that these four could only be Matthew, Mark, Luke and John: this is something which, for them, did not even need to be proved. By the time of Irenaeus, too, the main contents of the catholic canon were fixed and accepted throughout the Christian world. He does not give us a formal list, but it is plain that for him the fourfold Gospel, Acts, the Pauline corpus, I Peter, I John and Revelation were "scripture" (as also were I Clement and the *Shepherd* of Hermas).[3]

The earliest catholic list of New Testament books that has been preserved to us is that in the "Muratorian" canon, which probably represents the tradition of the Roman church at the end of the second century.[4] The one surprise in this list is the omission of I Peter (this omission, in view of the corrupt state of the text in the only extant copy of the list, could conceivably be accidental).[5] As it is, the list contains the four Gospels, Acts, the letters of Paul, Jude and John,[6] "John's Apocalypse and Peter's",[7] with the Wisdom of Solomon.[8] The *Shepherd* of Hermas, edifying as it is, is too recent to be reckoned canonical.[9] The writings of the Valentinians, Marcionites and Montanists are to be rejected.

[1] Cf. A. Baumstark, "Die syrische Übersetzung des Titus von Bostra und das 'Diatessaron'", *Biblica* 16 (1935), pp. 257 ff.

[2] Irenaeus, *Heresies* iii. 11.11.

[3] Irenaeus, *Heresies* iii. 3.2; iv. 34.2.

[4] A convenient edition is that in the series *Kleine Texte* edited by H. Lietzmann: *Das Muratorische Fragment und die Monarchianischen Prologe zu den Evangelien* (Berlin[2] 1933).

[5] T. Zahn thought that some words had fallen out after "John's Apocalypse and Peter's", and that the original text ran: "John's Apocalypse and Peter's *epistle. There is also another epistle of Peter,* which some of our people refuse to have read in church" (*Geschichte des neutestamentlichen Kanons* ii, Erlangen, 1890, p. 142; the italicized words are supplied by Zahn).

[6] "Two by the aforementioned John", says the list: if this means two in addition to I John, mentioned some lines earlier in connexion with the Gospel of John, these two will be our II and III John; otherwise we should have to conclude either that only one of the two shorter letters of John was included, or else that II and III John were reckoned together as one.

[7] The Apocalypse of Peter has been preserved (cf. *New Testament Apocrypha*, ed. E. Hennecke, W. Schneemelcher, R. McL. Wilson, E. T., ii, London, 1965, pp. 663-683); its lurid pictures of the torments of the damned are the source of much medieval imagery, e.g. of their portrayal in Dante's *Inferno*.

[8] We associate Wisdom with the Old Testament Apocrypha rather than with the New Testament, but in date it is closer to the New Testament than to the Old.

[9] Hermas is said to have been the brother of Pius I, bishop of Rome c. A.D. 150. He may have been an older brother, as the date of the *Shepherd* is probably nearer the beginning of the second century than the middle

As interesting as the contents of the list is the kind of argument put forward for the canonical acceptance of the various books. Luke was Paul's "legal expert", an official who issued decrees and similar documents in accordance with his superior's judgement;[1] thus Luke's writings are made to share Paul's authority. Luke's second volume is inappropriately called "the Acts of all the apostles" – possibly by way of anti-Marcionite emphasis but possibly also to make it clear that this was the only genuine book of apostolic Acts. In recent decades the five volumes of "Leucian" Acts had appeared – of Peter, John, Andrew, Thomas and Paul[2] – and the compiler of our list wishes it to be understood that it is to the canonical Acts, and not to these apocryphal works, that one must go in order to find an authentic record of the apostles' journeyings. Should anyone ask why Luke breaks off his narrative without tracing Paul's career to its end, the answer is that he narrated only those things which took place in his presence.[3] This same insistence on eyewitness testimony – a further token of the author's acquaintance with Roman law – appears in his treatment of the Gospel of John, in which, he maintains, the Evangelist recorded only "what we have seen with our eyes and heard with our ears and our hands have handled" – quoting I John 1:1.[4]

When he comes to deal with the canonicity of Paul's letters, he makes the quite astonishing statement that Paul wrote letters to seven churches in accordance with the pattern set by John, who did the same in the Apocalypse. Presumably the canonicity of John's seven letters depended on his being a prophet, and the authority of Paul's letters was established by analogy with John's.[5] The same implication that prophecy is the main criterion of canonicity appears in his remark about the *Shepherd* of Hermas. This obviously could not be accepted as an apostolic writing, but its character would have qualified it for inclusion among the prophets, had the prophetic list not been closed long since.

The principal criterion of New Testament canonicity imposed in the early church was not prophetic inspiration but apostolic authorship – or, if not authorship, then authority. In an environment where apostolic tradition counted for so much, the source and norm of that tradition were naturally found in the writings of apostles or of men closely associated

---

[1] Cf. A. Ehrhardt, *The Framework of the New Testament Stories* (Manchester. 1964), pp. 16 ff.; he deduces from the technical language of Roman law used here that the document must have been composed at Rome, and in Latin, perhaps under Pope Zephyrinus (197–217).

[2] Cf. *New Testament Apocrypha*, ed. E. Hennecke, W. Schneemelcher, R. McL. Wilson, ii, pp. 167–531.

[3] Two events are mentioned as unrelated by Luke for this reason – Paul's departure for Spain and Peter's execution in Rome. It is no accident that both of these are related in the "Acts of Peter".

[4] See p. 107.

[5] Cf. K. Stendahl, "The Apocalypse of John and the Epistles of Paul in the Muratorian Fragment", in *Current Issues in New Testament Interpretation*, ed. W. Klassen and G. F. Snyder (New York, 1962), pp. 239 ff.

with apostles. Mark and Luke, for instance, were known not to be apostles, but their close association with Peter[1] and Paul[2] respectively was emphasized. As for the epistles, however, the tendency was for canonicity to be tied to the ascription of apostolic authorship. The Letter to the Hebrews, for example, was known in the Roman church earlier than anywhere else[3] (so far as our evidence goes) but Rome was one of the last important churches to acknowledge it as canonical, just as Rome was one of the last important churches to ascribe Pauline authorship to it – not out of conviction, but out of an unwillingness to be out of step in this regard with Alexandria and the other great eastern churches.

This unwillingness to be out of step with other churches reminds us that another criterion of canonicity was catholicity. A document which was acknowledged only in one small corner of Christendom was unlikely to win acceptance as canonical; one which was acknowledged over the greater area of Christendom was likely to win still wider acceptance.

Throughout the third and fourth centuries the definition of the New Testament canon continued to become more and more precise until in 367 Athanasius[4] (followed by the Synod of Hippo in 393 and the Third Synod of Carthage in 397) listed as canonical the twenty-seven books which have been handed down to us. Until then it was customary to distinguish the (universally) acknowledged books and the disputed books, the spurious books (those laying false claim to apostolic authorship) and the heretical books which were erroneous and utterly to be repudiated. If a disputed book taught apostolic doctrine and was sufficiently ancient, it tended to be given the benefit of the doubt.[5] The authorship of Jude, for example, was uncertain but, as Origen said, it was "full of words of heavenly grace"[6] and so it ultimately gained admission. The *Shepherd* of Hermas, on the other hand, popular as it was and recommended for reading in church, was *known* to be of post-apostolic origin and so was ruled out on the score of insufficient antiquity.[7]

---

[1] Cf. Papias (quoted on p. 110).

[2] Eusebius mentions some who went so far as to suggest that, when Paul speaks of "my gospel" (Rom. 2:16; 16:25; II Tim. 2:8), he refers to the Gospel of Luke (*Hist. Eccl.* iii. 4.7).

[3] Clement of Rome (*c.* A.D. 96) knows the letter and quotes it – misinterpreting it in one place (I Clement 17:1) where he takes those who "went about in skins of sheep and goats" (Heb. 11:37) to be Elijah and Elisha – but he gives no inkling of its authorship nor does he treat it as an apostolic document.

[4] *Thirty-Ninth Festal Letter* (see p. 134). Athanasius includes the *Didachē* and the *Shepherd* of Hermas along with five of the Old Testament apocrypha as read in church but not canonical.

[5] Thus the Gospel of Peter was allowed to be read in the church of Rhossus in Syria, until Serapion, bishop of Antioch, discovered its Docetic tendency and put them on their guard against it (Eusebius, *Hist. Eccl.* vi. 12.2 ff.).

[6] Origen, *Commentary on Matthew* x. 17 (on Matt. 13:55).

[7] There were also practical considerations which made the contents of the canon better known among the rank and file of Christians; it was important for them to know which books might be appealed to in disputes with heretics and (in the last imperial persecution) which books might be handed over to the police for destruction and which must be guarded at the cost of one's life, if necessary.

But, as has already been said, these criteria of canonicity were largely devised to justify a tradition which already existed. Authority precedes canonicity: that is to say, the various writings do not derive their authority from their inclusion in the canon: they were included in the canon because their authenticity was recognized.[1] It is going too far to say, as Oscar Cullmann does, that "among the early Christian writings the books which were to form the future canon *forced themselves on the Church by their intrinsic apostolic authority,* as they do still, because the *Kyrios* Christ speaks in them"[2] – at least, if this is to be taken as a statement of history. "Intrinsic apostolic authority" is a difficult entity to define.

With our longer perspective we can say that the early church, in recognizing the books which make up the New Testament canon as uniquely worthy to stand alongside the sacred scriptures of the old covenant, was guided by a wisdom higher than its own. When we think of other early Christian documents more or less contemporary with the latest books of the New Testament – the Epistle of Clement of Rome, the Epistle of Barnabas, the *Shepherd* of Hermas, the Letters of Ignatius and the *Didache,* for example – we may be thankful that they did not succeed in gaining admission to the canon, although some of them were on the fringe of it for a considerable time. The question has been raised whether it is legitimate for us to defend the early church's decision about admission and exclusion with arguments quite different from those which were used at the time.[3] But we have no option if we accept the canon: we must defend our acceptance of it with arguments which *we* hold to be valid.

The Reformation and After

At the time of the Reformation the canon of Scripture, like everything else that was handed down by tradition, was subjected to scrutiny. In many of the traditions handed down through medieval times the Reformers recognized a close kinship to that "tradition of men" with which our Lord found fault because it displaced "the commandment of God".[4] The danger of this tendency, said Calvin, lies in the fact that "whenever holiness is made to consist in anything else than in observing the law of God, men are led to believe that the law may be violated without danger". Then he adds: "Let any man now consider whether this wickedness does not at present abound more among the Papists than it formerly did among the Jews."[5] And in many other places where the Gospels said "Pharisees"

---

[1] Of course their authority came to be recognized in a practical way from their presence in the canon, but this is a *ratio cognoscendi,* not the *ratio essendi.*

[2] O. Cullmann, "The Tradition", in *The Early Church* (London, 1956), p. 91.

[3] Cf. E. Flesseman-van Leer, "Prinzipien der Sammlung und Ausscheidung bei der Bildung des Kanons", *Zeitschrift für Theologie und Kirche* 61 (1964), pp. 404 ff.

[4] Mark 7:8 (see p. 24).

[5] *Commentary on a Harmony of the Evangelists,* E. T. by W. Pringle (Edinburgh, 1845), p. 251.

the Reformers read "Papists". Yet church tradition was not jettisoned completely by the mainstream Reformers: in doctrine and practice alike they went back beyond the Middle Ages to appeal to the fathers of the early centuries: Calvin himself was no mean patristic scholar and adduces patristic evidence freely and copiously in support of his arguments. But the fathers themselves were subject to the superior authority of Scripture. Calvin himself does not discuss the canon of the Scripture as distinct from its authority, which he defends alike against those who in practice made it subordinate to church tradition and those who rejected it in favour of their private revelations.[1] "Those who are inwardly taught by the Holy Spirit acquiesce implicitly in Scripture . . . Scripture, carrying its own evidence along with it, deigns not to submit to proofs and arguments, but owes the full conviction with which we ought to receive it to the testimony of the Spirit."[2] He does not explicitly make the inward testimony of the Spirit a criterion of canonicity, but if the question had been directly put to him how he knew (say) that the Hebrew and Aramaic text of Daniel was Scripture whereas the additions in the Greek version were not, he might well have done so. The apostolicity of II Peter is for him secondary,[3] but "it contains nothing unworthy of Peter, and . . . shows throughout the power and grace of the apostolic spirit . . . Certainly since the majesty of the Spirit of Christ expresses itself in all parts of the epistle, I have a dread of repudiating it, even though I do not recognize in it the genuine language of Peter."[4] This is, in effect, an appeal to the testimony of the Spirit for decision regarding a "disputed" book.[5]

Luther expressed himself more freely, if less systematically. He translated the apocryphal books along with the Hebrew Bible, but gave them the same inferior rank as Jerome did. The same inferior rank, indeed, was given with emphasis to one of the books of the Hebrew Bible: "I hate Esther and II Maccabees so much," he said, "that I wish they did not exist. There is too much Judaism in them and much heathen vice."[6] But within the New Testament also he assigned a lower rank to some books than to others. As is well known, in the list of books prefaced to his German New Testament he attaches serial numbers to the first twenty-three, which he calls elsewhere "the right certain capital books",[7] and

---

[1] *Institutio* i. 7.1–9.3.

[2] *Institutio* i. 7.5.

[3] "I conclude that if the epistle is trustworthy it has come from Peter; not that he wrote it himself, but that one of his disciples composed by his command what the necessity of the times demanded" (*Commentary on Hebrews and I and II Peter*, E. T. by W. B. Johnston, Edinburgh, 1963, p. 325).

[4] *Ibid.*

[5] Sebastian Castellio's treatment of Canticles as a secular lovesong (though he included it in his new Latin version of the Bible) was a principal reason for the Genevan ministers' declining to ordain him (*Calvini Opera* xi = CR 39, cols. 674 ff.).

[6] *Table Talk* (Weimar edition 1, p. 208; cf. *De servo arbitrio*, Weimar edition 18, p. 666).

[7] Preface to Hebrews, *Die deutsche Bibel*(Weimar edition 7, p. 345).

separates off the remaining four – Hebrews, James, Jude and Revelation – by a space and by the absence of serial numbers. In his prefaces to these books he indicates his reasons for relegating them to what was in essence deuterocanonical status. Hebrews, he reckoned, contained some "wood, straw and hay" along with the "gold, silver and precious stones" which were built into its fabric, and so it could not be placed "on a level with the apostolic epistles".[1] James contradicted the doctrine of justification by faith, and although it pressed home the law of God it bore no evangelical witness to Christ.[2] Jude, which he (mistakenly, no doubt) regarded as an abstract of II Peter, was "an unnecessary epistle to include among the capital books which ought to lay the foundation of faith"; it was also held against it that it included uncanonical teaching and history (a reference to the Enoch quotation and the dispute about the body of Moses).[3] Revelation "lacks everything that I hold as apostolic or prophetic"[4] – although the sharpness of this judgement, expressed in 1522, was subsequently mitigated.

To a large degree Luther's deuterocanonical books coincide with those which the early church ranked as disputed, but it was not the verdict of the early church that weighed with Luther so much as evangelical content. Therefore he had no difficulty about II Peter or II and III John, although their apostolicity was questioned in the early church. The criterion of canonicity – at least for protocanonicity, for inclusion among the "capital books" – was for Luther "what presses home Christ" (was Christum treibet).[5] Not the identity of the writer, but the character of the writing, is what counts. "That which does not teach Christ is not apostolic, even if Peter or Paul taught it. Again, that which does preach Christ is apostolic even if Judas, Annas, Pilate or Herod did it."[6] In this Luther shows himself a true disciple of Paul: "even if we, or an angel from heaven, should preach to you a gospel contrary to that which we preached to you, let him be accursed" (Gal. 1:8).

Luther's criterion is still widely accepted. When Dr. Norman Snaith delivered his Fernley-Hartley Lecture on The Distinctive Ideas of the Old Testament, he found that the distinctive ideas were those which were taken up and brought to perfection in the New Testament, not least in the letters of Paul, while "the true development from the Pauline theology is to be found in Luther and in John Wesley".[7] Some readers might find it a surprising coincidence that the finest flowering of the biblical revelation should be discerned in the tradition of which Dr. Snaith is himself

[1] Preface to Hebrews (Weimar edition 7, pp. 344 f.).
[2] Preface to James (Weimar edition 7, p. 387).
[3] Preface to Jude (Weimar edition 7, p. 387).
[4] Preface to Revelation (Weimar edition 7, p. 404).
[5] Preface to James (Weimar edition 7, pp. 384 f.).
[6] Preface to James (Weimar edition 7, pp. 384 f.).
[7] N. H. Snaith, The Distinctive Ideas of the Old Testament (London, 1944), p. 186.

such a worthy and devoted exponent; but I have no doubt he is right – although I too may not be entirely unbiased in this regard.

Quite similar is the argument of the late Edward J. Carnell that, since justification by faith is systematically expounded only in Romans and Galatians, "therefore, if the church teaches anything that offends the system of Romans and Galatians, it is cultic"[1] ("cultic" apparently having the sense of "sectarian" as opposed to "catholic"). Again: "whenever a passage conflicts with the teaching of Romans and Galatians, either the mind has failed to grasp its meaning, or the passage falls under the concept of progressive revelation".[2]

The Canon in the Twentieth Century

But we have received the twenty-seven books of the New Testament, and while individual readers or teachers may make distinctions between those among them which are "capital" and those which are of lower grade, our church tradition has made no such distinction – since the end of the fourth century. The statement of Article VI, that these twenty-seven are books "of whose authority was never any doubt in the Church", is not true if we press our quest back earlier than that date, but from then on it represents the general consensus, if we overlook some of the separated eastern churches. If, however, we are asked today why we accept these twenty-seven, or why we accept any specific one of them, do we give our tradition as a sufficient answer, or do we seek an answer more satisfactory to ourselves and to our questioners?

Some of us, theological students and the like, have studied the formation of the canon and can give a historical reason of sorts for our position. But what is the ordinary church member to say, especially if his church's formularies make no explicit statement about the canon? A Roman Catholic layman will appeal to the authority of the church, which has made clear pronouncements on this subject, but what does the ordinary free churchman say? Hardly, I suppose, "Because the church say so" – the only church he knows may be the local church to which he belongs, and it is unlikely ever to have made a pronouncement on the canon. Will he say, "Because my pastor says so, and he is a man of such piety and learning – in fact, he is a B.A.(Theol.) of Manchester – that he cannot be wrong"? Perhaps; but what if his pastor voices doubts about the canonicity of Jude or the apostolicity of II Peter? He is then quite likely to say, "My pastor, I fear, is a little unsound; he does not believe the whole Bible – and that is the result of his attending those classes in Biblical Criticism at Manchester University." But how does he know what "the

---

[1] E. J. Carnell, *The Case for Orthodox Theology* (London, 1961), p. 59.
[2] Carnell, *op. cit.*, p. 99.

whole Bible" is? Most probably by tradition – sound and reliable tradition, no doubt, but tradition none the less.

I turn now to a body of nineteenth-century origin unsurpassed in its professed adherence to *sola scriptura* and repudiation of the authority of tradition – the Exclusive Brethren – and cite no unlearned church member but their ablest scholar, William Kelly. William Kelly was no mean theologian, but he would have been the last man to acknowledge any debt to "mere" tradition.[1] Yet he "was the staunchest upholder of the entire Nicene and Athanasian doctrine"[2] and to him the New Testament canon was a *datum*. In his commentary on the Epistles of Peter, for example, he notes the doubts that some had expressed in his day about the authorship of II Peter, but takes a short and sharp line with them.

The Petrine authorship and divine inspiration of II Peter as of I Peter, he says, is apprehended by "any unbiased Christian"[3] – which is a good example of the pre-emptive strike in theological controversy. He refuses to admit catholic tradition as authority for the genuineness and canonicity of the document, but with equal vigour he rejects the Protestant assertion of private judgement; both alike tend to the deification of man and the dethronement of God. Perhaps he would have allowed the appeal to the inward witness of the Spirit, but he does not explicitly say so. What he does say is more peremptory, and he says it in criticism of Bishop Christopher Wordsworth's argument that, in view of the many pseudepigrapha circulating in Peter's name, it was the church's duty to suspend judgement on II Peter until adequate proofs of its authenticity were available.[4] "It is *never a duty*", says Kelly, "even for the simplest Christian, *to doubt Scripture,* but only to believe."[5] True: but how is the simplest Christian to know in the first instance what is Scripture and what is not? Kelly leaves this question unanswered, what is the more surprising in such an able thinker. Again, he may have held that the simplest Christian knows Scripture by the inward witness of the Spirit; but again, he does not explicitly say so. Even so, the Spirit's inward witness may assure me that what I hear or read is the word of God to me: it will hardly give an answer to questions of authorship or date.

It is noteworthy that, when it comes to textual criticism or straight exegesis, as distinct from the history of the canon, Kelly can use his private

---

[1] Except in so far as he was a faithful follower of J. N. Darby (see p. 14). "'Read Darby!' he used to say, to the last" (*Memories of the Life and Last Days of William Kelly,* ed. H. Wreford, London, 1906, p. 75). C. H. Spurgeon described him as "a man 'who, born for the universe, narrowed his mind' by Darbyism" (*Commenting and Commentaries,* London, 1887, p. 164).

[2] W. B. Neatby, "Mr. William Kelly as a Theologian", *Expositor,* 7th series, 2 (London, 1907), p. 79.

[3] *The Epistles of Peter* (London, 1923): *The Second Epistle of Peter,* p. 10. The commentaries on I and II Peter in this volume are paginated separately; that on II Peter was left unfinished at his death in 1906.

[4] C. Wordsworth, *The New Testament in the Original Greek,* ii (London, 1862).

[5] Kelly, *op. cit.,* p. 5.

judgement in as sound and uninhibited a manner as any other scholar –
though he is always apt, having established the true text or the proper
exegesis on a grammatico-historical basis, to turn his weapon round and
say that any spiritual and unprejudiced reader can see that this is the right
way of it.

To us the canon is something "received" – the books "disputed by
some" being handed down with, and carried by, those "acknowledged
by all".[1] Any talk of enlarging or contracting it at this time of day is
unrealistic. We may toy with the fancy that some discovery of the future,
like that of the Qumran or Nag Hammadi texts, may bring to light a lost
letter of Paul's – say his "previous" letter to the Corinthians[2] – or a copy
of the Gospel of Mark complete with its "lost" ending (supposing that it
was not the Evangelist's intention to finish at Mark 16:8). Would there
be a move to have such a document added to the canon? It is difficult to
see how this could be effected. For one thing, scholars would certainly
not be unanimous about its authenticity. For another thing, there is no
competent authority, acknowledged throughout Christendom, to decree
its addition. Even if we could imagine the Pope, the Ecumenical Patriarch
and the Presidents of the World Council of Churches and the International
Council of Christian Churches agreeing to recommend the addition, there
are some awkward nonconformists who would probably repudiate the
idea just because it was recommended by one or all of these. If the analogy
of history is relevant, it suggests that the common consensus of Christians
over several generations would have to precede any official pronouncement.

Suggestions that the canon might be augmented by the inclusion of
other "inspirational" literature, ancient or modern, arise from a failure
to appreciate what the canon actually is. It is not an anthology of inspirational literature. The question is not what is to be read in church: when
a sermon is read the congregation is treated to what is usually, in intention
at least, inspirational literature, and the same may be said of prayers
which are read from the Prayer Book or hymns which are read from the
hymn-book. It is a question of getting as near as possible to the source of
the Christian faith.

In a lecture delivered at Oxford in 1961 Professor Kurt Aland expressed
the view that, as the Old Testament canon underwent a *de facto* narrowing
as a result of the new covenant established in Christ,[3] so also the New
Testament canon "is *in practice* undergoing a narrowing and a shortening",
so that we can recognize in the New Testament as in the Old a "canon

---

[1] The terminology is Origen's: the universally acknowledged books are the ἀναντίρρητα
or ὁμολογούμενα, while the disputed ones are ἀμφιβαλλόμενα (quoted by Eusebius, *Hist.
Eccl.* vi. 25).
[2] Cf. I Cor. 5:9.
[3] The reference may be to those parts of the Old Testament directly cited in the New as
fulfilled in the gospel.

within the canon".[1] This is a natural attitude on the part of a scholar in the Lutheran tradition; we know how depreciatory is the judgement passed today by many scholars in this tradition on those parts of the New Testament which smack of "primitive catholicism".[2] The "actual living, effective Canon", as distinct from the formal canon, "is constructed according to the method of 'self-understanding'."[3] But if it is suggested that Christians and churches get together and try to reach agreement on a common effective canon, the difficulty is that the "effective" canon of some groups or individuals differs from that of others. If the inner canon to some consists of Romans and Galatians (with the two Corinthian epistles), to others it consists of the Captivity Epistles, to others of the Synoptic Gospels, to others of the Johannine Gospels and Epistles, and to others (one might be tempted to think) of the Apocalypse.

It would be precarious to try to name any part of Scripture – even the genealogical lists! – in which some believing reader has not heard the word of God addressing him effectively and in context. William Robertson Smith gave as his reason for believing in the Bible as the Word of God: "Because the Bible is the only record of the redeeming love of God, because in the Bible alone I find God drawing near to man in Christ Jesus, and declaring to us, in Him, His will for our salvation. And this record I know to be true by the witness of His Spirit in my heart, whereby I am assured that none other than God Himself is able to speak such words to my soul."[4] If he had been asked just where in the Bible he recognized this record and experienced this witness, he would probably not have mentioned every book, but he might well have said that the record of God's love and the witness of the Spirit were so pervasive that they gave character to the Old and New Testament canon as a whole. Other readers might bear the same testimony, but might think of other parts of the Bible than Robertson Smith had in mind. No wonder, then, that Professor Aland speaks of the necessity of questioning one's own actual canon and taking the actual canon of others seriously.[5]

The appeal to the testimony of the Holy Spirit is valid, but it will scarcely enable all to decide the precise limits of the canon. By an act of faith one may identify the New Testament canon as we have received it with the entire *paradosis* of Christ, to which, in Oscar Cullmann's view, all the apostles contribute, each passing on to another that part which he himself received.[6] This may be so, but it cannot be proved. It is better

---

[1] K. Aland, *The Problem of the New Testament Canon* (London, 1962), pp. 27 ff.

[2] E. Käsemann, "Paul and Early Catholicism", *New Testament Questions of Today*, E. T. (London, 1969), pp. 236 ff. See critique by H. Küng, *The Structures of the Church*, E. T. (London, 1965), pp. 142 ff.

[3] Aland, *op. cit.*, p. 29.

[4] W. R. Smith, *Answer to the Form of Libel now before the Free Church Presbytery of Aberdeen* (Edinburgh, 1878), p. 21.

[5] Aland, *op. cit.*, pp. 31 f.

[6] O. Cullmann, *The Early Church*, p. 73.

to say of the New Testament books what Hans Lietzmann said of the four Gospels in the early church, that "the reference to their apostolic authority, which can only appear to us as a reminder of sound historical bases, had the deeper meaning that this particular tradition of Jesus – and this alone – had been established and guaranteed by the Holy Spirit working authoritatively in the Church."[1] No doubt within "this particular tradition" diverse strands of tradition – indeed diverse traditions – may be detected, but although critical scholars may emphasize their diversity, the church, both ancient and modern, has been more conscious of their overall unity, in contrast to other interpretations which patently conflict with the New Testament witness but cannot substantiate a comparable claim to apostolic authority.

In the canon we have the foundation documents or the charter of the Christian faith. For no other document or group of documents from the earliest Christian generations can such a claim be made. (Even the most debatable of the "disputed" books in the New Testament canon has more of the quality of apostolic authority about it than the letters of Clement of Rome and Ignatius of Antioch or the *Shepherd* of Hermas.) The implications of this appeal to history, as it appears to be, will be considered later.[2] But what has been said is not tantamount to shutting the Holy Spirit up in a book or collection of books. Repeatedly new movements of the Spirit have been launched by a rediscovery of the living power which resides in the canon of Scripture. The New Testament "is not one of the paralysing and enslaving forces of the past, but it is full of eternal and present strength to make strong and to make free".[3]

---

[1] H. Lietzmann, *The Founding of the Church Universal*, E. T. (London, 1950), p. 97.
[2] See pp. 172 ff.
[3] A. Deissmann, *Light from the Ancient East*, E. T. (London, 1927), p. 409.

CHAPTER IX

TRADITION AND THE TEXT
OF SCRIPTURE

IN CONNEXION WITH THE TEXT OF SCRIPTURE AS WELL AS
with its canon the term "tradition" is widely used, though usually
in a different sense. The fact that the text has been "handed down"
to our day from the time of its original composition means that we are
dependent on textual tradition. Had the original texts survived – the actual
copy of Romans, for example, which Tertius wrote down at Paul's
dictation, or the copy of Philemon which another amanuensis wrote down
for him, but which included an IOU, written and signed by the apostle
himself[1] – then we should not be dependent on tradition, any more than
we are when confronted by (say) the Siloam inscription or the rescript of
Claudius at Delphi which mentions Gallio as proconsul of Achaia.

Textual Tradition of the Old Testament

Our earliest Old Testament manuscripts in Hebrew – those found
among the Qumran scrolls and fragments – bear witness to at least three
lines of tradition along which the text had been handed down.[2] There is
an Egyptian type of text, previously postulated as that on which the earliest
Greek version of the Old Testament (the Septuagint) was based; there is
a popular Palestinian type, exhibiting close affinities with the Samaritan
Pentateuch; there is a Babylonian type, the direct ancestor of what we
call the Masoretic text. But after the catastrophe of A.D. 70 only one of
these, the third, was perpetuated among the Jews. By contrast with the
variety of Hebrew text-types represented at Qumran (from the period
before A.D. 70), the third type only is represented among the manuscripts
found at Murabba'at and other outposts of the fighters in the second Jewish
revolt against Rome (A.D. 132–135). In the interval between the two
revolts the text of Babylonian provenance was standardized by Rabbi
Aqiba and his colleagues. We cannot be sure of the criteria on which they
decided that this text, and not its competitors, was to be standardized; we
are quite sure that, whatever their criteria were, they standardized the
best text of the three. Along with the written (consonantal) text, they
also standardized its vocalization, punctuation and interpretation, but
these were handed down for some centuries in oral tradition or, to use

[1] Rom. 16:22; Philem. 19.
[2] Cf. F. M. Cross, *The Ancient Library of Qumran and Modern Biblical Studies* (New York, 1958), pp. 124 ff.

the Hebrew word, *masorah* (also spelt *massorah*).[1] It was during this period of oral tradition that Jerome (*c.* A.D. 400) based his Latin translation of the Old Testament on the Hebrew Bible. He could read and translate the consonantal text; for those elements that were still matters of oral tradition he was dependent on his Jewish mentor Bar Hanina.[2] The fact that he had to rely on the aid of a Jew did nothing to commend his new translation to his more conservative fellow-Christians who had learned by tradition to accept the Greek Septuagint (on which the earlier Latin Old Testament was based) as a divinely inspired version. (Although the Septuagint was the work of Jewish translators, it was taken over so completely by the Christians that from the beginning of the second century onwards the Jews abandoned it to them.)

From the end of the fifth or beginning of the sixth century this oral tradition began to be recorded in written form. The men who were charged with recording the *masorah* in this way are called the Masoretes (Massoretes).[3] They were not innovators; they were preservers of tradition. By elaborate systems of signs and notes they superimposed on the consontal text the vocalization, punctuation and interpretation which had been fixed in the oral tradition. There were various schools of Masoretes, some in Babylonia and others in Palestine, using different forms of notation to record the tradition. The school which ultimately possessed the field was that of Tiberias, where two illustrious families of Masoretes, the families of Ben Asher and Ben Naphtali, flourished in the late ninth and early tenth centuries. The most important Masoretic codices of the Hebrew Bible, dated between A.D. 895 and 1008, exhibit the Ben Asher edition, which succeeded to a large extent in dislodging that of Ben Naphtali.

The printing of the Hebrew Bible began in 1477;[4] it was printed in its entirety in 1488, at Soncino, near Cremona, in North Italy. In 1524–25 there was printed at Venice, under the superintendence of Jacob Ben Chayyim, an edition of the Hebrew Bible which was to become for nearly four centuries the "received text" on which were based the main Protestant vernacular translations of the Old Testament after that date.[5] These printed editions were based on rather late manuscripts with mixed texts; they have been superseded by the critical editions of the twentieth century.

[1] From the verb *māsar*, "hand down" (see p. 21).
[2] Jerome, *Epistle* 84:3.
[3] Cf. P. Kahle, *Masoreten des Ostens* (Leipzig, 1913); *Masoreten des Westens* (Leipzig, 1927. 1930); *The Cairo Geniza* ([1]London, 1947; [2]Oxford, 1959).
[4] In 1477 the Hebrew Psalter was printed at Bologna; in 1482 the Pentateuch and five *Megillôt*, also at Bologna; in 1485–86 the Prophets, at Soncino; in 1486–87, the Writings, at Naples.
[5] It was a rabbinical Bible (i.e. containing Targums and Hebrew commentaries in addition to the text), printed by Daniel Bomberg. Luther's German Old Testament was based on an edition of the Hebrew Bible printed at Brescia in 1494.

Textual Tradition of the New Testament

As for the New Testament, its textual tradition can be traced back much closer to the time when the documents themselves were composed.[1] The bulk of later manuscripts exhibit the "common" or "Byzantine" text, which can be traced back to the second half of the fourth century A.D. Earlier than that are the Alexandrian, the "Western", and one or two other types of text, while earlier still are the types of text represented by the oldest known papyri, which are dated between the middle of the second and middle of the third centuries. The establishment of the various lines of tradition, and the evaluation of the evidence as presented by the respective groups of witnesses – texts, lectionaries, versions, citations – belong to the discipline of New Testament textual criticism.

Like the earliest printed editions of the Hebrew Bible, the earliest printed editions of the Greek New Testament were based on manuscripts of recent date and inferior worth[2] (two qualities which do not inevitably go together). Such were the New Testament volume of the Complutensian Polyglot (printed in 1514 but not published until 1520, when its companion volumes were ready) and the successive editions of Erasmus's Greek Testament (1516, 1519, 1522, 1527 and 1535). It was Erasmus's third edition that formed the basis of Luther's German New Testament (1522) and Tyndale's English New Testament (1525–26). The edition of the Greek Testament which later became standard in England was that printed at Paris in 1550 by Robert Estienne, an edition so free from misprints that Estienne claimed to have an angel as his compositor. The printing house of Elzevir at Leyden took this edition as the basis for two editions which they issued in 1624 and 1633. The Latin preface to the 1633 edition assures the reader that he has in his hands "the text which is now received by all" without alteration or corruption.[3] From this piece of publisher's blurb comes the term "the received text", which is applied more generally to the text of most of the early printed editions.

From the eighteenth century to the present day there have been continuous attempts, represented by many critical editions, to establish a more accurate text than the "received text", based on manuscripts which are both earlier and more reliable[4] than those on which the earliest printed

---

[1] An up-to-date summary may be found in K. Aland, "Novi Testamenti Graeci Editio Maior Critica: Der Gegenwärtige Stand der Arbeit an einer neuen grossen kritischen Ausgabe des Neuen Testaments", *New Testament Studies* 16 (1969–70), pp. 163 ff.

[2] Erasmus was in such a hurry to have his first edition printed (1516) that when the Greek manuscript he was following failed in the last chapter of Revelation, he translated the remaining verses back into Greek from the Latin Vulgate; at least two of his Greek words persisted throughout the history of the Received Text (C. H. Turner, *The Early Printed Editions of the Greek Testament*, Oxford, 1924, pp. 15 ff.).

[3] "Textum ergo habes nunc ab omnibus receptum" (whence *Textus Receptus*).

[4] Again, early date and reliable text are two qualities which do not necessarily go together

editions were based. While the Authorized Version of 1611, like its pre-decessors from Tyndale onwards, reproduces the "received text", the Revised Version of 1881 is based to a large extent on the Alexandrian revision attested by the Vatican and Sinaitic codices of the fourth century, and the Revised Standard Version and New English Bible of our own day represent an "eclectic" text, no single early text-type being followed to the exclusion of the others – which corresponds to the present position in New Testament textual study.[1]

The Reformation and After

When the churches of the Reformation repudiated the authority of Rome and the ecclesiastical tradition that went with it, and made their appeal to *sola scriptura*, they found themselves faced before long with a question which had not been so important previously. What was this *scriptura* to which they appealed? Was it conveyed to them in immediate directness from the prophets and apostles? If not, how was it conveyed?

The answer, of course, was that it was conveyed through a process of copying and recopying stretching over many centuries – a process of manuscript tradition which led to a good deal of textual variation. But the earliest Reformers were not greatly troubled about textual variants. Even before their time, John Purvey, editor of the second Wycliffite Bible, knew that a pure text must first be established if a reliable version was to be produced: the translator's first task therefore, he said, was "to make one Latin Bible some deal true" by comparing existing Latin copies, which varied considerably one from another; and then, on the basis of such a Latin Bible, to construct an English version.[2] So, too, in the six-teenth century the great Reformed scholars found no theological problems in variant readings; to decide between them was a matter of judging the evidence.

This was John Calvin's attitude, for example, whether the variation was between readings in New Testament manuscripts or between the Septuagint and Masoretic traditions. Thus the Masoretic text of Genesis 46:27 and Exodus 1:5 mentions Jacob's descendants who went down to Egypt as 70 persons in all; the Septuagint version gives the number as 75, and it is this latter reading that is given in Stephen's speech in Acts 7:14. On this Calvin says:

> In saying that Jacob came into Egypt with seventy-five people, Stephen does not agree with Moses, whose reckoning is only seventy. Jerome considers that Luke has not given an exact account of what Stephen said, but took this

[1] Cf. R. V. G. Tasker, *The Greek New Testament, being the text translated in the New English Bible, 1961* (Oxford and Cambridge, 1964), pp. vii ff.
[2] From John Purvey's *General Prologue* (1395–6).

number from the Septuagint translation of Moses' account (Gen. 46:27), either because, being a proselyte, he did not know Hebrew, or because he wished to concede this to the Gentiles, among whom that was the accepted reading. Furthermore it is not certain whether the Greek translators put down that number on purpose, or whether later on it crept in by error . . . It certainly seems very likely to me that the Septuagint translators correctly translated what Moses had written. For it is not possible to say that their minds were wandering, seeing that Deut. 10 (v. 22), where that particular number is repeated, agrees with Moses, considering that in Jerome's day at least that verse was being read without any controversy; for those copies which are printed today have it different.[1] Therefore I conclude that this discrepancy arose by an error on the part of copyists. But this was not such an important matter that Luke should have confused the Gentiles over it, when they were used to the Greek reading. And it is possible that he himself did write down the true number, but somebody erroneously changed it from that of Moses. For we know that the New Testament was handled by those who were ignorant of Hebrew, but thoroughly conversant with Greek. Therefore, to make the words of Stephen agree with the verse in Moses' account, it is probable that the wrong number in the Greek version of Genesis was transferred to this place also. If anyone is to persist in disputing about this, let us allow him a superiority of wisdom.[2]

Calvin mentions the various possibilities which could account for the difference between the two readings. What he could not know, because it has been discovered only in recent years, is that the variation arose first in the Hebrew tradition, before the Greek translation was made; the Septuagint translators, whose version was followed by Stephen or Luke, translated the Hebrew text which lay before them. But Calvin is not greatly troubled by the textual variation one way or the other.[3]

Similarly Calvin's disciples, who pronounced the Geneva Bible in 1560, did not imagine that by drawing their readers' attention to variant readings which they noted in their margin they were confusing their minds or disturbing their faith.[4]

But when, later in the century, the Council of Trent (1546) declared the "ancient and vulgate edition" of the Latin Bible to be alone authentic,[5] and a standard text of this edition was promulgated first by Pope Sixtus

---

[1] In Deut. 10:22 the Septuagint reading is "seventy", as in the Masoretic text (although Codex A reads "seventy-five" in conformity with the Greek text of Gen. 46:27; Ex. 1:5).

[2] *Calvin's Commentaries: The Acts of the Apostles 1–13*, E. T. by J. W. Fraser and W. J. G. McDonald (Edinburgh, 1965), pp. 181 ff.

[3] A Qumran fragment of Exodus in Hebrew (4Q Ex^a) agrees with the Septuagint against the Masoretic text in Ex. 1:5 by reading 75, not 70.

[4] Cf. B. M. Metzger, "The Geneva Bible of 1560", *Theology Today* 17 (1960), pp. 339 ff.; "The Influence of Codex Bezae upon the Geneva Bible of 1560", *New Testament Studies* 8 (1961–62), pp. 72 ff.; he refers also to N. Pocock, "Some Notices of the Genevan Bible", *The Bibliographer* 6 (1884), pp. 105 ff.

[5] Sessio 4: *Decretum de Definitione et Usu Sacrorum Librorum*. Cf. E. F. Sutcliffe, "The Council of Trent on the *Authentia* of the Vulgate", *JTS* 49 (1948), pp. 35 ff.

V (1590) and then with the authority of Clement VIII (1592), it was possible for Roman Catholics to charge their separated brethren with having no such standard for deciding which was the true reading among several variants as they themselves had. Whether it was the effect of this charge or not, a certain sensitiveness on the score of variant readings manifests itself among some seventeenth-century heirs of the Reformation. This can be seen in the reaction to the *Biblia Sacra Polyglotta* (London, 1655–57) edited by Brian Walton, later Bishop of Chester. Walton's work contains the first systematic collection of New Testament variant readings. John Owen, Dean of Christ Church, Oxford, under the Commonwealth, and a theologian of portentous stature, appreciated many of the scholarly features of Walton's work but did not approve of his *apparatus criticus*. He expressed his disapproval in *Considerations on the Prolegomena and Appendix to the Late Polyglotta* (Oxford, 1659), in terms like the following:

> What use hath been made, and is as yet made, in the world, of this supposition, that corruptions have befallen the originals of the Scripture, which those various lections at first view seem to intimate, I need not declare. It is, in brief, the foundation of Mohammedanism . . . the chiefest and principal prop of Popery, the only pretence of fanatical antiscripturists, and the root of much hidden atheism in the world.[1]

And again:

> We went from Rome under the conduct of the *purity* of the originals. I wish none have a mind to return thither under the pretence of their *corruption*.[2]

To Owen's *Considerations* Walton lost no time in issuing a spirited reply, *The Considerator Considered,* "wherein, amongst other things, the Certainty, Integrity, and Divine Authority of the Original Texts, is defended against the Consequences of Atheists, Papists, Antiscripturists, &c. inferred from the Various Readings, and Novelty of the HEBREW POINTS, by the Author of the said CONSIDERATIONS". The significance of this reference to the Hebrew points will be dealt with below.[3] Walton argued particularly, as he had already done in his *Prolegomena,* that the existence of variants does not prove the corruption of the originals, and in fact that the variants do not affect any matter of moment.[4] In any case, he says, the only security against "the uncertainty arising from these

---

[1] *The Works of John Owen,* ed. W. H. Goold, xvi (London, 1853, reprinted London, 1968), p. 348. These *Considerations* formed an addendum to Owen's treatise *Of the Divine Original, Authority, Self-evidencing Light, and Power of the Scriptures* (pp. 281 ff.)

[2] *Op. cit.,* p. 370.

[3] See pp. 159 ff.

[4] J. H. Todd, *Memoir of the Life and Writings of the Right Rev. Brian Walton,* ii (London, 1821), p. 71.

varieties" would be "to make one Copy a standard for all", and this is "a meer chimera, a groundless fancy, and a vain imagination of that which never was since the *autographa* were in being".[1]

The same kind of objection to the publicizing of variant readings appears in J. W. Burgon's comment on the numerous marginal notes in the Revised New Testament of 1881 which tell the reader what "some" or "many ancient authorities" read:

> The effect which these ever-recurring announcements produce on the devout reader of Scripture is the reverse of edifying; is never helpful; is always bewildering.[2]

But, put like this, the objection is little better than a theological way of saying that "where ignorance is bliss, 'tis folly to be wise".

Burgon indeed thought that the Revisers in these notes were needlessly publicizing scribal errors, a charge which John Owen had laid against Brian Walton;[3] but he himself was not bewildered. He knew too much about textual criticism for that, and in his mastery of the bearing of lectionary evidence and patristic citations on the history of the New Testament text he had few rivals in his day. He appealed confidently to "Catholic Antiquity",[4] which he believed could be traced back to the second half of the fourth century A.D., and in his eyes Catholic Antiquity conclusively vindicated the trustworthiness of the common (Byzantine) text or, as he called it, the "traditional text".[5] For Burgon to call this text "traditional" was to praise it, not to disparage it. The state of textual knowledge in the 1880s was such that Burgon was able to present a powerful case, a case which could be answered only by a scholar who had covered the ground as painstakingly as he himself had done. Some who attempted to refute him without this equipment succeeded only in having their incompetence exposed: the one man who could have answered him – F. J. A. Hort – chose not to do so. Perhaps Hort, like Burgon himself, was willing to leave the question to "the verdict of succeeding days".[6] The verdict of succeeding days has had the advantage of much more and earlier evidence than was available to either Hort or Burgon, and while it has by no means left Hort unscathed, it has shown that the

---

[1] *Op. cit.*, p. 73. By *autographa* are meant the original documents, many of which, however, were not strictly autographs, since their contents were dictated, not written by the author (e.g. the oracles of Jeremiah and the letters of Paul).

[2] J. W. Burgon, *The Revision Revised* (London, 1883), p. 5.

[3] Owen, *op. cit.*, pp. 364 ff.

[4] Burgon, *op. cit.*, pp. xxv, xxvii.

[5] Cf. the titles of his posthumously published books *The Traditional Text of the Holy Gospels* (London, 1896) and *The Causes of the Corruption of the Traditional Text of the Holy Gospels* (London, 1896), both edited by Edward Miller.

[6] *The Revision Revised*, p. 382 (a quotation from Pindar); cf. J. R. Harris's chapter, "The Verdict of Succeeding Days", in *Sidelights on New Testament Research* (London, 1908), pp. 36 ff.

"Catholic Antiquity" to which Burgon appealed went back as far as he traced it, but no farther – that the "traditional text" which he regarded as authentic represents a tradition originating in the second half of the fourth century.

In more recent times Burgon's case has been defended anew by an American scholar, Dr. E. F. Hills, who appeals not to Catholic Antiquity but to the words of Jesus. When our Lord said "It is easier for heaven and earth to pass away, than for one dot of the law to become void" (Luke 16:17),[1] and undertook to be with His disciples always as they made disciples in His name and taught them to observe all that He had commanded (Matt. 28:19 f.), He was in effect, according to Dr. Hills, promising "that a trustworthy text of the sacred books shall be preserved in His Church down through the ages until the last day".[2] This is doubtful exegesis, but if we grant it for the sake of the argument, we have still to identify this "trustworthy text". For general purposes it might be said that the New Testament text has been preserved with sufficient fidelity to accomplish its purpose – that, in fact, the way of life through faith in Christ is set forth so clearly that it cannot be obscured even by the most tendentious translation of the most corrupt edition. But Dr. Hills means more than this: his argument is that the trustworthy text is to be found in the Byzantine manuscripts, "because it is that form of the Greek New Testament which is known to have been used in the Church of Christ in unbroken succession for many centuries, first in the Greek Church and then in the Protestant Church". He continues:

And all orthodox Christians, all Christians who show due regard for the divine inspiration and providential preservation of Scripture, must agree with Burgon in this matter. For in what other way can it be that Christ has fulfilled His promise always to preserve in His Church the true New Testament text?[3]

This argument has the tactical advantage of discrediting in advance those who take a different view, by suggesting that they are not orthodox or consistent Christians. But when they are told that they "must agree with Burgon", they may well reply in Shylock's words:

On what compulsion must I? Tell me that.

[1] Cf. Matt. 5:18.
[2] E. F. Hills, in preface to new issue of J. W. Burgon, *The Last Twelve Verses of the Gospel according to S. Mark* (London, 1871; reprinted Evansville, Indiana, 1959), p. 18. Cf. his *The King James Version Defended! A Christian View of the New Testament Manuscripts* (Des Moines, 1956).
[3] Preface to Burgon, *Last Twelve Verses*, p. 21. The appeal to the Greek church is precarious; it could be used to support the authority of the Septuagint against the Masoretic text of the Old Testament. Cf. Origen, *Letter to Africanus*, 4 (arguing against those who appealed from the Septuagint to the Hebrew Bible): "Are we to suppose that Providence, which in the sacred scriptures has ministered to the edification of all the churches of Christ, had no thought for those bought with a price, for whom Christ died?"

Besides, the argument proves too much: it could equally well be used (and no doubt would readily have been used by Burgon) to defend the divinely imparted authority of the historic episcopate and even more doubtful institutions. The exegesis on which it is based resembles nothing so much as the use that is made of the words of Christ to Peter in Matt. 16:18 f. to prove that the Church is incapable of holding or teaching error and that the Pope, as Peter's successor, exercises a dominically bestowed primacy over his fellow-bishops. Burgon's faith in the "traditional text" was bound up with his faith that the church, as the recipient of the Spirit who was to lead her children into all the truth, was guided continually to reject depraved manuscripts and retain those which were substantially reliable – those which exhibited the common text.

Tradition may command our respect as that which has been delivered to us, but it cannot be appealed to as an authority. History and evidence must be heard; "honest obedience" must be yielded to "truth of testimony" and "truth of rendering".[1] B. B. Warfield, a conservative of the conservatives in the interpretation of Scripture according to the Westminster Confession, found the "singular care and providence" of God by which, in the words of that Confession, the Old and New Testaments in Hebrew and Greek have been "kept pure in all ages",[2] manifested in

the multiplication of copies of the Scriptures, the several early efforts towards the revision of the text, the raising up of scholars in our own day to collect and collate manuscripts, and to reform them on scientific principles – of our Tischendorfs and Tregelleses, and Westcotts and Horts.[3]

To the same effect another scholar who stands in the Warfield tradition, Professor J. H. Skilton, has declared that "textual criticism, in God's providence, is the means provided for ascertaining the true text of the Bible".[4] The textual critic, working at his task in a spirit of commitment to truth, performs a valuable and indeed essential service in the church, which cannot be by-passed by any appeal to tradition.

The Battle of the Vowel-Points

In the immediate post-Reformation age there was another problem, more acute, in the mind of some people, than that of variant readings in New Testament manuscripts or the differences between the Masoretic, Samaritan and Septuagint editions of the Old Testament. This was the problem presented by the Hebrew points.[5]

[1] H. Alford, *The New Testament . . . revised* (London, 1870), p. vii.
[2] Westminster Confession of Faith i. 8.
[3] B. B. Warfield, *The Westminster Assembly and its Work* (New York, 1931), p. 239.
[4] J. H. Skilton, in *The Infallible Word*, ed. N. B. Stonehouse and P. Woolley (Philadelphia, 1946), p. 162.
[5] Cf. J. Bowman, "A Forgotten Controversy", *Evangelical Quarterly* 20 (1948), pp. 46 ff.

These points were the dots and strokes devised by the Masoretes – ultimately, the Masoretes of Tiberias – to help readers of the Hebrew Bible to pronounce the text correctly. Among the most important sets of points were those which indicated the vowels. The Hebrew alphabet originally consisted of consonantal letters only, and although a few of the letters came to be used secondarily to denote certain important vowels, most of the vowels had no written notation before the age of the Masoretes. To readers who were familiar with Hebrew this did not matter greatly; since they knew the language they knew which vowels to pronounce when they saw the consonantal letters. But an increasing number of readers were none too conversant with the language, and they would find visible representations of the vowel-sounds a useful crutch. (The general principle of the Hebrew vowel-points, though not the identical pointing, is reproduced in Pitman's shorthand.) The Masoretes did not invent the vowel sounds, but "received" them as part of their tradition: what they did was to add signs or points to the text of Scripture as visible representations of the traditional vowel sounds.[1] The earliest Reformers, like Luther and Calvin, knew this quite well; they took it, as they took the variant readings, in their stride. But some of their successors found themselves embarrassed by these Hebrew points. The points represented the stereotyping of *masorah,* and what was *masorah*? It was simply tradition – something that had been handed down. And whose tradition? The tradition of unbelieving Jews. But – and here the spokesmen of the Counter-Reformation were not slow to point the moral – surely it was preposterous to abandon *Christian* tradition, as the Reformers had done, and then have to rely on *Jewish* tradition! Who could tell how many corruptions the Jewish Masoretes and scribes had introduced, deliberately or inadvertently, into the sacred text? *Sola scriptura,* indeed! This *scriptura,* in the Old Testament, consisted of the Hebrew text (for the Reformers would not appeal to the secondary authority of versions when the original text was available), but this Hebrew text consisted of the letters, which to be sure went back to the sacred authors, *plus* the vowel points which were indispensable for the understanding and interpreting of the letters – and these vowel points were added at a relatively late date on the basis of Jewish tradition! The Catholics, on the other hand, had their "ancient and vulgate edition", translated indeed from the Hebrew (at a date antecedent to the addition of the vowel points), but certified as authentic by the *magisterium* of the church. The Reformed churches, they insisted, had no comparable certainty.

Some of the Reformed party were uncomfortably alive to this dilemma (as they felt it to be) and undertook to argue that the points, far from being of recent, man-made origin, were coeval with the consonantal letters

---

[1] The Jewish scholar Elias Levita (1486–1549) had conclusively established the post-Talmudic date of the vowel-points in his *Masōreth ha-Masōreth* (Venice, 1538).

(or at latest were added by Ezra) and equally inspired by God.[1] John
Owen took this line,[2] and in defending it he invoked the authority of the
great Talmudical scholar John Lightfoot. John Lightfoot adduced copious
examples of the ineptitudes (by his seventeenth-century standards) of
which the rabbis were capable and, tarring the Masoretes of Tiberias with
the same stick, expressed his judgement thus:

> The pointing of the Bible savours of the work of the Holy Spirit, not of wicked,
> blind, and mad men.[3]

It is surprising that a man of John Lightfoot's learning could not distinguish between vowel sounds and their written representation: he pours
scorn on the idea that a language could ever have been devoid of vowels.
To him a language without vowels was like a baby without swaddling
bands, liable to grow all out of shape without their restricting control.[4]
But no one ever suggested that the Hebrew language lacked vowels
before the Masoretic age; the fact simply was that these vowels had for the
most part been unrepresented in written form before then.

The climax of this dogmatic conviction, expressed by Lightfoot, Owen
and others, was reached in 1675 when the Helvetic Consensus Formula
provided that no man should be licensed to preach the gospel without
first professing his belief in the divine inspiration of the Hebrew vowel
points. But it was a forlorn cause, as the arguments of Ludovicus Cappellus
and other scholars quickly and decisively proved.

There have not been wanting, however, sturdy Protestants of another
stripe who, far from claiming excessive antiquity or authority for the
Hebrew points, repudiated them and the tradition to which they belonged,
and undertook to vocalize the consonantal text on quite different principles. Ferrar Fenton, for instance, an amateur Bible translator at the

---

[1] The most learned defender of this position was the lexicographer John Buxtorf (1564–
1629); he assailed Elias Levita's arguments in his *Tiberias* (Basel, 1620), and was thought by
many to have refuted him; but he himself was refuted by Ludovicus Cappellus (*Arcanum
punctationis revelatum*, Amsterdam, 1624; *Critica Sacra*, Paris, 1650). Buxtorf on his deathbed
charged his son to give Cappellus the answer which he was unable to give himself, but his
son's successive attempts to do so were demolished by Cappellus time after time. The first
scholar in Britain to affirm the Masoretic origin of the points, twenty years before Brian
Walton did so in his *Biblia Sacra Polyglotta*, was a St. Andrews graduate, John Weemes, in
*Exercitations Divine proving the Necessitie, Majestie, Integritie, perspicuitie and sense of the Scrip-
tures* (London, 1636), Exercitation XV: "That the points were not originally with the Letters
from the beginning."

[2] "And as I shall not oppose them who maintain that they are coevous with the letters . . .
so I nowise doubt but that, as we now enjoy them, we shall yet manifest that they were completed by . . . the men of the great synagogue, Ezra and his companions, guided therein by the
infallible direction of the Spirit of God" (Owen, *op. cit.*, p. 371). Owen deprecated the argument for the recency of the points in Walton's *Prolegomena* as "this brand brought yet nearer
to the church's bread-corn" (*op. cit.*, p. 289).

[3] So Owen (*op. cit.*, p. 384) translates the Latin of Lightfoot's *Centuria Chorographia* (Cambridge, 1658), ch. 81, p. 146.

[4] J. Lightfoot, *Works* ii (London, 1684), p. 1014.

beginning of this century, indicated his independent line in this matter by such forms as Aisebal (for the common Jezebel) and Alisha (for the common Elisha).[1] W. A. Wordsworth, an original commentator on Isaiah and other prophets, held that the Masoretes were liable to the same rebuke as those scribes to whom our Lord said, "You have taken away the key of knowledge and made the word of God of none effect by your tradition" (Luke 11:52);[2] thus he did not hesitate to re-read "a son is given" *(bēn nittān)* in Isa. 9:5 as "the son of Nathan" *(ben nātān)*, in the light of our Lord's descent from David through Nathan in Luke 3:31.[3] And in recent years a good man could be seen walking along the streets of Manchester holding aloft on a pole a banner with the strange device YHVH ALHYM – the latter form being his vocalization and pronunciation of the Hebrew word for "God", commonly transliterated 'Elohim. (He did not show the vocalization of the former word, but told inquirers that it was to be pronounced Yavá, with the stress on the second syllable.)[4]

Tradition – Jewish, Christian, or any other – may be right or it may be wrong. It must be tested by evidence. The validity of the Masoretic pointing has to be critically assessed, and this is a further reminder that biblical criticism is a necessary ministry – not so important as interpretation, but preparatory to it. If the Masoretic tradition is generally (and properly) admitted to be substantially right, this is not because it is tradition but because the evidence confirms it.

[1] F. Fenton, *The Holy Bible in Modern English* (London, 1903).
[2] W. A. Wordsworth, *En Roeh* (Edinburgh, 1939), p. 3.
[3] W. A. Wordsworth, *op. cit.*, p. 94.
[4] He also, Athanasius-like, announced the "true" date of Easter year by year; he was, in fact, a Quartodeciman (though perhaps he did not realize this).

CHAPTER X

TRADITION TODAY

IN THE ECUMENICAL CLIMATE OF TODAY TRADITION HAS
become a subject of live interest and debate, and it has become important to understand the diversity of role and significance accorded to
tradition in varying Christian communities.

Eastern Orthodoxy

In the Orthodox Church of the East, tradition is the concept which
embraces the whole of Christian existence. The idea of any tension
between Scripture and tradition is foreign to Orthodoxy: Scripture is
part of what is handed down, as also are Councils and Creed, liturgy and
icons, canon law and everything that goes to make up the church's life
and thought. And this indivisible tradition is a living thing, whereby (for
example) the early fathers are felt to be contemporary witnesses, for in
it the Holy Spirit gives substance to the gospel and pours the love of God
into the hearts of believers. "If we do not love one another, we cannot
love God; and if we do not love God, we cannot make a true confession
of faith and cannot enter into the inner spirit of Tradition, for there is
no other way of knowing God than to love Him."[1] Tradition, in effect,
is identical with the witness of the Spirit.[2]

Western Catholicism

But in western Christendom tradition has not been accorded this all-
embracing role; perhaps that is one reason for the Orthodox failure to
discern any difference in fundamental principle between Protestants and
Roman Catholics. Alexis Khomiakov could describe all Protestants as
"crypto-Papists"[3] and the Pope as "the first Protestant".[4] For in the west
the custom has grown up of regarding tradition as unwritten tradition in
distinction from Holy Writ. (The distinction, in fact, is ancient: when once

[1] T. Ware, The Orthodox Church (Harmondsworth, 1963), p. 215, commenting on the introduction to the Creed in the Byzantine Liturgy: "Let us love one another, that with one mind
we may confess Father, Son and Holy Spirit, Trinity one in essence and undivided." There
is no better introduction in English to the Orthodox Church than this "Pelican Original"
by Timothy Ware (now Archimandrite Kallistos).
[2] G. Florovsky, "Sobornost: the Catholicity of the Church", in The Church of God, ed.
E. L. Mascall (London, 1934), p. 64.
[3] Letter in W. J. Birkbeck, Russia and the English Church (London, 1895), p. 67 (cited by T.
Ware, op. cit., p. 9).
[4] As cited by T. Ware, op. cit., p. 10.

the canon of Christian Scripture was defined, the church accorded it the normative status of "constitutive tradition", alongside which the continuing and developing teaching ministry or *magisterium* filled the role of "interpretative traditions".)[1] But it was in the age of the Reformation and Counter-Reformation that the relation between the two, the nature of their respective authority, was formally defined, largely because of the Reformers' appeal from the church's tradition to the canonical Scriptures. This was one of the major concerns of the Council of Trent, and in this as in other respects we cannot do justice to the terms in which its decrees were formulated unless we bear in mind what those positions were against which the Tridentine theologians reacted so vigorously.

The affirmation of the Council on the subject of Scripture and tradition represents a compromise in more ways than one. The only traditions to which authority is ascribed are those which can be described as apostolic – those, that is to say, for which apostolic origin can be claimed and which have not been allowed to fall into disuse.[2] Some of the fathers present would have liked to include ecclesiastical traditions, but they were in the minority. By apostolic traditions were meant unwritten traditions, in which the divine revelation had been handed down as well as in the canonical writings. The finally approved decree recognized that the gospel,

> promised of old through the prophets in the holy scriptures, was first promulgated by our Lord Jesus Christ, the Son of God, with His own mouth, and then commanded to be preached by His apostles to every creature as the source both of all saving truth and of all rules of conduct.[3]

It then goes on to affirm that the Council,

> clearly perceiving that this truth and these rules are contained in written books and unwritten traditions which, received from the mouth of Christ Himself by the apostles, or from the apostles themselves at the dictation of the Holy Spirit, have come down to us, passed on as it were from hand to hand, and following the example of the orthodox fathers, receives and venerates with equal feelings of piety and equal reverence all the books of the Old and New Testaments, since one God is the author of both, and also the traditions themselves, pertaining to faith and conduct alike, since they were dictated either orally by Christ or by the Holy Spirit, and preserved in the catholic church in continuous succession.[4]

An earlier draft, following a proposal of Cardinal del Monte, one of

---

[1] See pp. 116 ff.
[2] The giving of the chalice as well as the bread to the laity was indubitably an apostolic practice, but had fallen into disuse in the west, as also had the exchange of the "holy kiss" II Thess. 5:26).
[3] Session 4: *Decretum de Canonicis Scripturis.*
[4] *Ibid.*

the three papal legates at the Council, stated that the saving truth was contained "partly in written books, partly in unwritten traditions".[1] This clearly implied that not all of the truth was contained in Scripture: some of it was there, but some of it was not to be found there, but in the unwritten traditions. This did not commend itself to some of the fathers, who maintained that the whole of saving truth was contained in Scripture; the agreed form of words therefore represents a calculated ambiguity, to which all could conscientiously subscribe. This ambiguity has been as helpful in our own day as it was in 1546.

The Vatican Council of 1869–70 contented itself with repeating the Tridentine decree on this subject:

> This supernatural revelation, according to the faith of the universal church, as declared by the holy Synod of Trent, is "contained in written books and unwritten traditions which, received from the mouth of Christ Himself by the apostles, or from the apostles themselves at the dictation of the Holy Spirit, have come down to us, passed on as it were from hand to hand."[2]

But Vatican II paid much more attention to it, and its Constitution on Divine Revelation is one of the most important of its documents. After an admirable introduction on the nature and purpose of divine revelation the Constitution comes to its transmission:

> As for those things which God had revealed for the salvation of all peoples, He has most graciously arranged that they should remain in their entirety for ever and be transmitted to all generations. Therefore Christ the Lord, in whom the whole revelation of God Most High is consummated, commanded the apostles to preach to all men that gospel which, promised in advance through the prophets, He Himself fulfilled and promulgated with His own mouth . . . This command was faithfully carried out by the apostles who, by their oral preaching, their example, and their ordinance, delivered those things which they had received . . . and also by those apostles and apostolic men who, under the inspiration of the Holy Spirit, committed the message of salvation to writing.
>
> But that the gospel might be forever preserved entire and alive in the church, the apostles left bishops as their successors, "delivering to them their own teaching office". Therefore this sacred tradition and sacred scripture of both Testaments are like a mirror in which the church beholds God during her pilgrimage on earth . . . until she is brought to see Him as He is, face to face . . .
>
> Thus the apostolic preaching, which is expressed in a special way in the inspired books, was to be preserved by a continuous succession until the end of time. Therefore the apostles, delivering what they themselves had received, admonish the faithful to hold fast the traditions which they have learned either by spoken word or by letter [II Thess. 2:15] and to contend earnestly for the faith once for all delivered to them [Jude 3]. But what was delivered by the

---

[1] Cf. G. H. Tavard, *Holy Writ or Holy Church* (London, 1959), pp. 195 ff.
[2] *Constitutio Dogmatica de Fide Catholica*, cap. 2: *De Revelatione*.

apostles embraces all those things which contribute to holiness of life and increase of faith in the people of God, and so the church, in her teaching, life and worship, perpetuates and transmits to all generations all that she is, all that she believes.

This tradition which stems from the apostles develops in the church by the Holy Spirit's aid . . . The utterances of the holy fathers testify to the living presence of this tradition . . . Through the same tradition the entire canon of sacred books becomes known to the church, and the sacred letters themselves are more thoroughly understood and unceasingly rendered active . . .

Therefore sacred tradition and the sacred scripture are closely interconnected and communicate one with another. For since both emanate from the same divine source, they somehow merge into one and tend towards the same end. Sacred Scripture is the voice of God inasmuch as it was consigned to writing by the inspiration of the Divine Spirit; but it is by sacred tradition that the word of God, entrusted to the apostles by Christ the Lord and the Holy Spirit, is transmitted in its entirety to their successors . . . Therefore both are to be received and venerated "with equal feelings of piety and equal reverence".

Sacred traditions and sacred Scripture constitute one sacred deposit of God's word committed to the church . . . The function of authentically interpreting the word of God, written or delivered by tradition, has been exclusively entrusted to the living teaching office of the church, whose authority is exercised in the name of Jesus Christ . . . It is plain, therefore, that sacred tradition, sacred Scripture and the church's teaching office, according to God's most wise counsel, are so interconnected and associated together that one cannot stand without the others, and all together, in their several ways, under the action of the one Holy Spirit, contribute effectively to the salvation of souls.[1]

Doubtless there were discrepant views to be reconciled at Vatican Council II as much as at Trent and Vatican I, and an outsider, reading what is said about Scripture and tradition in this Constitution, might be pardoned for thinking at times that the positive affirmations about Scripture were made by one party and that those about tradition were added by another. In this he would probably be mistaken, but it is difficult to suppose that Vatican II would have been able to formulate the doctrine of Scripture so freely if the "partly . . . partly" wording had been adopted at Trent. Thanks to the wording which was adopted in 1546, the fathers at Vatican II could say that, while tradition *transmits* the word of God, Scripture *is* His word, since

in the composition of the sacred books God chose men who, while employed by Him, so used their own faculties and powers, as He acted in and through them, that as true authors they delivered in writing all those things, and only those things, that He Himself willed.[2]

The church accordingly

---

[1] *Constitutio Dogmatica "De Divina Revelatione"*, cap. 2: *De Divinae Revelatione Transmissione*, § § 2–10. The phrases within quotation-marks are repeated from the corresponding Tridentine decree.

[2] *Ibid.*, cap. 3: *De Sacrae Scripturae Divina Inspiratione et de eius Interpretatione*, § 11.

has always held, and still holds, the Scriptures to be, along with sacred tradition, the supreme rule of her faith since, having been inspired by God and once for all consigned to writing, they impart unchangeably the word of God Himself, and cause the voice of the Holy Spirit to sound in the words of the prophets and apostles. Therefore all the church's preaching, like the Christian religion itself, must be nourished and controlled by the sacred Scripture. For in the sacred books our Father in heaven meets His children and converses with them in great love; moreover there is such great power and virtue in the word of God that it abides as sustenance and strength for the church, and for the church's children the reinforcement of faith, the food of the soul, the pure and perennial wellspring of spiritual life.[1]

The natural implication of this noble language is that all the divine revelation given through prophets and apostles is recorded in the Scripture,[2] while it is the province of tradition to preserve and transmit it from generation to generation (so that "the church, as the ages revolve, constantly tends towards the fullness of divine truth, until the words of God reach their consummation in her"),[3] and the province of the church in her teaching office to interpret what has thus been revealed, recorded and transmitted.

In not dissimilar vein Fr. Congar treats tradition not as something additional to Scripture (in the sense that it transmits apostolic doctrine not contained in Scripture) but as another way of imparting the truths of Scripture – Scripture itself being "absolutely sovereign".[4] Tradition is a *thésaurisation* or constant accrual of meditation on the biblical text made by one generation after another, "the living continuity of faith quickening the people of God" – a sort of *midrash* or *gemara,* in fact.[5] The existence of such a tradition is undoubted: many parts of Scripture mean more to Christians today than they did to their predecessors in the early centuries A.D. because of what they have meant to intervening generations of Christians. (It is equally true that they often meant something to Christians in the early centuries A.D. that they could not mean today – but that is another story.) Psalm 46 has a special significance in the Lutheran tradition (in the form of *Ein' feste Burg*) and Psalm 90 has acquired additional meaning in English history (in the form *O God, our help in ages past*).[6] But tradition of this kind cannot have such independent authority as has classically been ascribed to tradition in the church: it is entirely dependent on Scripture. The interpretation of Scripture, even if it accrues

---

[1] *Ibid.,* cap. 6: *De Sacra Scriptura in Vita Ecclesiae,* § 21.
[2] Cf. K. Rahner's reference to Scripture's "unique position" as "the permanent and unrepeatable *norma normata* for all subsequent dogmatic utterances" ("Was ist eine dogmatische Aussage?" *Catholica* 15, 1961, p. 180).
[3] *Constitutio Dogmatica "De Divina Revelatione",* cap. 2, § 8.
[4] Y. M.-J. Congar, *La Tradition et les Traditions,* ii (Paris, 1963), p. 177.
[5] Y. M.-J. Congar, *La Tradition et les Traditions,* i (Paris, 1961), pp. 16 ff.
[6] Cf. R. Prothero's work mentioned on p. 86, n. 2; also J. T. Stoddart, *The Old Testament in Life and Literature* (London, 1913); *The New Testament in Life and Literature* (London, 1914).

at compound interest over the centuries, cannot get more out of Scripture than is there already – implicitly if not expressly.

Historic Anglicanism

The historical Anglican position appears in the association of Articles VI and XX – the former laying it down that

> Holy Scripture containeth all things necessary to salvation: so that whatsoever is not read therein, nor may be proved thereby, is not to be required of any man, that it should be believed as an article of the Faith, or be thought requisite or necessary to salvation;

while the latter states:

> The Church hath power to decree Rites or Ceremonies, and authority in Controversies of Faith: And yet it is not lawful for the Church to ordain anything that is contrary to God's Word written, neither may it so expound one place of Scripture, that it be repugnant to another. Wherefore, although the Church be a witness and a keeper of holy Writ, yet, as it ought not to decree anything against the same, so besides the same ought it not to enforce any thing to be believed for necessity of Salvation.[1]

The insistence in both these Articles that only what is taught in Scripture may be held "necessary for salvation" is in line with Luther's insistence on *sola scriptura*;[2] it is the same insistence which finds expression in William Chillingworth's memorable asseveration: "*The Bible*, I say, the *Bible* only, is the religion of Protestants"[3] – an asseveration which "epitomized the refusal of non-Roman Christians to accept the equation of Scripture and oral tradition required by the Council of Trent."[4]

The more thorough-going Reformers went farther than the Anglicans and Lutherans, who allowed themselves considerable latitude in the ordering of "rites or ceremonies". Calvin and his followers in that "most perfect school of Christ"[5] established at Geneva, together with many of the English Puritans, held that in matters of church order, as much as in

---

[1] Cf. also Article XXI, according to which General Councils, being assemblies of fallible men, "may err, and sometimes have erred, even in things pertaining unto God", so that "things ordained by them as necessary to salvation have neither strength nor authority, unless it may be declared that they be taken out of holy Scripture".

[2] See p. 13, n. 1.

[3] W. Chillingworth, *The Religion of Protestants: a Safe Way to Salvation* (Oxford, 1638), Answer vi, para. 56.

[4] N. Sykes, "The Religion of Protestants", *Cambridge History of the Bible* iii, ed. S. L. Greenslade (Cambridge, 1963), p. 175. Cf. the Inter-Varsity Fellowship statement *Evangelical Belief*, first edition (London, n.d., but before 1940), p. 10: "By using the word 'infallibility' in reference to Holy Scripture, we mean that it is in itself a true and complete guide, and requires no external correction either by Church or Tradition."

[5] John Knox, *Letter to Anne Locke*, December 9, 1556, *Works* iv (Edinburgh, 1895), p. 240.

matters of faith and morals, positive Scriptural authority must be forth-coming. Where faith and morals were prescribed in detail, and church order in some degree circumscribed, on this basis, as in the Westminster Confession and related documents, liberty of prophesying and practising alike was effectively prevented from straying beyond authorized bounds.

The greater latitude permitted by the Articles in ordering rites or ceremonies might be exploited in a variety of ways, just as the insistence on *sola scriptura* might coexist with a wide range of conflicting private interpretations. The consensus of thought and action which developed in the Church of England was due in part to uniformity of liturgy, but even more to a pervasive attitude which was summed up thus by that supreme exponent of the Anglican *via media*, Richard Hooker:

> What Scripture doth plainly deliver, to that the first place both of credit and obedience is due; the next whereunto, is whatsoever any man can necessarily conclude by force of Reason; after these, the voice of the Church succeedeth.[1]

This collocation of reason alongside Scripture and "the voice of the Church" (which is at least one phase of tradition) has characterized Anglicanism in all its comprehensiveness. When today Dr. John A. T. Robinson confesses his indebtedness to his Anglican heritage, he explains that the Anglican "conception of authority is not single-stranded but the three-fold cord, not easily broken, of Scripture and tradition and reason" and that he himself is therefore "by nature a man of continuities rather than discontinuities, of evolution rather than revolution, of both-and rather than either-or".[2]

Anglican – Methodist Conversations

This emphasis on reason must not be rejected as though it were an appeal to rationalism; if we consider the possibilities that may become actual when Scripture is interpreted unreasonably or tradition is defended or rejected on irrational grounds, we may well be grateful for this emphasis – even if "reason" is capable of being understood in a variety of ways. This emphasis can be heard in the interesting discussion of the relation between Scripture and tradition which forms part of the 1963 Report on *Conversations between the Church of England and the Methodist Church*.[3] Here is it acknowledged that "Holy Scripture is and must always

---

[1] *Laws of Ecclesiastical Polity* v (London, 1597), 8. 2. Hooker was arguing not only against the Tridentine placing of tradition on the same level of authority as Scripture, but also (and more particularly) against the Genevan and Puritan insistence that the imposing of any church ordinance not authorized by Scripture was sinful.
[2] J. A. T. Robinson, "Not Radical Enough?" in *The Christian Century*, November 12, 1969, p. 1446.
[3] *Conversations* (London, 1963), Part II, chapter 2, pp. 15 ff.

be the supreme standard of faith and morals in the Church because it embodies the testimony of chosen witnesses to God's saving action";[1] but the fact that we live in an age much later than that unique and unrepeatable saving action demands the operation of tradition "in the sense of the handing down of the faith from one generation to another".[2] What is primarily to be handed down is "the apostolic testimony of scripture";[3] this tradition "should be the norm for all other tradition".[4] Approval is expressed of the definition of tradition which commended itself to the second Faith and Order Conference (Edinburgh, 1937) – "the living stream of the Church's life".[5] But in itself this tradition exercises no authority, provides no means of diagnosing "virus, poison in the blood stream",[6] or of prescribing a remedy for it. In certain forms of tradition, however, there is the requisite authority – first, in Holy Scripture which, among other things, acts as a "saving salt" in the church's life; then, the appeal to primitive Christianity; next, the church's "continuous theological conversation" from the early fathers to the present day; liturgies, hymns and works of devotion and edification; the appeal to reason and history, as expressed today in biblical scholarship. "Though we must not leave the solution of our problems about tradition to biblical scholars and Church historians, they have an evident importance here."[7]

Without disagreeing with the substance of these words (in which there is much that commands general agreement), the four Methodist dissentients[8] added a caveat on this subject of Scripture and tradition:

> All Churches have traditions, for no body of men can exist long without accumulating them, but they are of mixed value, containing both truth and falsehood, good and evil. They are thus not without use, but must continually be sifted, and tested by scripture. It is true that scripture interprets (and not infrequently condemns) tradition rather than that tradition interprets scripture. In a word, tradition represents the worldliness of the church, scripture points to its supernatural origin and basis. All Christians have much to learn from the past, but it is their perpetual obligation to bring their inherited customs, institutions and traditions to the bar of scripture, by which Christ rules in his Church.[9]

The statement that "tradition represents the worldliness of the church, scripture points to its supernatural origin and basis" is a remarkable one which makes the reader stop and think. The dissentients are not the sort of men to "conclude with an implied denial of the work of the Holy Spirit in the whole 1900 years of Christian history", as one critic has put it.[10] No

[1] *Ibid.*, p. 15.   [2] *Ibid.*, p. 17.   [3] *Ibid.*
[4] *Ibid.*   [5] *Ibid.*   [6] *Ibid.*, p. 18.
[7] Ibid., pp. 18ff.
[8] C. K. Barrett, T. E. Jessop, T. D. Meadley and N. H. Snaith.
[9] *Conversations*, pp. 57 f.
[10] B. Drewery, "Scripture and Tradition in Modern British Church Relations", in *Holy Book and Holy Tradition*, ed. F. F. Bruce and E. G. Rupp (Manchester, 1968), p. 152.

men could be more conscious of the vitality of the Spirit's work. But when we consider those features in church life and history which minister to spiritual pride and claims to the superiority of one group over another, they are features which belong to tradition. Scripture, with its emphasis on the sovereignty of God's grace, does not encourage the people of God to have a good conceit of themselves; tradition too often does – and this is of the very essence of worldliness. Even the most biblicist and (in intention) anti-traditionalist groups are prone to this temptation. In the best tradition of Qumran they believe that the key of knowledge has been entrusted to them and that they are the only people who really understand Scripture (sometimes, indeed, the smaller the group the more confidently does it make this claim); and it calls for an exceptional endowment of Christian humility to keep this belief from engendering a highly refined sense of one-upmanship. Pride in tradition – a conviction that the "denominational distinctives" of this body or that have preserved in special purity an essential and non-negotiable element in true Christianity – may be a form of worldliness all the more subtle for not being immediately recognizable as such, and no doubt the dissentients had Methodist as well as Anglican "worldliness" in mind when they expressed themselves thus.

The Montreal Report

In the same year (1963) as saw the publication of the Anglican-Methodist Report, the second section of the Fourth World Conference on Faith and Order (meeting at Montreal) presented its report on this subject of Scripture and tradition.[1] Probably the most important feature of this report is found in the working definitions which it put forward:

First: *tradition* (uncapitalized and singular) is the general category, including the process of transmission *(traditio)* and the content of what is transmitted *(res tradita)*. By this on-going activity the Christian past is renewed in the present and made available to the future. On the other hand, experience shows that there is a form of tradition which fossilizes the past and betrays its heritage.

Second: *traditions* (uncapitalized and plural) are the several patterns of tradition by which congregations, denominations and wider associations of churches have acquired their distinctive qualities and characteristics.

Third: *the Tradition* (capitalized, singular and preceded by the definite article) is the history in and by which the people of God live; it gathers up the history of Israel, centres in the history of our Lord and continues in the history of the church. The norm of the Tradition is Holy Writ;

[1] *The Fourth World Conference on Faith and Order*, ed. P. C. Rodger and L. Vischer (London, 1964), paras. 45 ff. For an interesting comparison of this document with the Constitution on Divine Revelation of Vatican Council II, see E. Flesseman-van Leer, "Present-day Frontiers in the Discussion about Tradition" in *Holy Book and Holy Tradition*, pp. 154 ff.

the essence of reformation is the bringing of *traditions* into closer conformity with *the Tradition*.

But in view of the Scriptural content and authority of this Tradition, the bringing of traditions into closer conformity with it cannot be other than the principle of reformation in accordance with the word of God. Without this principle of continuous reformation, without the abiding witness and guidance of the Spirit, we have fossilization where we might have had renewal.

The Appeal to History

The Tradition, then, is defined in terms of history – sacred history, indeed, but real history none the less: real history interpreted as the vehicle of God's saving revelation to His people. History is decried today in those quarters where it is fashionable to think of the "dead past" as a millstone round the neck of the living present, impeding progress towards the radiant future.[1] It is true that the invocation of the past can be a menace: we may think of the response which some of our fellow-citizens in the United Kingdom make when 1690 and all that is called to mind.[2] The kindly, tolerant people of England are perpetually bewildered by the inordinate sense of history which characterizes their neighbours with whom they have to share the islands of Great Britain and Ireland. It was the petrifying misuse of the past that Paul had in mind when he spoke of "forgetting what lies behind and straining forward to what lies ahead" (Phil. 3:13).

But the past is not dead: it is part of the continuous life of mankind. It is not only that, as Thucydides said in defence of his recording the history of the Peloponnesian War, "one man is not very different from another" and "what has happened once is likely to happen again".[3] It is that the past has played an irrevocable part in making the present what it is, so that the present is unintelligible apart from the understanding of the past. If our world is one world, it is so both in the sense that we are involved in all mankind alive at this time and in the sense that we are involved in our ancestors as much as our posterity will be involved in us. And, for the Christian, history is the arena of the witness of the Spirit, by whose vital presence the once-for-all act of God which launched the Christian era and is documented in the New Testament retains its dynamism from generation to generation and is effective in human life today.

The history of Christian beginnings inevitably takes on fresh significance as it is reapplied and reinterpreted in the experience of successive

[1] Cf. J. H. Plumb, *The Death of the Past* (London, 1969).

[2] Or, if the author throws two or three stones in his own ancestral glass house, when 1314, 1327 and 1707 are called to mind.

[3] Thucydides, *History* i.84.4; i.22.4; cf. iii.82.2

generations that receive it as their heritage. Thus it remains potent and relevant. But it is necessary that the history as received should be checked from time to time against the history *wie es eigentlich gewesen*,[1] lest the two should part company irretrievably.

We must not be afraid of the appeal to history, whether our appeal is dismissed as irrelevant or condemned as illegitimate. In England a century ago we had Cardinal Manning denouncing it as treason and heresy – treason, because it rejects the living voice of the church today, and heresy, because it denies that voice to be divine.[2] Be it so: where the living voice of the church collides with history, history tends to be victorious in the long run.

From a very different point of view we have been warned more recently against the appeal to history by the venerable voice of Professor Bultmann.[3] History, he warns us, is a precarious and shifting authority: the gospel of justification by faith excludes justification by history as decisively in the twentieth century as it excluded justification by works in the sixteenth. True: history does not save us; even the historical Jesus does not save us except in so far as the Spirit makes effective in us the act of God accomplished for us when "Christ died for our sins in accordance with the scriptures . . . and was raised the third day in accordance with the scriptures". True also that the salvation accomplished by that historic act and made effective by the Spirit is an eternal salvation, just as the sacrifice then offered once for all is the eternal sacrifice. But the redemptive power of this eternal sacrifice depends on its having been offered in time, by the Saviour who "suffered under Pontius Pilate". The appeal to history is not to be avoided, even if it does involve a measure of "risk". Whatever risk it involves, it is nothing like the risk involved in an appeal to tradition isolated from history, or in an appeal to faith *in vacuo*. Let tradition and faith, church doctrine and church practice, canon and text, and the gospel narrative itself, be tested and validated by historical inquiry as far as such inquiry can take us: we shall be the gainers, not the losers.

Above all, the church's faith in Christ and proclamation of Christ must not be detached from the historical Jesus, lest her faith and proclamation should prove to lack foundation. An interest in the historical Jesus is not

---

[1] Leopold von Ranke's resolve to narrate history "as it actually occurred" (preface to *Geschichten der romanischen und germanischen Völker, 1494–1535* [Berlin, 1824] has been called in question in recent years; as a result especially of R. G. Collingwood's *The Idea of History* (Oxford, 1946), the attainability of pure objectivity in the writing of history is widely doubted. Attainable or not, it is a goal to be aimed at. See review of *The Idea of History* by D. M. Mackinnon in *JTS* 48 (1947), pp. 249 ff.

[2] H. E. Manning, *The Temporal Mission of the Holy Ghost* (London, 1865), p. 226, cited by G. Salmon, *The Infallibility of the Church* (London, 1888), p. 42. (Manning became a cardinal in 1877.)

[3] Cf. R. Bultmann, "The Significance of the Historical Jesus for the Theology of Paul", *Faith and Understanding*, E. T. i (London, 1966), p. 241.

that endeavour to know Christ after the flesh which Paul renounces: the Christian with a historical conscience can and should ask historical questions about the one whom he has believed, and material to answer his questions is present in abundance in the New Testament. When Emil Brunner, in one of his earlier works, says that "Jesus of Nazareth, the rabbi, the so-called historical Jesus, was an object of no interest for the early Christians, and it is of no interest today for those who have preserved some understanding of what Christian faith means",[1] his statement must be denied in both its parts. The tradition which is maintained in life by the risen Lord through the agency of His Spirit is the tradition which originates with the historical Jesus. With R. C. Moberly, "Councils, we admit [only we do not just admit it; we assert it], and Creeds, cannot go behind, but must wholly rest upon the history of our Lord Jesus Christ."[2]

[1] E. Brunner, *The Word and the World*, E. T. (London, 1931), pp. 87 ff.
[2] R. C. Moberly, "The Incarnation as the Basis of Dogma", in *Lux Mundi*, ed. C. Gore (London, 1889), p. 243.

BIBLIOGRAPHY

Aland, K., *The Problem of the New Testament Canon* (London, 1962).

Aland, K., and others, *The Gospels Reconsidered* (Oxford, 1960).

Amand de Mendieta, E., *The "Unwritten" and "Secret" Apostolic Traditions in the Theological Thought of St. Basil of Caesarea* (Edinburgh, 1965).

Anderson, H., *Jesus and Christian Origins* (New York, 1964).

Baird, J. A., *Audience Criticism and the Historical Jesus* (Philadelphia, 1969).

Barr, J., *Old and New in Interpretation* (London, 1966).

Barrett, C. K., *Jesus and the Gospel Tradition* (London, 1967).

Bartlet, J. V., *Church-Life and Church-Order during the First Four Centuries* (Oxford, 1943).

Bauer, W., *Rechtgläubigkeit und Ketzerei im ältesten Christentum* (Tübingen, 1964).

Bentzen, A., *King and Messiah*, E. T. (London, 1955).

Betz, O., *Offenbarung und Schriftforschung in der Qumransekte* (Tübingen, 1960).

Betz, O., *What de we know about Jesus?* E. T. (London, 1967).

Black, M., *The Scrolls and Christian Origins* (London, 1961).

Bruce, F. F., *Biblical Exegesis in the Qumran Texts* (London, 1960).

Bruce, F. F., *This is That* (Exeter, 1969).

Bruce, F. F., and Rupp, E. G. (ed.), *Holy Book and Holy Tradition* (Manchester, 1968).

Bultmann, R., *The History of the Synoptic Tradition*, E. T. (Oxford, 1963).

Burgon, J. W., *The Last Twelve Verses of the Gospel according to S. Mark* (London, 1871), reprinted with introduction by Edward F. Hills (Evansville, Ind., 1959).

Burney, C. F., *The Poetry of our Lord* (Oxford, 1925).

Butler, B. C., *The Church and Infallibility* (London, 1954).

Campenhausen, H. von, *Tradition and Life in the Church* (London, 1968).

Carnell, E. J., *The Case for Orthodox Theology* (London, 1961).

Congar, Y. M.-J., *La Tradition et les Traditions*, i (Paris, 1961); ii (Paris, 1963).

Cross, F. L. (ed.), *The Jung Codex* (London, 1955).

Cross, F. M., *The Ancient Library of Qumran and Modern Biblical Studies* (New York, 1958).

Cullmann, O., *The Early Church*, E. T. (London, 1956).

Daube, D., *The Exodus Pattern in the Bible* (London, 1963).

Davies, W. D., *Christian Origins and Judaism* (London, 1962).

Davies, W. D., *Paul and Rabbinic Judaism* (London, 1948).

Davies, W. D., *The Setting of the Sermon on the Mount* (Cambridge, 1964).

Dibelius, M., *From Tradition to Gospel*, E. T. (London, 1934).

Dibelius, M., *Gospel Criticism and Christology* (London, 1935).

Dodd, C. H., *According to the Scriptures* (London, 1952).

Dodd, C. H., *The Apostolic Preaching and its Developments* (London, 1936).

Dodd, C. H., *Gospel and Law* (Cambridge, 1951).

Dodd, C. H., *Historical Tradition in the Fourth Gospel* (Cambridge, 1963).

Dodd, C. H., *History and the Gospel* (London, 1938).

Dodd, C. H., *The Interpretation of the Fourth Gospel* (Cambridge, 1953).

Dodd, C. H., *New Testament Studies* (Manchester, 1953).

Dodd, C. H., *The Old Testament in the New* (London, 1952).

Dugmore, C. W. (ed.), *The Interpretation of the Bible* (London, 1944).

Easton, B. S., *Christ in the Gospels* (New York, 1930).

Ebeling, G., *The Word of God and Tradition*, E. T. (London, 1968).

Ehrhardt, A., *The Apostolic Ministry* (Edinburgh, 1958).

Ehrhardt, A., *The Apostolic Succession in the First Two Centuries of the Church* (London, 1953).

Ehrhardt, A., *The Framework of the New Testament Stories* (Manchester, 1964).

Flesseman-van Leer, E., *Tradition and Scripture in the Early Church* (Assen, 1955).

Fridrichsen, A., and others, *The Root of the Vine* (London, 1953).

Gärtner, B., *The Temple and the Community in Qumran and the New Testament* (Cambridge, 1965).

Gärtner, B., *The Theology of the Gospel of Thomas* (London, 1961).

Gerhardsson, B., *Memory and Manuscript* (Lund and Copenhagen, 1961).

Gerhardsson, B., *Tradition and Transmission in Early Christianity* (Lund and Copenhagen, 1964).

Grant, F. C. (ed.), *Form Criticism* (New York, [2]1962).

Grant, R. M., *The Bible in the Church* (New York, 1948), revised edition, *A Short History of the Interpretation of the Bible* (London, 1965).

Grant, R. M., *The Formation of the New Testament* (London, 1965).

Grant, R. M., *Gnosticism and Early Christianity* (New York, 1959).

Grant, R. M., and Freedman, D. N., *The Secret Sayings of Jesus* (London, 1960).

Gundry, R. H., *The Use of the Old Testament in St. Matthew's Gospel* (Leiden, 1967).

Hanson, A. T., *Jesus Christ in the Old Testament* (London, 1965).

Hanson, R. P. C., *Origen's Doctrine of Tradition* (London, 1954).

Hanson, R. P. C., *Tradition in the Early Church* (London, 1962).

Harnack, A., *The Constitution and Law of the Church in the First Two Centuries*, E. T. (London, 1910).

Harnack, A., *Marcion* (Leipzig, 1924).

Harnack, A., *Neue Studien zu Marcion* (Leipzig, 1923).

Harnack, A., *The Origin of the New Testament*, E. T. (London, 1925).

Harris, J. Rendel, *Sidelights on New Testament Research* (London, 1908).

Harris, J. Rendel, *Testimonies*, i (Cambridge, 1916); ii (Cambridge, 1920).

Higgins, A. J. B., *The Tradition about Jesus* (Edinburgh, 1969).

Hooke, S. H., *Alpha and Omega* (London, 1961).

Hunter, A. M., *Paul and his Predecessors* (London, 1961).

Jeremias, J., *The Central Message of the New Testament* (London, 1965).

Jeremias, J., *The Eucharistic Words of Jesus*, E. T. (Oxford, 1955).

Jeremias, J., *The Parables of Jesus*, E. T. (London, 1954).

Jeremias, J., *Unknown Sayings of Jesus*, E. T. (London, [2]1964).

Käsemann, E., *Essays on New Testament Themes*, E. T. (London, 1964).

Käsemann, E., *New Testament Questions of Today*, E. T. (London, 1969).

Käsemann, E., *Das wandernde Gottesvolk* (Göttingen, 1938).

Klausner, J., *The Messianic Idea in Israel*, E. T. (London, 1956).

Koch, K., *The Growth of the Biblical Tradition*, E. T. (London, 1969).

Küng, H., *The Structure of the Church*, E. T. (London, 1965).

Lightfoot, J. B., *Essays on "Supernatural Religion"* (London, 1889).

Lindars, B., *New Testament Apologetic* (London, 1961).

Manson, T. W., *Ethics and the Gospel* (London, 1960).

Manson, T. W., *The Sayings of Jesus* (London, 1949).

Manson, T. W., *Studies in the Gospels and Epistles* (Manchester, 1962).

Manson, T. W., *The Teaching of Jesus* (Cambridge, [2]1935).

Manson, W., *Jesus the Messiah* (London, 1943)

Montefiore, H. W., and Turner, H. E. W., *Thomas and the Evangelists* (London, 1962).

Moore, G. F., *Judaism in the First Centuries of the Christian Era* (Cambridge, Mass., 1927-30).

Morrison, K. F., *Tradition and History in the Western Church, 300–1140* (Princeton, 1969).

Mowinckel, S., *He That Cometh*, E. T. (Oxford, 1956).

Neilsen, E., *Oral Tradition* (London, 1954).

Nineham, D. E. (ed.), *The Church's Use of the Bible Past and Present* (London, 1963).

Nixon, R. E., *The Exodus in the New Testament* (London, 1963).

Perrin, N., *The Kingdom of God in the Teaching of Jesus* (London, 1963).

Perrin, N., *Rediscovering the Teaching of Jesus* (London, 1967).

Pickering, F. P., *Literatur und darstellende Kunst im Mittelalter* (Berlin, 1966).

Prestige, G. L., *Fathers and Heretics* (London, 1954).

Rahner, K., and Ratzinger, J., *Revelation and Tradition*, E. T. (London, 1966).

Reid, W. Stanford, *Calvin and Tradition* (Redhill, 1966).

Riesenfeld, H., *The Gospel Tradition and its Beginnings* (London, 1957).

Robinson, J. A. T., *Twelve New Testament Studies* (London, 1962).

Rohde, J., *Rediscovering the Teaching of the Evangelists*, E. T. (London, 1968).

Salmon, G., *The Infallibility of the Church* (London, [2]1890).

Sanders, E. P., *The Tendencies of the Synoptic Tradition* (Cambridge, 1969).

Sasse, H., *Holy Church or Holy Writ?* (Sydney, 1967).

Schmidt, K. L., *Der Rahmen der Geschichte Jesu* (Berlin, 1919).

Seeberg, A., *Der Katechismus der Urchristenheit* (Leipzig, 1903).

Selwyn, E. G., *The First Epistle of St. Peter* (London, 1946), Essay II (pp. 363 ff.).

Shelley, B., *By What Authority?* (Exeter, 1966).

Snaith, N. H., *The Distinctive Ideas of the Old Testament* (London, 1944).

Stendahl, K., *The School of St. Matthew* (Lund, [2]1968).

Streeter, B. H., *The Primitive Church* (London, 1929).

Tavard, G. H., *Holy Writ or Holy Church* (London, 1959).

Taylor, V., *The Formation of the Gospel Tradition* (London, 1933).

Theron, D. J., *Evidence of Tradition* (London, 1957).

Turner, H. E. W., *The Pattern of Christian Truth* (London, 1954).

Vermes, G., *Scripture and Tradition in Judaism* (Leiden, 1961).

Ware, T., *The Orthodox Church* (Harmondsworth, 1963).

Widengren, G., *Tradition and Literature in Early Judaism and in the Early Church* (Leiden, 1963).

Wilson, R. McL., *Gnosis and the New Testament* (Oxford, 1968).

Wilson, R. McL., *The Gnostic Problem* (London, 1958).

Wilson, R. McL., *Studies in the Gospel of Thomas* (London, 1960).

Wood, A. Skevington, *Captive to the Word* (Exeter, 1969).

Wood, A. Skevington, *The Principles of Biblical Interpretation* (Grand Rapids, 1967).

INDEX

ABBA, 53
Abd al Masih, Y., 90
Abraham, 40, 85
Abrahams, I, 48
Acts (of the Apostles), 139, 141
Acts (apocryphal), 141
Adultera, Pericope de, 87
Aesop, 94
Agrapha, 87, 89, 110
Akbar (mogul), 97
Aland, K., 148 f., 153
Albright, W. F., 50
Alexandria, 114, 118, 142
Alexandrian text, 153 f.
Alford, H., 159
Allegorization, 76, 118, 119
Amand de Mendieta, E., 127
Ambrosiaster, 113
Amphictyony, 40
Angel of Yahweh, 85
Anglican-Methodist Conversations, 18, 169 f.
Antioch, Syrian, 33
Antipas, Herod, 57, 81
Apocalypse (of John), 79, 111, 141, 145, 149
Apocrypha, 129, 133, 134, 135, 144
Apollinarius, 111
Apollos, 74 f.
Apophthegms, 43, 59
Apostles, 121, 122, 123
Apostolic Church Order, 124
Apostolic Constitutions, 123, 125
Apostolic succession, 112 ff.
Apostolic Tradition, 112 ff., 125 ff.
Apostolicity, 92, 137, 141 f.
Aqiba, 22, 26, 86, 151
Aramaic, 105, 122
Arendzen, J. P., 124
Arianism, 126
Aristion (elder), 109

Ariston (of Smyrna), 109
Artaxerxes I, 133
Articles, Thirty-Nine, 116, 135, 146, 168
Asceticism, 120
Asia (province), 113
Athanasius, 129, 134, 142
Audet, J. P., 134
Augustine (of Hippo), 135
Authorized Version, 84, 154
Autographs, 157

BABYLONIA, 152
Bacon, B. W., 32
Bagatti, P. B., 16
Bailey, D. S., 27
Baird, J. A., 43
Baptism, 115, 121, 126
Baptismal confession, 115
Barclay, W., 132
Bar Hanina, 152
Barnabas, Epistle of, 120, 143
Barr, J., 28
Barrett, C. K., 39, 46, 48, 70, 137, 170
Bartlet, J. V., 120, 124
Baruch, Apocalypse of, 111
Basil (of Caesarea), 127
Bauer, W., 114
Baumstark, A., 140
Beasley-Murray, G. R., 51
Beatitudes, 97 ff.
Beersheba, 40
Begrich, J., 42
Ben Asher, 152
Ben Chayyim, J., 152
Ben Naphtali, 152
Benoit, P., 70
Bentzen, A., 133
Bernard (of Clairvaux), 83
Bethel, 40, 85
Betz, O., 76
Biblicism, Biblicists, 13, 20, 171
Birkbeck, W. J., 163
Bishops, 113, 120, 122, 123, 124, 125, 126, 165

Black, M., 126
Bologna, 152
Bomberg, D., 152
Bonar, H. 35
Botte, B., 126
Bowman, J. 159
Bowra, C. M., 46
Brandon, S. G. F., 48
Brescia, 152
Bridal chamber, Mystery of, 101
Brinker, R., 40
Bruce, F. F., 76, 84, 137
Brunner, E., 174
Büchsel, F., 33
Bultmann, R., 39, 43, 47, 51, 59, 64, 173
Bunyan, J., 130
Burgess, W. H., 18
Burgon, J. W., 157, 158, 159
Burkitt, F. C., 45, 55, 114
Burney, C. F., 65
Burning Bush, 85
Buxtorf, J., 161
Byzantine liturgy, 163
Byzantine text, 153, 157 f.

CAESAREA PHILIPPI, 52, 91
Caiaphas, 123
Caird, G. B., 36
Callistus I (pope), 125
Calvin, J., 18, 143 f., 154 f., 160, 168
Canon, 129 ff., 166
Canons of Hippolytus, 126
Canticles (Song of Songs), 83, 133, 134, 144
Capernaum, 63
Cappellus, L., 161
Capper, W. M., 16
Carlston, C. E., 54
Carnell, E. J., 118, 146
Carroll, L., 13
Carthage, Synod of, 135, 142
Castellio, S., 144
Catholic Antiquity, 157 f.